Y0-DVY-016

REVIEW 8

REVIEW

Volume 8   1986

Edited by

James O. Hoge
*Virginia Polytechnic Institute
and State University*

James L. W. West III
The Pennsylvania State University

University Press of Virginia
Charlottesville

THE UNIVERSITY PRESS OF VIRGINIA
Copyright © 1986 by the Rector and Visitors
of the University of Virginia

This journal is a member of (CELJ) the Conference of Editors of Learned Journals

First published 1986

ISSN 0190-3233
ISBN 0-8139-1113-3

Printed in the United States of America

Funding for *Review* is provided by the generous gifts of Mr. and Mrs. Henry J. Dekker, Mr. and Mrs. J. S. Hill, and Mr. Adger S. Johnson to the Virginia Tech Foundation, and by a grant from the College of Liberal Arts, The Pennsylvania State University. Additional support is provided by the *Review* Association, a group of major universities which support the aims and purposes of the series. Member universities are as follows:

>   City College of New York
>   Columbia University
>   University of Colorado
>   Duke University
>   University of Minnesota
>   University of Virginia

Contents

Using Hardy's Notebooks   1
   by Dale Kramer
     Review of *The Literary Notebooks of Thomas Hardy*, ed. Lennart A. Björk, 2 Vols.

Jane Austen and History   21
   by James Thompson
     Review of Margaret Kirkham, *Jane Austen: Feminism and Fiction*; John Halperin, *The Life of Jane Austen*; David Monaghan, ed., *Jane Austen in a Social Context*; Mary Poovey, *The Proper Lady and the Woman Writer: Ideology as Style in the Works of Mary Wollstonecraft, Mary Shelley, and Jane Austen*; LeRoy Smith, *Jane Austen and the Drama of Woman*; Janet Todd, ed., *Jane Austen: New Perspectives*

Understanding Modernism   33
   by Harvey Gross
     Review of Michael H. Levenson, *A Genealogy of Modernism: A Study of English Literary Doctrine, 1908-1922;* Jeffrey M. Perl, *The Tradition of Return: The Implicit History of Modern Literature*; Ricardo J. Quinones, *Mapping Literary Modernism: Time and Development*

The "Wordsworth Industry" Revisited   47
   by John E. Jordan
     Review of David McCracken, *Wordsworth and the Lake District: A Guide to the Poems and Their Places;* Kenneth R. Johnston, *Wordsworth and* The Recluse;

James A. W. Heffernan, *The Re-Creation of Landscape: A Study of Wordsworth, Coleridge, Constable, and Turner*

Shakespeare and the Stage   59
  by Donald Gwynn Watson
    Review of Peter Thomson, *Shakespeare's Theatre*; Alan C. Dessen, *Elizabethan Stage Conventions and Modern Interpreters*; David Bevington, *Action Is Eloquence: Shakespeare's Language of Gesture*; John Barton, *Playing Shakespeare*; Philip Brockbank, ed., *Players of Shakespeare*; Joseph H. Summers, *Dreams of Love and Power: On Shakespeare's Plays*; Jean E. Howard, *Shakespeare's Art of Orchestration: Stage Technique and Audience Response*

The Stanford *Falesá* and Textual Scholarship   79
  by David H. Jackson
    Review of Barry Menikoff, *Robert Louis Stevenson and The Beach of Falesá: A Study in Victorian Publishing with the Original Text*

Ben Jonson, Realist   93
  by Alastair Fowler
    Review of Anne Barton, *Ben Jonson, Dramatist*

"No Such Scarecrows in Your Father's Time":
A New Tennyson Bibliography   101
  by P. G. Scott
    Review of Kirk H. Beetz, *Tennyson, A Bibliography, 1827-1982*

Contents ix

Authorial Revision 119
   by James McLaverty
      Review of Hershel Parker, *Flawed Texts and Verbal Icons: Literary Authority in American Fiction*

Homophobia in English Culture 139
   by Seymour Kleinberg
      Review of Louis Crompton, *Byron and Greek Love: Homophobia in 19th-Century England*; Eve Kosofsky Sedgwick, *Between Men: English Literature and Male Homosocial Desire*

Authorship in America during the Progressive Period 149
   by James L. W. West III
      Review of Christopher P. Wilson, *The Labor of Words: Literary Professionalism in the Progressive Era*

Samuel Johnson's Enthusiasm for History 157
   by James L. Battersby
      Review of John A. Vance, *Samuel Johnson and the Sense of History*

Framing Caws 189
   by Gerhard Joseph
      Review of Mary Ann Caws, *Reading Frames in Modern Fiction*

Literary Stepchildren: Nineteenth-Century Dramatists 197
   by Brenda Murphy
      Review of *Plays by Dion Boucicault*, ed. Peter Thomson; *Plays by Augustin Daly*, ed. Don B. Wilmeth and Rosemary Cullen

Wordsworth and the Genius of Burke 205
   by Jeffrey C. Robinson
      Review of James K. Chandler, *Wordsworth's Second Nature: A Study of the Poetry and Politics*

Living at a Gallop 215
   by R. C. Terry
      Review of *The Letters of Anthony Trollope*, ed. N. John Hall, 2 Vols.

Styron and Evil 231
   by Robert K. Morris
      Review of John Kenny Crane, *The Root of All Evil: The Thematic Unity of William Styron's Fiction*

Five Feminist Studies of Shakespeare 241
   by Burton Hatlen
      Review of Linda Bamber, *Comic Women, Tragic Men: A Study of Gender and Genre in Shakespeare*; Irene G. Dash, *Wooing, Wedding, and Power: Women in Shakespeare's Plays*; Peter Erickson, *Patriarchal Structures in Shakespeare's Drama*; Marilyn French, *Shakespeare's Division of Experience*; Marianne L. Novy, *Love's Argument: Gender Relations in Shakespeare*

Popular Criticism 265
   by Martin Roth
      Review of David Geherin, *The American Private Eye: The Image in Fiction*; Sinda Gregory, *Private Investigations: The Novels of Dashiell Hammett*

Contents

A Book for a Parlour-Window 273
  by O M Brack, Jr.
    Review of Laurence Sterne, *The Life and Opinions of Tristram Shandy, Gentleman*, 3 Vols. Vols.1-2: The Text, ed. Melvyn New and Joan New; vol. 3: The Notes, ed. Melvyn New with Richard A. Davies and W. G. Day

Contributors 303

Editorial Board

Felicia Bonaparte
City College, CUNY

Jerome H. Buckley
Harvard University

Paul Connolly
Yeshiva University

A. S. G. Edwards
University of Victoria

Ian Jack
Cambridge University

Robert Kellogg
University of Virginia

James R. Kincaid
University of Colorado

Cecil Y. Lang
University of Virginia

James B. Meriwether
University of South Carolina

Hershel Parker
University of Delaware

Martin Roth
University of Minnesota

George Stade
Columbia University

John L. Sharpe III
Duke University

G. Thomas Tanselle
John Simon Guggenheim Memorial Foundation

Stanley Weintraub
The Pennsylvania State University

Using Hardy's Notebooks

Dale Kramer

Lennart A. Björk, ed. *The Literary Notebooks of Thomas Hardy*. 2 volumes. New York: New York University Press, 1985. xliv, 428 pp.; xliv, 591 pp.

In 1974 *The Literary Notes of Thomas Hardy* was published as the first volume of a two-volume set.[1] The second volume never appeared in that format; but now the New York University Press has printed a revised version of that first volume, the remaining material Björk had promised more than a decade ago, and also an additional notebook not mentioned in the 1974 promises. Possibly because reviewers and journal editors were waiting for the completion of the project, there were few substantive or extended (which I have seen, at least) reviews of Volume I.[2] My comments here encompass both the decade-known material and that which was published for the first time in 1985.

The edition prints several notebooks now in the Thomas Hardy Memorial Collection in the Dorset County Museum, Dorchester, compiled by Hardy over a number of years but with a common purpose. They contain quotations and pieces of information Hardy had gleaned in his reading, and which he evidently thought he might be able to draw upon in his writings. "Literary Notes I" and "Literary Notes II" are made up mostly of quotations from and paraphrases of historical, literary, philosophical, scientific, and antiquarian subjects (toward the end there are a few pasted-in clippings of printed material). A third notebook lacks its first few leaves, and has as its only title the date "1867" on the front flyleaf; evidently the appeal for Hardy of the quotations he placed in it is their stylistic flair in phrasing. Björk's 1974 edition prints the first 1339 items in "Literary Notes I" and the entire "1867" notebook (245 items—in the 1985 edition still, as in 1974, separately enumerated, references to them distinguished from the items in the larger listing by a prefatory "A"). Björk's announced second volume presumably was to have included the remainder of "Literary Notes I" (items 1340 through 1649 in the present edition) and all of "Literary Notes II" (items 1650-2482). Sometime after 1974 Björk decided to incorporate another notebook, named "Literary Notes III," which had been added to the Thomas Hardy Memorial Collection in 1972. This comprises items 2483-2641—mostly clippings of quite long journal articles and reviews on subjects similar to those paraphrased and quoted in "Literary Notes I and II," with a few handwritten entries interspersed.

These notebooks form a large share of what survives of Hardy's efforts to collect and store information he might draw upon or use to jog his own thinking about philosophical matters or art or aesthetics or history. Apart from them, there are, basically, only (1) those notes which he printed in his *Life*;[3] (2) several notebooks published in 1979 by Richard Taylor in *The Personal Notebooks of Thomas Hardy* (a notebook on the history of art—the "Schools of Painting Notebook"—the "Trumpet-Major Notebook," and two "memoranda" notebooks of *aperçus*, diary jottings, memories, and other such personal reflections);[4] (3) two books of clippings and facts in the Dorset County Museum still unpublished—one headed "Facts from Newspapers, Histories, Biographies, & other chronicles—(mainly Local)," the other simply "Press Cuttings"; and (4) two notebooks in the private collection of R. L. Purdy—an 1865 notebook entitled "Studies, Specimens &c" and a photocopy of a "Poetical Matter" notebook. In addition, one might be inclined to place in this list *The Architectural Notebook of Thomas Hardy*,[5] although its note material is minuscule compared to its architectural drawings. A fairly small mountain of material for a writer who is thought to reflect so much of the thinking—especially the more adventurous thinking—of his times.[6]

There are explanations for the relatively small amount of material a modern scholar has to work with in reconstructing

Using Hardy's Notebooks

what Björk, quoting David DeLaura, calls "the complex contemporary matrix of Hardy's writing" (p. xxx).[7] The most obvious is that in contrast to the work of such writers as Charles Reade, who based his massive novels of information and action on vast research, Hardy's writings are fundamentally personal, not expository. Hardy himself no doubt felt it necessary to bone up on facts and opinions to dignify his narratives or to deepen their range, but it is questionable whether his success depends to any degree upon this material or whether many of his readers have read him for the information they gain (on any other subject than Wessex or Dorset, that is).[8]

A secondary, but more pragmatic, explanation for the sparse evidence of Hardy's background reading is that before his death Hardy burned large amounts of papers in his garden. We can only hypothesize about what was destroyed, but almost certainly it included a good deal of correspondence, possibly foul drafts of his stories and poems, unquestionably clippings and notes and magazines and newspapers of the kind that somehow pile up in studies. The very notebooks which Björk is editing may in part amount to what was withheld from such bonfires. Toward the end of "Literary Notes II" the entries were evidently copied or pasted in the 1920s although many date from two decades earlier. Items 2452-56, made of material published in 1926, are followed by many dating from ca. 1908; e.g., item 2477—a quotation about poetry from *TLS* of 1908, written in to follow a cutting from 1927. Some of the Hardy bonfires also oxidized the materials drawn upon and quoted in the *Life* but which (naturally) have never surfaced in their original forms in libraries or auction rooms. After he died, selecting material for still additional bonfires occupied Sydney Cockerell, one of Hardy's executors, and Florence Hardy, the other executor as well as the author's wife.

A third explanation is perhaps primarily contributory to the first and second. Although Hardy resisted the identification all his life, in fact he was an autodidact, whose education was acquired in the interstices of an apprenticeship in architecture and a budding if never blooming career in that field. Hardy's sensitivity about his rise from an inauspicious background—

although he never hid it, and remained faithful to his rural family—is understandable given the class-based society he moved in during most of his adult life; and even when he "retired" to Max Gate the steady influx of visitors reminded him that although ensconced in Dorset he was still very much a part of his nation's intellectual and social life. The present notebooks do not contain much essentially rudimentary information of the sort that is in the "Schools of Painting Notebook," but to think that Hardy may have destroyed similar information that he might have felt he would have absorbed naturally as a youth had he had the education of a grammar school and a moderately intellectual middle class life—evidences that would reveal he was forced to "cram" as an adult for the allusive knowledge he felt was needed by a novelist—does not discredit his talent or sincerity.

An essential question is the value of such an edition as this, which is, after all, comprised of material written by writers other than the one who is highlighted by the existence of the edition.[9] In considering the place of these Literary Notes in Hardy's career, the obvious preliminary remark is that practically none of the entries in these volumes is a direct reflection of Hardy's own opinion, and there are only a few notations by Hardy evaluating the passages he copied. The surviving notes can be looked upon as the cream of Hardy's reading and reflection, containing invaluable clues about the way his genius draws upon or reacts to others' ideas or expressions; or as the detritus of his reading, insignificant in that he did not find an opportunity to use most of them and in that they do not convey any information personal enough to make him uneasy about their survival. In either case, they comprise a record of ideas or information that—at one time, at the minimum—struck Hardy as interesting or potentially useful. The ones made *after* Hardy had already used similar ideas in his writings point to underlying personal interests as much as potential literary exploitation; others, such as the great number of items dealing with freedom of the will which continued to accumulate into the last year of Hardy's life, point to Hardy's restless curiosity about issues without resolutions. If we are willing to grant that the human mind is constantly accreting impressions, these notebooks invaluably reveal the sources of discrete salient ideas and images, some of which may have affected Hardy's subsequent thinking and feeling more than others, even though there is no way of knowing the nature of the impact or the precise impression itself that any given quotation may have imparted to Hardy. Hardy once referred to "the author's idiosyncratic mode of regard":[10] this mode can be as instrumental in responding to another's writing as it is in formulating perceptions into words for others to read.

Certainly there is God's plenty within the entries for analysis, categorization, and deduction of parallels with Hardy's fiction, parallels that can range from the purely structural to an ingrained correspondence between the citation and Hardy's own thought processes. The very first entry, Hardy's schematic rendition of Charles Fourier's theory of psychology and human nature, instances both kinds of potential influence. Fourier was one of the nineteenth century's scientifically inclined humanists who believed he could intellectually render the complexities of human psychology into discernible interactive elements (such as Passions, Will, Intellect—in one of the schema Hardy made); among many other such thinkers whose words Hardy transcribed in these notebooks are Comte (about whom more later) and Herbert Spencer. Hardy appears to have made the schema based on Fourier around 1863, when he was only twenty-three years old. This sort of mechanistic view of humanity was rife during the period, so perhaps Fourier was not even a central influence. Nevertheless, Hardy's early portrayal of character obviously suggests he held a confidence similar to Fourier's that a personality could be grasped by noting its constitutive dichotomous elements, a confidence that permeates the presentation of every character (and thematic idea) in a relatively early novel like *Far from the Madding Crowd* (Boldwood's symmetrical existence is composed of "enormous antagonistic forces" tenuously held in "perfect balance" [Wessex Edition, p. 137]; "Bathsheba's was an *impulsive* nature under a *deliberative* aspect. An *Elizabeth in brain* and a *Mary Stuart in spirit*, she often performed actions of the *greatest temerity* with a manner of *extreme discretion*" [p. 149; my italics]). The schematic thinking seen in Fourier clearly was attractive to Hardy, for throughout his career his prose style inclined toward regularity and a closed syntax—although this stylistic preference became more and more at odds with a subtlety that refused absolute certitudes, the resulting indeterminacy achieving immensely powerful effects in mutually incompatible meditations upon free will and nature in *Tess of the d'Urbervilles*. Along these lines, and as another instance of deep-seated parallelism one can perhaps adduce John Henry Newman, whose *Apologia pro Vita Sua* Hardy read in 1865. Hardy could not accede to Newman's insistence upon the inherent validity of the first link in his reasoning, that God must exist; but Newman's advocacy of the concept that securing certitude on all consequent links "was the result of an *assemblage* of concurring & converging probabilities" confirmed Hardy's belief in a mode of perception that exceeded logic and realism. And the resemblance in Hardy's and Newman's dedication to their life-work (fiction, and religion) as at base a moral rather than intellectual performance is only modestly made discordant by the stark contrast between Newman's fear of intellectualism because it led to liberalism (see item 8) and Hardy's following of the promptings of the more adventurous thinkers of his time not only into liberalism but into radicalism. It is not insignificant that after the first entry given to Fourier the next eighteen are from *Apologia*—a sign of Hardy's memorializing in the notes copied in the mid-1870s the impact that Newman had made on him earlier.

In what other general ways, and what particular, can the publication of these entries contribute to the late-twentieth-century's study of the novelist-poet? First, there are numerous essentially minor "discoveries" or parallels with novels (primarily) that give us a glimpse into the ways that Hardy marshalled his instincts, his "genius," and his perseverance in shaping a novel into his distinctive tone. The novel for which Björk finds the notebooks most directly relevant is *The Return of the Native*—not surprising in that he sets the occasion for Hardy's beginning to take notes in the spring of 1876 to be the "mixed reception of *Ethelberta*" (p. xix), the novel

Using Hardy's Notebooks

immediately preceding *The Return of the Native*. At this time Hardy also followed the advice of Leslie Stephen, to take a rest from novel-writing. Björk notes that "approximately one third of the 'Literary Notes' appears to be from the interval between the completion of *The Hand of Ethelberta* and the start on *The Return of the Native*" (p. xxi), a novel which "by critical consensus marks the beginning of a new phase in Hardy's literary career, a phase both ideologically and aesthetically more ambitious than the previous one" (p. xiv). There are, then, more reflections of his note-taking in this novel than in any of the others, and Björk's introduction and notes are especially strong in detailing these parallels and echoes, such as entry 604: "*Link between extinct animals & those present now*—The Dodo, last seen in <17th cent.>" Björk points us to the way this nugget of knowledge appears in fiction, in *The Return of the Native*: "He [Diggory Venn] was one of a class rapidly becoming extinct in Wessex, filling at present in the rural world the place which, during the last century, the dodo occupied in the world of animals" (Wessex Edition, p. 9). One can go beyond Björk's identification of the notebook item to observe that the novel's passage illustrates Hardy's characteristic labored manner of allusion: stiff and—when we know its source—artificial and imposed upon the context. Yet, in the fiction how superbly this kind of interposition of information confirms the quality of the novel and the authority of the author. The laboredness of the simile of animal and human underscores the parallel Hardy was conscious of throughout his career that sentient beings were not solely those of the *homo sapiens* species. That the deliberateness of Hardy's drawing on this sort of knowledge is not accidental may be confirmed by the note to item 1133, where Björk quotes Hardy's approval of the idea that a reader "may be a picker-up of trifles of useful knowledge, statistics, queer historic fact, such as sometimes occur in the pages of Hugo" (and had he been interested in a general defense of his endeavor Björk might well have gone on to quote further from this passage Hardy's assertion that an author "may even wish to brush up his knowledge of quotations from ancient and other authors by studying some chapters of *Pelham* and the disquisitions of Parson Adams in *Joseph Andrews*").[11]

Several other such citations of material bearing upon *The Return of the Native* are identified in the notes. But of course the value of such an edition must lie not in our willingness to be cued by the editor but in the availability of evidence for our own searchings. In the case of *The Return of the Native* the numerous quotations from Comte (items 618-20, 640-769 are nearly all from *Social Dynamics*) remind us of Hardy's indebtedness to such early nineteenth-century writers. For example, many of the entries from *Social Dynamics* concerning the stage Comte terms Fetichism refer to Greek culture—a not irrelevant consideration considering the classical echoes in the novel. The note to items 737-39 expounds Comte's famous idea of the three stages of intellectual development. The quotations contain many echoes of Clym's Comte-based philosophy of programmatic evolution in social existence. For instance, Hardy as narrator indicates that Clym's mistake in returning to his birthplace to educate the heath-people is that human nature requires that social reform follow a necessary sequence (Book Third, Chapter 2). In attempting to skip the stage of social effort to leapfrog directly to that of aesthetic effort Clym violates a permutation of Comte's theory which bears in interesting ways on one of the interpretive cruxes of the novel. "*Strong Passion, or Disease* may produce temporary retrogression through the 3 stages, or 1 or 2 of them—as from Positivism to Theologism" (item 751): this is exactly what is happening to Clym at the end of the novel, and this note suggests that in the Comte-founded orientation of the novel Clym's retrogression to a form of Christianity may not have been intended to be permanent.

The notebooks are also relevant for Hardy's other, later novels, although it is not always possible to know whether a given note was made before, during, or after the writing of the novel in question. *Tess of the d'Urbervilles* is connected in so many subtle ways to social and intellectual interests of the late nineteenth century that it is difficult to think that anyone could now write a history-of-ideas essay on *Tess* without mining these *Literary Notebooks* for perspectives. There are citations dealing with Brazil and with matters that Angel learns of in Brazil (items

1472, 1657), with stillborn baptism (item 1779), Malthusianism (items 1459 and note), primitive religion (item 1465, identified by Björk as similar to Tess's argument to Alec "that he had mixed in his dull brain two matters, theology and morals, which in the primitive days of mankind had been quite distinct" [Wessex Edition, p. 421]), and the way in which one "remembers," like Tess, the experiences of one's ancestors (item 1519). As elsewhere, Positivism runs through the novel like a motif: item 1650, a Frederic Harrison quotation from an 1888 essay, seems particularly matched to *Tess of the d'Urbervilles*— not so much through verbal echoes as through substantive concerns, i.e. religion of humanity or anthropomorphism, and the abandonment of dogmatic Christianity while clinging to its transcendentalism (cf. Angel). There are also passages that reflect closely upon the novel's basis in a mentalist concept of essential reality. For instance, item A-175 ("the world is only a cerebral phenomenon") is Hardy's translation from F. A. Aulard's "Essai sur les idées philosophiques et l'inspiration poétique de Leopardi."Björk notes that this comes from a section on "Leopardi and Schopenhauer" but despite his ear for most echoes does not mention how closely it parallels Hardy's "the world is only a psychological phenomenon" (*Tess of the d'Urbervilles*, p. 108). What is of special interest is that the notebook entry is Hardy's own translation, suggesting the closeness of this passage to the concept of consciousness which dominates this novel. Another major parallel, however, is not missed by Björk, who points out the possible influence of Zola's *Abbé Mouret's Transgressions* on *Tess of the d'Urbervilles*, including item A-187 (from the "1867" notebook) on the lush description of the garden Tess walks through. (The note to A-187 sketches in general the novel's parallels with *Tess*.) The bearing upon *Tess* of Walter Pater's *Marius the Epicurean* is less certain, and Björk appropriately does not mention the ways in which Hardy's absorption of this novel (including items 1549 and 1552) might have contributed something to the central importance of individual consciousness, nor how item 1559 might be thought to have some bearing on the presentation of Tess's situation (although I think it does not). Item 1559 reads: "*The fatality* wh. seems to haunt any signal beauty, whether moral or phy.^{cal}, as if it were in itself something illicit & isolating; the suspicion & hatred it so often excites in the vulgar—[this forms] a constant tradition of somewhat cynical pagan sentiment, from Medusa & Helen downwards." This quotation certainly is not foreign to Hardy's thinking about retribution and social standing, as his stress on the beauty of Eustacia, and more particularly on the townspeople's resentment of Lucetta in *The Major of Casterbridge*, indicates. But there is less relevance to *Tess of the d'Urbervilles*, for Tess is not hated or envied by others because of her beauty. This suggests that while Hardy may have been alert to ideas, his own concepts of his material prevailed. (And, of course, there is some ambivalence in the novel itself as to whether Tess is even exceptionally attractive or essentially only a milkmaid arbitrarily chosen by fate to suffer.)

Entries especially relevant for *The Woodlanders* range from trivial matters—such as a reference to Robert Dudley, Earl of Leicester (item 74), whose wife Amy appears in Chapter 31 as one of several women made unhappy by men; and the quoting of Carlyle's phrase "The Grand, & the Little Toilette, [of Marie Antoinette]" (item 621) which Hardy draws on ironically to describe the process of tree-barking in Chapter 19—to such items as 817 that apply to large characterizing issues in the novel: "*It has been said* that Spinozism or transcendentalism in poetic production becomes Machiavellism on reflection." Although again we do not have Hardy's judgment of the phrase, that he was aware of his view of Spinoza's philosophy gives us at least an approach to the quandary of understanding Hardy's presentation of Fitzpiers: that is, although Fitzpiers is apparently presented straightforwardly as a student of transcendentalism, this does not mean Hardy is *approving* him. Rather, this passage confirms Fitzpiers as an opportunist and exploiter of others. (It is odd that Björk, in his discussion of Spinoza in the note to items 112-13, does not refer to this later item in order to resolve the point he raises there as to how Hardy conceived of Fitzpiers. But perhaps Björk, like too many readers, gives little attention to *The Woodlanders*: in a general discussion

Using Hardy's Notebooks   11

of Shelley [item 1175n.], Björk refers to Angel Clare and Sue Bridehead but not to Fitzpiers, who not only is associated with Shelley in his idealism but quotes him at length.)

It is hardly surprising that Hardy ranged widely in the reading of contemporary periodical criticism. No doubt one of the reasons he reflected so much of his times' concerns is that he consciously "studied up on" them. Clearly he was not merely a casual reader. The range of his reading is much too impressive. He read (or at least quoted from, which in his case must mean the same thing) the following journals, among others: *Fortnightly Review, Nineteenth-Century, Spectator, Review of Reviews, Cornhill, Nation, National Observer, Contemporary Review, Church Quarterly Review, Harper's New Monthly Magazine, Athenaeum, New Quarterly Magazine, North American Review, Blackwood's, Proceedings of the Society for Psychical Research, Longman's, English Review, Periodical, Literature, Edinburgh Review, Macmillan's Magazine, T.P.'s Weekly, Quarterly Review, Graphic, Speaker, Bookman, Mind*, and of course the *Times Literary Supplement*. On a totally non-scientific count, I'd say that the journal that Hardy initially draws material from the most frequently is the *Saturday Review*, in later years the *Academy*, while the most frequently copied or pasted newspaper was initially *The Times* and later the *Daily Chronicle*. Apart from the periodicals, most of the citations come from books, naturally, and not a few from encyclopedia articles.

There are sub-patterns indicating something of the way Hardy collected these materials. For instance, items 871-73 are taken from different articles in the same issue of *Edinburgh Review*, revealing that—naturally—many of these notes are the result of chance reading of material being published rather than of Hardy's deliberately searching out particular information. Likewise, items 1632-34 and 1637-47 are all from six 1888 issues of *Revue des deux mondes*. Hardy read in these journals frequently. From them he gleaned not only many general literary allusions and concerns, but many discussions of philosophy and essays on Comte, Hegel, Schopenhauer, and others.

The usableness of an edition like this, and the contribution the notebooks can make to an understanding of Hardy's writings, depend upon the editor's concept of his responsibility and its fulfillment. Björk is an industrious and searching editor. He satisfies superbly the first obligations of an editor of quotations: the entries in Hardy's notebooks are with remarkably few and minor exceptions accurately transcribed and printed, and the sources of the quotations are, again with only few exceptions, identified. Especially in the first publication in 1974, he compares Hardy's citations and notes quite carefully with the original passages whenever he can find them, and many of these comparisons survive in the 1985 edition. To take only one example: in the note to item 664 in the Comte section he quotes a Comtean passage to clarify Hardy's extraction. Also, Björk examines various editions for the precise source of Hardy's extracts (e.g., in the note to item 1015, he discusses several editions of Arnold's *Essays in Criticism,* succinctly considering three editions [1865, 1869, 1875] Hardy may have read for passages located near each other). Hardy appears to have used *different* editions of *Essays in Criticism* for some of these entries, raising interesting questions as to when the pieces from which the different entries were drawn were read, and as to whether Hardy owned several editions of the same works.

Also, Björk is informative about the reflections in Hardy's works of many of these items, not only direct quotations but echoes, as in item 93, a *verbal* echo between *A Laodicean* and a Biblical passage. In the note to item 301 he points out a similarity in *idea* between a Bishop Butler statement and one in the *Life* concerning the disadvantages of emotions. Moreover, he is well acquainted with the different versions of Hardy's novels. Time and again he is able to pinpoint an influence upon a passage that had been deleted previous to the Wessex Edition. For several instances, see the notes to the following— item 79: Björk notes the bearing of a quotation to a deleted passage in *The Return of the Native*; item 123: to a deleted passage in *A Pair of Blue Eyes*; item 136: to a deleted passage in *A Laodicean*; item 597: to several revisions within one passage in *The Return of the Native*; item 669: to different revisions in *Tess of the d'Urbervilles* regarding Fetichism; item 1269: to a passage referring to Huxley in the first edition of *Tess of the d'Urbervilles.*

Using Hardy's Notebooks

The introduction to the edition, a slightly expanded version of that to the 1974 edition, succinctly limns ways the edition can be used. Moreover, this edition is distinguished, as was the 1974 edition, by the inclusion of numerous "pocket lectures," or summary notes, on many writers, on influences upon Thomas Hardy, and on topics many of the notes deal with (e.g., on Hardy's attitude toward St. Paul [670n.]). These notes are one of the edition's finest features. They are in themselves valuable both biographically and critically, and they allow the reader of the edition to make many connections and deductions. Björk has collated other of Hardy's notebooks to see if Hardy double-copied some items. He did double-copy item 118 of "Literary Notes I," which is also in "Memoranda" notebook.[12] Items 2431 and 2589 are near-exact duplications of a passage from D. G. Ritchie's *Philosophical Studies*. The later one is typed (by Florence, Björk presumes). Among many further instances of repetitions, all noted by Björk: item 2595 on Monism is a repetition of item 2441; item 2609 is a typed duplication of 2430 (Huxley on Hume and Freedom of the Will); item 2611 is a repetition of 1401 (Morley on "classic"). This situation suggests the rather minor point that Hardy did not always discard what he had copied into his notebooks and that he did not always remember he had already copied a clipping into the notebooks.

Perhaps it is inevitable in a work of this sort, edited by a single person, that there will be gaps in material annotated and a bias toward certain kinds of entries. For instance, the historical citations are given short shrift (e.g., many of the references to the French Revolution in Carlyle [items 770 ff.]). Such information could be supplied in a mere word or phrase or brief sentence, but it might go far toward explaining what in the historical items might have struck Hardy's interest. The entries involving poetry and literature are much more fully annotated (e.g., the entry on George Sand, 477n., encompasses a wide range of searching of documents by and about Hardy's views of Sand; it also provides the context of a citation within the Sand novel being quoted, *Mauprat*, including [in 1974] a long quotation). Thus, Björk's own interests naturally tend to portray Hardy more as a purely literary man than a man keenly attuned to and concerned by the intellectual and social interests of the day. None of this is to criticize that which is given, only to wish for more.

Given that a portion of this edition has had prior publication, I need to explain the differences in presentation between the 1974 edition and the 1985 edition. Apart from any differences within the citations themselves, the most noticeable—indeed, striking—difference between the two jobs of editing is that the annotations of 1985 are considerably briefer than those of 1974, both the annotations being reprinted in 1985 and those written for the material not printed in 1974. In the first type—annotations whose fuller versions were published in 1974—the greater economy is sometimes the result of making entries more concise rather than of cutting material (e.g., the note to item 2, from Newman), but more frequently reduction is attained by deleting material, such as Björk's commentary, the passages from the books which Hardy's entries are paraphrases of, or nearby passages which clarify or add details to the passages Hardy copied or paraphrased. Again, this can be illustrated from the Newman entries. Reduced or cut drastically for 1985 is amplifying material in the notes to items 6, 8, 10, 11, 13 (particularly to be regretted), 14, 15, 16, 17, and 19. Providing in 1974 the context from which Hardy copied sentences, and other information, made reading that edition frequently exciting and genuinely informative. Readers of the entries appearing first in 1985 will simply have to locate the passages in the sources in order to have the same sort of experience—an effort which, of course, is not likely to be made often. Also, the 1974 edition of the "1867" notebook frequently gives the original passages from which Hardy's translations are made. The 1985 edition usually does not. The cutting of the 1974 citations was presumably done to reduce the cost of the present edition, but it is a pity to lose this benefit of Swedish respect for scholarship.

Equally noticeable and perhaps even a greater pity (since interested readers can always spend the extra money to buy from Sweden the 1974 partial edition) is that the annotation of material first published in 1985 is much sparser than that for

Using Hardy's Notebooks

entries first published in the 1974 edition (even taking into account the 1985 deletions and reductions of the 1974 annotations). The following chart—using a page-count based on the 1985 edition—indicates the comparative brevity of post-1974 editorial commentary:

	Text	Notes
Published in 1974:		
LN I: Items 1-1339	160 pages	148 pages
"1867": Items 1-245	23 pages	19 pages
Published in 1985:		
LN I: Items 1340-1649	67 pages	22 pages
LN II: Items 1650-2482	247 pages	57 pages
LN III: Items 2483-2641	199 pages	9 pages

It is immediately seen that—even in the more restrictive 1985 format from which this page-count was made—the material which was published in 1974 is annotated on nearly a page-for-page ratio.[13] Even allowing that a greater *number* of items (mostly short) made up the 1974 text, and thus required more space proportionately just for bibliographic data, the new annotations appear to be a bit on the cursory side. Certain questions have to be asked—whether the remaining notebook material could have been a feasible publishing project without the revision and re-issue of the 1974 edition, and whether reprinting the 1974 volume makes an extraordinary call upon libraries' and individuals' purchasing budgets. Would it not have generally been more useful to have completed the publication of Hardy's research-and-note takings by publishing the "Facts" notebook instead of reprinting the 1974 material? Had that been done, it would have been more justifiable to change the 1974 title *Literary Notes* to *Literary Notebooks* in 1985, to emphasize that only new material was being offered for purchase.

Apart from those issues, other questions concerning the 1985 edition similarly press for answers. For example, why is the Textual Introduction reprinted letter-for-letter in these two volumes? Since part of the 1974 edition is reproduced here in Volume I (items 1-1339), and part in Volume II (the "1867" notebook), the publishers surely hoped and assumed that buyers of the 1985 edition would be buying both volumes, and simultaneously. Thus, printing the thirty-six-page section a second time, in Volume II, is gratuitous.

The publishers could also be asked to justify the quality of their product as a physical object. These two volumes are not well-made. After my first reading of Volume I (a somewhat lengthy exercise but one not physically taxing upon the book), the spine was cracked, and the top and bottom of the spine and the corners were frayed. The inside of the volume continues to look good; but ordinary library use is going to require within a short time that the volumes be re-bound. The contrast with the handsome Swedish bindings, still bright and firm after a decade of reference, is depressing.

But the most disappointing aspect of the 1985 edition is its failure to contain the analytical index which Björk in 1974 had indicated was "best left to the second volume."[14] The 1985 edition offers only a name-index, a single list of names of authors Hardy copied and paraphrased, and persons being referred to in the entries. It is not as complete as the several name-indexes (one for place-names; one for cited titles; one for "persons and groups"—both references and cited authors) in the 1974 edition. Both editions index Hardy's works referrred to in the notes (of course). It would have been useful had the 1985 name-index also contained, at a minimum, cited material—i.e., names of books and articles as well as the names of their authors.

An analytic index is crucial if this kind of project is to be made as useful as its contents justify. There are, obviously, pitfalls in an analytic index, predominantly the biases of the indexer. But the benefits would far outweigh the potential liabilities and make tolerable the shortcomings. Although a good index requires immense labors and time from the editor, it saves time and labor exponentially for everyone else. As things stand, the present index helps only with the study of specific human and individual influences on Hardy. To benefit from this important and essential publication (a judgment which no one working with Hardy would deny), one must read the entire range of readings and make notes about relevant matters. To

Using Hardy's Notebooks

develop a study of an *idea* in relation to Hardy, one must read the entire edition—and of course this must be repeated with any given idea or subject.

To indicate even a few of the broad topics that deserve multiple entries in an analytic index is, in practical terms, to suggest the immense value of the edition (at least potential value, since the absence of a good index means that fewer are likely to benefit from it than would otherwise be the case): pessimism, realism, idealism, naturalism, Positivism, Post Impressionism, aesthetics, suicide, Greek and Roman customs, Monism, Nature (or nature), evolution, relativity (several quotations refer to Einstein), music, myth, pragmatism. Very many of the entries deal with scientific information—more, it would seem, along the order of things Hardy would like to know (or remember) than anything he was likely to use in fiction or poetry. Similarly, without a good index the extent of Hardy's note-taking on socialism (or near-communism) is in effect "lost," as well as his attention to other political and social matters, because Hardy makes little use of them in creative contexts (although some have distinct substantive echoes in *Jude the Obscure*). Someone writing on feminism in Hardy would find an analytic index immensely helpful as a guide to many items. For example, items 1918-21 and their notes on differences between men and women as copied from George Egerton's *Keynotes* (published in 1893) and item 1923 on women as treacherous (or loyal). Item 2516, a complete essay named "The Woman of the Future," considers feminism and the history of sex role divergences: an intelligent statement, at once skeptical of claims of prehistoric matriarchies and sympathetic to aspirations to equality of opportunity that toward the end of the twentieth century still await fulfillment. Item 2522, a review about women in Greece and Rome, refers to contemporary (1907) feminism. (It also compares Hardy's *Tess of the d'Urbervilles* and Euripides.) There are also such items as 1267: "From those high windows behind the flower-pots young girls have looked out upon life, which their instincts told them was made for pleasure, but which year after year convinced them was, somehow or other, given over to pain" (a quotation from *John Inglesant*, which although not noted by Björk in this context has some bearing upon Hardy's description in *Jude the Obscure* of the gender-based fate of the women in the dormitory sleeping-room). While reading the edition I took notes on various topics such as those above. On one issue of close interest to Hardyans, tragedy, I noted some forty-one relevant items, many of which can be back-traced by looking up items in a name-index listed under "Aeschylus," "Shakespeare," and "Nietzsche," but not every reader will think to also look up items listed under "Vaughan," "Dryden," "Alfieri," or "Pater."

But such strictures as these, justified I think by the high expectations of work of this sort, do not lessen the achievement of this edition. Now, on to the "Facts" notebook.

Notes

1. *The Literary Notes of Thomas Hardy*, Volume I, in two fascicles ("Text" and "Notes"), edited by Lennart A. Björk (Göteborg, Sweden: Acta Universitatis Gothoburgensis, 1974).

2. Nor, despite the general praise accorded it in the reviews it received, has there been much commentary based on its contents in the secondary literature on Hardy since then. Björk himself, in "Hardy's Reading," *Thomas Hardy Annual No. 1,* ed. Norman Page (London: Macmillan, 1982), pp. 225-28, comments helpfully both on the 1974 material and on material that had not yet appeared.

3. Originally published under the name of his second wife Florence, but since the early 1940s recognized as having been written primarily by Hardy: *The Early Life of Thomas Hardy, 1840-1891* and *The Later Years of Thomas Hardy, 1892-1928* (London and New York: Macmillan, 1928 and 1930). These volumes were combined in *The Life of Thomas Hardy, 1840-1928* (London: Macmillan; New York: St. Martin's Press, 1962), the edition which Björk uses, and so are cited here as *Life*. Michael Millgate's recent edition of this autobiography, *The Life and Work of Thomas Hardy* (London: Macmillan; Athens: Univ. of Georgia Press, 1985), restores passages omitted from the typescript by Florence Hardy and removes (to an appendix) the additions to the typescript inserted by Florence and her advisers, thereby presenting Hardy's autobiography in the form prepared by Hardy himself.

4. *The Personal Notebooks of Thomas Hardy*, ed. Richard H. Taylor (London: Macmillan; New York: Columbia Univ. Press, 1979).

5. *Architectural Notebook*, ed. C.J.P. Beatty (Philadelphia: George S. Macmanus, 1966).

Using Hardy's Notebooks 19

6. The Dorset County Museum contains much still unpublished material of other sorts collected and retained by Hardy and his heirs—address books, reviews of his works and assessments of his career in journals, interviews in newspapers and journals, Emma Hardy's writings, music, visitor books, and other miscellanea. Some of these warrant publication, but none so much as those in (3) and (4) in the categories described above in the text, in particular the "Facts" notebook, comprising 200 and more folio leaves containing mostly handwritten excerpts from newspaper accounts of murders, suicides, ironic turns of fortune, crimes, trials, aristocratic and royal doings, and the like.

7. From DeLaura, " 'The Ache of Modernism' in Hardy's Later Novels," *ELH*, 34 (1967), 380. (Björk's citation to p. 280 in both 1974 and 1985 is erroneous.)

8. In "The Profitable Reading of Fiction," Hardy could be taking such a stand himself: "But though we are bound to consider by-motives like these [facts, quotations, "trifles of useful knowledge"] for reading fiction as praiseworthy enough where practicable . . . . Our true object is a lesson in life, mental enlargement from elements essential to the narratives themselves and from the reflections they engender" (rpt. in *Thomas Hardy's Personal Writings: Prefaces, Literary Opinions, Reminiscences*, ed. Harold Orel [Lawrence: Univ. of Kansas Press, 1966], pp. 113-14).

9. The material in these notebooks has long been known to exist, of course, and they have been drawn on by many scholars and critics who have been able to view them in the original or in microfilm copies held in many research libraries; but this does not alter the question of the value that justifies their being printed in full, with scholarly annotation.

10. Björk cites this as from *Life*, p. 255. I am unable to find it there, but I accept the phrase as Hardy's. Its gist occurs elsewhere in Hardy's critical writing: "Style, as far as the word is meant to express something more than literary finish, can only be treatment, and treatment depends upon the mental attitude of the novelist . . . . A writer who is not a mere imitator looks upon the world with his personal eyes, and in his peculiar moods; thence grows up his style, in the full sense of the term" ("The Profitable Reading of Fiction"; in Orel, *Thomas Hardy's Personal Writings*, p. 122).

11. "The Profitable Reading of Fiction," p. 113.

12. See Taylor, *Personal Notebooks of Thomas Hardy*, pp. 18-19.

13. In the format of 1974, "Literary Notes I" takes up 167 pages of text and the notes 183 pages; the "1867" notebook has 23 pages of text and 25 pages of notes.

14. *Literary Notes* (1974), p. ix.

Jane Austen and History

James Thompson

Margaret Kirkham. *Jane Austen: Feminism and Fiction.* Sussex: The Harvester Press/Totowa, N.J.: Barnes and Noble, 1983. xvii, 187 pp.

John Halperin. *The Life of Jane Austen.* Baltimore: The Johns Hopkins University Press. 1984. 399 pp.

David Monaghan, ed., *Jane Austen in a Social Context.* Totowa, N.J.: Barnes and Noble, 1981. 199 pp.

Mary Poovey. *The Proper Lady and the Woman Writer: Ideology as Style in the Works of Mary Wollstonecraft, Mary Shelley, and Jane Austen.* Chicago: University of Chicago Press, 1984. xxii, 287 pp.

LeRoy Smith. *Jane Austen and the Drama of Woman.* New York: St. Martin's Press, 1983. 205 pp.

Janet Todd, ed. *Jane Austen: New Perspectives. (Women in Literature.* NS Vol. 3. New York: Holmes and Meier, 1983. 293 pp.)

Austen studies have by now taken on all of the qualities of a well developed industry. Her six novels remain unusually popular for a writer studied by specialists as well as common readers, tempting one to think of Austen as something of a female Shakespeare, in that scholarly and popular interest seems to run merrily along separate but energetic lines. As is to be expected, the focus of more recent studies has become more and more particularized, from Jane Austen and education, to Austen and music, Austen and revolution,[1] and finally Austen and feminism. One happy consequence of this increasing specificity is fewer general interpretations, though it is true that there is no abating of the endless stream of introductions or general guides to Austen's fiction issued from smaller English presses. Two recent biographical offerings of this sort are *Jane Austen in Kent,* and *A Goodly Heritage, a History of Jane Austen's Family.*[2]

The number of new essays is obviously much greater and proportionately more burdensome, having reached the stage enjoyed or endured for a long time now in Shakespeare, Milton, Faulkner, and Joyce studies. At this point no one can seriously hope to read, absorb, and respond to all that is regularly produced by the field. Various responses to this situation are apparent in the notes to the works reviewed here: some try diligently to account for and acknowledge all predecessors (as does LeRoy Smith, for example), which can result in a full though cumbersome apparatus. Others make little attempt to acknowledge the work done before them. In *Jane Austen: New Perspectives,* for example, Jane Nardin's essay, "Children and Their Families in Jane Austen's Novels," focuses on parental inadequacy, yet there is no note to Mary Burgan's suggestive essay, "Mr. Bennett and the Failures of Fatherhood in Jane Austen's Novels."[3] A more serious omission mars an article which Zelda Boyd contributes on "The Language of Supposing," which is presented without reference to or apparent knowledge of Darrel Mansell's excellent book on the subject, *The Novels of Jane Austen.*[4] Margaret Kirkham appears not to know that Alison Sulloway published an essay on Austen and Wollstonecraft seven years before her own treatment of the subject.[5]

This flood of material takes the form of commentary or of criticism, for there has not been anything of substance added to the corpus of her work for decades, not even letters, with the single exception of B. C. Southam's attribution and publication of Austen's play based on *Sir Charles Grandison.*[6] Criticism, however, has been aided and abetted by recent works in women's studies and feminist literary history, criticism, and theory. It has certainly not hindered Austen studies to assert more forcefully than ever that Jane Austn is the first important or significant or major or masterful or full-fledged or what-honorific-you-will female author in English. As Janet Todd puts it, "Jane Austen is the first indubitably great woman writer in English."[7] Heightened interest in Austen as a woman writer has contributed to the more pervasive trend towards historicizing her novels. By and large, we appear to have abandoned the notion that because they were written on a lap-desk in a back parlor, hidden away from noisy nieces and nephews or nosy neighbors, and guarded by the squeaky hinge at Chawton Cottage, these novels were therefore sui generis, and so their history and origins do not need to be studied in order for us to understand them fully, as we do with the work of Milton or Wordsworth.

It is by now commonplace to credit Alistair Duckworth's *The Improvement of the Estate* with transforming Austen studies.[8] Duckworth's careful historicizing of Austen's novels has served as a powerful inhibition to the timeless and ahistorical Austen, such that subsequent students have been forced to consider the historical forces which shape her fiction. Before, when commenting on Austen's skill, it was common to observe how "universal" her novels seem. In an editon of three minor works, Margaret Drabble writes, "One looks in vain for obscure points of meaning or social detail in *Lady Susan*. There are none"; that is to say, only a pedant would think that Austen's fiction needs any sort of historical understanding, and so difference between her world and ours collapses in smug or cozy familiarity.[9] Tony Tanner writes similarly, though a bit more cautiously, in his edition of *Pride and Prejudice:* "It is perhaps worth commenting on just how little [one] requires, or would profit from, annotation in this book. References to topical events, or other writers, are almost totally suppressed, in spite of the fact that this was the age of Napoleon and the heyday of Romanticism. This perhaps contributes to the element of timelessness in the novel, even though it unmistakably reflects a certain kind of society at a certain historical moment."[10] With the exception of R. W. Chapman's standard Oxford Illustrated Austen, most editors of Austen say much the same thing. Such unexamined familiarity, however, has been thoroughly challenged by Marilyn Butler, in her detailed studies of the political climate in which Austen and other novelists, jacobin and conservative, wrote between 1790 and 1820.[11]

Though Austen studies have become increasingly historicized, what is meant by "History" or, often, appropriate "historical context," remains as vague and as various as ever.[12] It is not as if a previously innocent, aesthetically pure and timeless Austen has "fallen" into history but rather that Austen has fallen into a variety of conflicting histories, and the conflict is not simply between literary and social history. It is symptomatic of the problem here that intelligent and informed commentators such as Kirkham and Butler disagree violently about whether Austen is conservative or progressive, distantly dismissive or impassioned by the contemporary Man/Woman debate stirred up by Mary Wollstonecraft.[13] To employ Frederic Jameson's theory of the political unconscious, the history which gets exposed and restored to Austen's text varies enormously, for what passes under the name of history ranges from explorations of class conflict on down to the more ordinary annotation to the obscure social details which Drabble denies to Austen.[14]

The differing uses of history are particularly noticeable when comparing several recent studies of Austen and feminism under review here. Margaret Kirkham's *Jane Austen: Feminism and Fiction* and LeRoy Smith's *Jane Austen and the Drama of Woman* could not be more different, though both are concerned with Austen's focus on women: Kirkham's study centers largely around the contemporary debate, Wollstonecraft and her attack on Rousseau, whereas most of the authorities which Smith brings to bear are twentieth-century figures writing on the psychology of gender. As a consequence, Kirkham's interest is considerably more political, for she explores complex issues of repression (she notes, for example, that the Mansfield case, to which *Mansfield Park* may allude, was a celebrated legal decision dealing with slave ownership in England). Smith's interests however, are more psychological, for he is concerned with the "drama of woman," a phrase, from Simone de Beauvoir, which is, I think, significantly singular: it is not dramas of women because the drama is always the same, for all women, for all time. Kirkham focuses on the debate in the 1790s, arguing that

Austen and History

it was not possible for one to be as intelligent and informed as Austen evidently was and not be affected by and drawn into the polarization over the Rich/Poor and Man/Woman questions. Austen was born, lived, and died during a period of striking political upheaval, a time of revolution, war, and jacobinism, the period of Mary Wollstonecraft, Thomas Paine, William Cobbett, and, above all, the making of the English working class. As Kirkham puts it, "Jane Austen's heroines are not self-conscious feminists, yet they are all exemplary of the first claim of enlightenment feminism: that women share the same moral nature as men, ought to share the same moral status, and exercise the same responsibility for their own conduct" (p. 84).

This is not the argument which Smith makes. He does not argue from Austen's familiarity with Wollstonecraft or the Man/Woman controversy but rather from Austen's own insight into and quarrel with the patriarchical society into which she was born. Support for this moderate position is found "above all, on the evidence of the novels themselves" (p. 19), which leads into interpretations of each of the six novels.[15] Disapproval of patriarchy, however, comes to be presented as natural and eternal, basic to female nature: "All of the daughters of *Mansfield Park* are in danger of being forced to omit love from the pattern of courtship and adopt unnatural and self-defeating patterns of behaviour" (p. 116); "Fanny Price defends the birthright of every human being" (p. 128); *Emma* "ends in achievement of a true freedom and equality" (p. 132). The repetition of such words as "natural," "true," and "birthright" suggests that Austen's heroines are seeking timeless and eternal goals of "selfhood" and "personal fulfillment," desires which ought to be recognized as timebound and contemporary. Smith writes, "Austen describes a potential in women that is substantially modern in character" (p. 38), and in this fashion, the novels come to be about modern idealizations of the personal potential. Austen projects "a world of possibility in which the growth of sensitivity and candour points the way to mutual understanding, respect and accommodation between her male and female principals. Austen's vision . . . is a belief that individual men and women can attain mutual happiness through a discovery of the real self, their own and others' — a knowledge that her principals acquire and that unites them in a true society" (p. 45).

The path to this happiness, as one might expect, is by way of love, a subject in which Smith finds little complexity or ambiguity: "But Austen does not tailor or subvert the theme of love to accommodate social or economic realities. Personal integrity, independent of or in conflict with the pursuit of economic security, is championed, vindicated, and maintained" (p. 31). The views of John Halperin and Mary Poovey on the subject of love are very different. If Kirkham and Smith reveal moderate and more extreme sides of feminist literary criticism, the gulf is substantially wider between Poovey and Halperin.[16] Of all the work on Austen under consideration here, Halperin's *Life of Jane Austen* is the most traditional and conservative, while Poovey's *The Proper Lady* is the most innovative and theoretically sophisticated. This contrast is especially glaring over the issue of love. Halperin's overall task as biographer is one of demystifier, and so he describes Austen as neurasthenic, paranoid, disloyal, detached, "a caustic, disappointed woman," secretive, "emotionally cold," sneering, heartless, malicious, priggish, "incapable of love" — in short Jane Austen was "a woman deficient in feeling." According to Halperin, Austen's hostility can be explained as rage at her status as spinster, and so love is still paramount in Halperin's view of life and works, for the overall thesis of his biography is still *amor vincit omnia*. At bottom, Austen always wanted to get married but the right man never asked: "Where was the man for her? She found them only in her novels — in extraordinary men like Darcy, Henry Tilney, and Mr. Knightley. The men she met in real life suffered by comparison" (p. 72). While carefully acknowledging all of the limitations which circumscribed Jane Austen's life because she was a woman, Halperin nevertheless claims that she was bitter and unfulfilled because she lacked a man. This argument is not based on new evidence so much as on assertion: "It is impossible to believe that Jane Austen could ever have expected to remain a spinster or chosen such a fate willingly" (p. 54);

Austen and History

"Clearly enough, Darcy is the sort of man she [Jane Austen] was looking for" (p. 71). A remark in a letter — "there will be nobody worth dancing with, and nobody worth talking to" — is interpreted thus: "That is a note of sexual desperation, surely" (p. 82). "Jane Austen's own despondency is clear in this" — that is, it is clear in Catherine Moreland's having "reached the age of seventeen, without having seen one amiable youth who could call forth her sensibility" (p. 110). Emma's remarks on old maids lead to this conclusion: "If any of this is even remotely autobiographical, we may be excused for thinking that Jane Austen might never have been in love — that it was not her 'way' or in her 'nature,' as the passage above has it, to be in love with anyone. She may have been a woman incapable of love" (pp. 272-73).

Unlike Smith and Halperin, who seem to regard love as something natural and unchanging, Mary Poovey explores love and marriage as ideological phenomena, historical and timebound concepts and institutions which are determined by the material conditions of class:

> Romantic love purports to be completely "outside" ideology. It claims to be an inexplicable, irresistible, and possibly biological attraction that, in choosing its object, flouts hierarchy, the priorities, and the inequalities of class society. Romantic love seems to defy self-interest and calculation as completely as it ignores income and rank; as a consequence, if it articulates (or can be educated to articulate) an essentially unselfish, generous urge toward another person, it may serve as the agent of moral reform. . . . But it is crucial to recognize that the moral regeneration ideally promised by romantic love is as individual and private as its agent. In fact, the fundamental assumption of romantic love — and the reason it is so compatible with bourgeoise society — is that the personal can be kept from the social, that one's "self" can be fulfilled in spite of — and in isolation from — the demands of the marketplace. [p. 236]

Such insight leads to remarkably sophisticated discussions of the role of love and propriety in the novels, as here of *Pride and Prejudice*:

Elizabeth's eventual love for Darcy is legitimate because it springs not from the vanity we ordinarily associate with romantic expectations, but precisely from the mortification of pride. Yet because Elizabeth only belatedly realizes that she loves Darcy, her humbling does not entail a rejection of romantic love. Indeed, unaccountable, uncontrollable romantic love continues to play a role in *Pride and Prejudice* — in *Darcy's* desire for Elizabeth. This passion, which Austen notes but does not dwell on, is the subtextual force behind much of the action. . . . Romantic love remains the unexamined and unaccountable source of power in a novel preoccupied with various forms of social and psychological power and powerlessness. It not only overcomes all obstacles; it brings about a perfect society at the end of the novel. [p. 201]

Poovey's over-arching subject is the ideological relationship between propriety and sexuality, and the Proper Lady is the term given to a collective cultural image of idealized female (or more commonly feminine) behavior, which is, above all, decorous, self-effacing, and diffident. This insistence upon modesty, though, represses as it acknowledges female sexuality, a paradox which is neatly demonstrated in Colonel Brandon's narrative of the two Elizas in *Sense and Sensibility*: "The anxieties Brandon unwittingly reveals suggest that Austen at least intuits the twin imperatives that anchor patriarchal society: men want women to be passionate, but, because they fear the consequences of this appetite, they want to retain control over its expression" (pp. 191-92). Analysis of literary texts in terms of social expectations or definitions is not dissimilar from more traditional studies which examine Austen's appropriation of popular material like Hannah More's treatises on the education of women.[17] But Poovey sees the likes of John Gregory's *A Father's Legacy to his Daughters* or James Fordyce's *Sermons to Young Women*, as well as Wollstonecraft's *Mary*, as ideological constructs, whose idealized images of women are determined by the same economic base. Eighteenth-century women's fiction as a whole, and especially sentimental fiction with its stress on appropriately feminine feeling, is a conservative institution, replicating and recommending idealized models of behavior. The radical Wollstonecraft and conservative Austen

Austen and History

then present not dissimilar strategies for stabilizing the inherent tensions between the self-assertion of writing and the self-effacement or passivity demanded of the daughter, sister, or wife. By choosing such different figures, Poovey is able to demonstrate forcefully that however different the social situation and politics of each woman writer may be in this period, each one must respond to and somehow accommodate in her life and writing the cultural or ideological stereotypes of female conduct which dominate her class.

Finally, both recent collections of essays on Jane Austen, David Monaghan's *Jane Austen in a Social Context* and Janet Todd's *Jane Austen: New Perspectives*, are solid, useful volumes. The idea of considering Austen in a social context is perhaps not as radical as David Monaghan makes it out to be in his introduction, and in fact some of the essays in that volume do not have much to do with the subject. Marilyn Butler's essay on volume form is, as usual, informed and interesting, but it is not particularly social. The essay most directly on social history and social class, Ann Banfield's "The Influence of Place: Jane Austen and the Novel of Social Consciousness," seems the most forced, coming to this startling conclusion about *Mansfield Park*'s Fanny Price: "Social consciousness requires the assertion of self, of equality, and requires crossing the gulf of class — an act which reveals the barriers of class in overcoming them" (p. 39).[18] Janet Todd's collection is larger, longer, and more varied, with essays which range from relatives' reminiscence to Alistair Duckworth and Joel Weinsheimer's theoretical discussions of the state of Austen criticism. Overall, this is an excellent collection, a first-rate introduction to the state of Austen studies at the moment. The volume also illustrates some of the variety and versatility of recent feminist literary criticism. In this regard, Janet Todd's essay on Virginia Woolf's attitude towards Austen deserves mention, as does Nina Auerbach's suggestive essay on monstrosity in *Mansfield Park*. Though this admission does not reflect especially well on our profession, I found historian David Spring's essay on class in Austen (with his justification for the category of pseudo-gentry) the single most useful and informative piece in either volume.

Despite its mass Austen studies still have a long way to go before we can begin to restore and uncover the repressed history embodied in the novels. What passes for history too often is still conventional background study or annotation, as opposed to any real recovery of the forces that formed Austen's life and work. LeRoy Smith writes, "By virtually unanimous agreement Austen is a social novelist" (p. 19). Nevertheless, we have paid precious little attention to the details of that society. Raymond Williams's frustratingly brief model for such study in *The Country and the City* has been available for us for more than a decade. But only when such hard-core historical works as E. P. Thompson's *The Making of the English Working Class* are seen as *necessary* for a full understanding of *Pride and Prejudice*, will we be in a position to evaluate Austen as a social novelist.

Notes

1. See, for example, D. D. Devlin, *Jane Austen and Education* (New York: Barnes and Noble, 1975); Patrick Piggott, *The Innocent Diversion: A Study of Music in the Life and Writings of Jane Austen* (London: Douglas Cleverdon, 1979); Robert K. Wallace, *Jane Austen and Mozart: Classical Equilibrium in Fiction and Music* (Athens: Univ. of Georgia Press, 1983); Warren Roberts, *Jane Austen and the French Revolution* (New York: St. Martins, 1979).

2. David Waldron Smith, *Jane Austen in Kent* (Westerham, Kent: Hurtwood Publications, 1981); George Holbert, *A Goodly Heritage, A History of Jane Austen's Family* (Manchester: Carcanet New Press, 1983).

3. Mary Burgan, "Mr. Bennett and the Failures of Fatherhood in Jane Austen's Novels," *JEGP*, 74 (1975), 536-52.

4. Darrel Mansell, *The Novels of Jane Austen* (New York: Barnes and Noble, 1973).

5. Alison Sulloway, "Emma Woodhouse and *A Vindication of the Rights of Women*," *Wordsworth Circle*, 7 (1976), 320-32.

6. Brian Southam, ed., *Jane Austen's "Sir Charles Grandison"* (Oxford: Clarendon Press, 1980).

7. "Who's Afraid of Jane Austen," *Austen: New Perspectives*, p. 112.

8. Alistair Duckworth, *The Improvement of the Estate* (Baltimore: Johns Hopkins Univ. Press, 1971).

9. Margaret Drabble, ed. *Lady Susan/The Watsons/Sanditon* (Baltimore: Penguin Books, 1974), p. 215.

Austen and History

10. Tony Tanner, ed. *Pride and Prejudice* (Baltimore: Penguin Books, 1972), p. 397.

11. Marilyn Butler, *Jane Austen and the War of Ideas* (Oxford: Oxford Univ. Press, 1975); *Romantics, Rebels and Reactionaries: English Literature and its Background, 1760-1830* (New York: Oxford Univ. Press, 1982); in this regard, see also Warren Roberts's full-length study of Austen and the French Revolution.

12. This is much the same point which Alistair Duckworth makes in his essay, "Jane Austen and the Conflict of Interpretations," *Austen: New Perspectives*, pp. 39-52.

13. The two historians who have essays in these collections complain that literary students do not have sufficient historical knowledge to talk intelligently about Austen's society and social class, but the issue at hand is a much more basic question of what kinds of historical information ought to be brought to bear on this literature; see Christopher Kent, " 'Real Solemn History' and Social History," *Austen in a Social Context*, pp. 86-104; David Spring, "Interpreters of Jane Austen's Social World," *Austen: New Perspectives*, pp. 53-72. Both of these historians, rather oddly I think, regard their own material and discipline, that is, their particular interpretation of social history, as uncontroversial and not as open to debate as literary interpretation.

14. Frederic Jameson, *The Political Unconscious, Narrative as a Socially Symbolic Act* (Ithaca: Cornell Univ. Press, 1981), pp. 17-102.

15. Smith explicitly rejects the more radical readings of a subversive Austen with a conservative disguise or "cover story" from Sandra M. Gilbert and Susan Gubar, *The Madwoman in the Attic: The Woman Writer and the Nineteenth-Century Literary Imagination* (New Haven: Yale Univ. Press, 1979), pp. 146-183.

16. John Halperin's study is a biography, and so it is somewhat unfair to consider it on equal grounds with these other full-length critical studies. However, a good portion of *The Life of Jane Austen* is devoted to interpretation of the novels, and much of that interpretation is not terribly sophisticated: *Pride and Prejudice* "is about the difference between true and false moral values. It is about the difference between the appearance of things, the ways in which they may be perceived, and their true reality, the ways in which they exist" (p. 69). It should be pointed out as well that Mary Poovey's book also treats Mary Wollstonecraft and Mary Shelley, and the particular excellence of this study lies in Poovey's ability to see these three very diverse writers in a consistent light, an aspect of *The Proper Lady* which does not receive justice here.

17. See, for example, Joyce Hemlow, "Fanny Burney and the Courtesy Books" (*PMLA* 65, [1950], 732-61); Hazel Mews, *Frail Vessels, Woman's Role in Women's Novels* (London: The Athlone Press, 1969); Kenneth Moler, *Jane Austen's Art of Allusion* (Lincoln: Univ. of Nebraska Press, 1968); David Monaghan, "Jane Austen and the Position of Women," *Austen in a Social Context*, pp. 105-21.

18. Raymond Williams's discussion of Austen is cited in the notes to this essay, but it has not been attended to very carefully. See *The Country and the City* (New York: Oxford Univ. Press, 1973), pp. 108-19, particularly p. 117: "All her discrimination is, understandably, internal and exclusive. She is concerned with the conduct of people who, in the complications of improvement, are repeatedly trying to make themselves into a class. But where only one class is seen, no classes are seen."

Understanding Modernism

Harvey Gross

Michael H. Levenson, *A Genealogy of Modernism: A Study of English Literary Doctrine, 1908-1922*. Cambridge: Cambridge University Press, 1984. xi, 250 pp.

Jeffrey M. Perl, *The Tradition of Return: The Implicit History of Modern Literature*. Princeton: Princeton University Press, 1984. xii, 325 pp.

Ricardo J. Quinones, *Mapping Literary Modernism: Time and Development*. Princeton: Princeton University Press. ix, 303 pp.

1. *The Quarrel of Modernism with History*

Three recent books on Modernism by Michael Levenson, Jeffrey Perl, and Ricardo Quinones not only provoke our interest in the various movements, schools, and other emanations from the Modernist *Zeitgeist*; they also mark the reappearance of that consistently maligned and perennially lamented discipline: literary history. A generation or more ago, René Wellek and Austin Warren, in their influential *Theory of Literature* (1949), observed, "Most leading histories of literature are either histories of civilization or collections of critical essays. One type is not a history of *art*; the other not a *history* of art."[1] In the decades following *Theory of Literature* that loose and benign hegemony we call the New Criticism struck antihistorical or ahistorical postures. The various formalisms maintained belief in the "historical" simultaneity of all literary work; such a stance recalled the Crocean doctrine that understood history as "the self-knowledge of the living mind."[2] When that living mind possessed the wit and imagination of Northrop Frye, there followed the staggering performance of the *Anatomy of Criticism* where the totality of western literature appears in recurring types, genres, and myths. Diachronic history gives way to the great succession of cycles, to the Eternal Return of forms and themes.

During the 60s and 70s we witnessed in the movements of structuralism, semiotics, and deconstruction elaborate refinements of the anti-historical approaches to literary study. "Theory," to use the currently privileged and fashionable term, prefers not to deal with a writer's *oeuvre* in its historical development and particularity but rather with his "texts." Unfortunately our theorists have become mired in the Slough of Despond of ontology; there is no agreement on where a text has its true *situs:* on the printed page, in the intentions of the writer, or through the interpretive activity of reader and critic. While there is much talk of texts and "textuality," literary texts themselves have achieved a disembodied, ghostly existence. If the New Criticism established the aesthetic autonomy of the text, current "theory" has performed a magician's act of transmogrification: it has separated the text from its historical matrix, and substituted the concerns of philosophy for the primary critical acts of analysis, interpretation, and judgment.

The displacement of history from the newest criticism continues a tradition of Modernism itself: the late nineteenth-century perception that history had become unfathomable, even dangerous. Hegel's concept of history as a "rational" process, organic, eschatological, and ultimately redemptive, was challenged by beliefs that viewed history as contingent, a malign and meaningless power. Nietzsche saw history as an enemy to the human capacity for action; by confronting men with the grandeur of the past, history diminished their status and turned them into gray-headed epigones. As the nineteenth century moved toward its end, the cries of anguish grew louder: the pressures of unremitting technological innovation and cultural change had, to use Carl Schorske's image, cut "the diachronic line, the cord of consciousness that linked . . . present pursuits . . . to past concerns . . . ."[3] It seemed difficult, perhaps impossible to sift the facts and make the connections that once constituted historical truth. To Henry Adams, "his historical

Understanding Modernism

neck broken by the sudden irruption of forces totally new," history was indeterminate energy rather than a discipline offering insight and hope.[4]

From Nietzsche's Untimely Meditation *Vom Nutzen und Nachteil der Historie für das Leben* (*On the Use and Disadvantage of History for Life*, 1874) to Michel Foucault's assertion that "the notion of discontinuity assumes a major role in the historical disciplines,"[5] we can trace the development of the idea that modernity and history are ontological contradictions. If we acknowledge the tangled and inchoate nature of the modern world — its heterogeneity, its baffling complexity, its confusions of belief and ideology — we realize that history no longer fulfills its traditional functions of memory, interpretation, and critique. Nor does history, as Hegel argued, reveal and justify God's ways to men. Nietzsche declared the hour was too late to read history as a theodicy: "Interpreting history in honor of some divine reason, as a continual testimony of a moral world order and ultimate moral purposes . . . that is *all over now*."[6]

The crisis in historical thought I have been describing marks the starting point for a theory of Modernism. Thus Ricardo Quinones, in his *Mapping Literary Modernism: Time and Development* remarks: "The primary Modernist encounter is with history, and not only with history as a discipline of knowledge but with historical values, the very flow and continuities of life itself, or, at least, the particular Western construction that was placed on that flow since the time of the Renaissance. At their points of departure, following Nietzsche, Modernists rejected historical values and historical knowledge as linear development. This is the substance of the Modernist quarrel with the nineteenth century" (p. 256). Professor Quinones's critical discipline is literary history, his particular "approach" that of comparative literature. If it seems ironic that the instrument for understanding Modernism is a discipline rooted in the methodologies of historical investigation, we must recognize that the Modernist assault on history was, in part, a normal conflict of the generations; and that the assault was polemical and hyperbolic. More important, it is a central insight of the three scholars whose books are reviewed here that the works of Modernism have entered into history, and into the established literary order. Modernism can no longer be denounced as a program aimed at the overthrow of tradition, or a doctrine of anarchic innovation and ceaseless stylistic experimentation. As a literary and cultural force Modernism has achieved its own integrity and evolved its own traditions.

Quinones understands Modernism as a total European phenomenon; he has peopled the world of his discourse with Hans Castorp and Stephen Dedalus, with Joseph K. and Paul Morel. His comparatist method reveals, for example, the close intellectual proximity of Mann's Naphta to the anti-humanist program of T. E. Hulme: "Hulme's accusations are precisely the charges that Naphta levels at Settembrini (indicating that Mann's perception of the crisis of humanism was indeed integral to Anglo-American as well as to continental literature): 'Doesn't your monism bore you? . . . Dualism, antithesis, is the moving, the passionate, the dialetic principle of all Spirit. All monism is tedious . . . . You don't want even Absolute Spirit. You only want to have spirit synonymous with democratic progress' " (p.145).

Cruical to Quinones's argument is his correct insistence that Modernism was not merely a diachronic extension and expansion of nineteenth-century Romantic tendencies into the twentieth century, but rather a unique development with its own themes and styles: "If one were to follow a line of continuous development from Romanticism one could arrive at Tennyson or Thomas Hardy, but one could never arrive at Leopold Bloom or *The Waste Land*. Despite historical indebtedness and beyond any unconscious assimilation, something new was being done. To slight that change is to diminish the stature of all innovators as well as to ignore the importance of discontinuity, mutation itself, in historical development" (p. 127). The dialectic of stability and change, of tradition and innovation, of continuity and discontinuity that Quinones outlines has its great antecedent in the *Preface* to Hegel's *Phenomenology of Spirit*. In his rendering of the titanic struggle of ideas and actions that brought

Understanding Modernism

on the French Revolution, Hegel introduces his metaphor of gestation and birth:

Our epoch is a birth-time and a period of transition. The spirit of man has broken with the old order of things . . . and is in the mind to let them all sink into the depths of the past . . . it is here as in the example of the birth of a child; after a long period of nutrition in silence, the continuity of the gradual growth in size, of quantitative change, is suddenly cut short by the first breath drawn—there is a break in the process, a qualitative change—and the child is born. In like manner the spirit of the time, growing slowly and quietly ripe for the new form it is to assume, disintegrates one fragment after another of the structure of the previous world.[7]

Theodor Adorno has written a brilliant gloss on this, one of Hegel's most penetrating texts. Adorno writes: "Hegel taught that wherever something new becomes visible, immediate, striking, authentic, a long process of formation has preceded it and it has now merely thrown off its shell. Only that which has been nourished with the life blood of the tradition can possibly have the power to confront it authentically; the rest becomes the helpless prey of forces which it has failed to overcome sufficiently within itself."[8]

"Only that which has been nourished with the life-blood of the tradition can possibly have the power to confront it authentically . . . ." This assertion might stand as a motto at the head of all discussions of the connections between historical break and continuity, of Modernism and its dependence on the past. Adorno is speaking specifically of Arnold Schoenberg's breakthrough, during the years 1906-1909, to a new musical idiom and syntax which repudiated the traditional balance between consonance and dissonance and the three-hundred-year hegemony of tonal harmony. Schoenberg's successful confrontation of the tonal tradition was possible because his creative development absorbed then transcended the musical inheritance of the late nineteenth century and its sources in the "schools" of both Brahms and Wagner. Similarly, Eliot's re-shaping of the idiom and syntax of Anglo-American poetry rested on his discovery of a "useable past" in the compositional methods of French Symbolism and the loosened rhythms of the

Jacobean dramatists. It is worth emphasizing that Schoenberg and Eliot made their challenges to tradition within two or three years of each other; this fact gives substance to Ortega's belief in the "compact unity" of historical epochs and the appearance of distinct period styles in all the arts.[9]

2. *Myth: The Backward Look*

> ... not forgetting
> Something that is probably quite ineffable:
> The backward look behind the assurance
> Of recorded history, the backward half-look
> Over the shoulder, towards the primitive terror.
>
> — T. S. Eliot, *The Dry Salvages*

Adorno explains that tradition is not only the artist's conscious remembrance and employment of the historical past, but is also the potent "recollection of something unconscious, indeed repressed."[10] Under the layers of recorded history lie the deeper strata of myth and primitive culture — strata that were penetrated by Frazer and Freud in *The Golden Bough* and *Totem and Taboo*. Freud maintained that the fear-dominated psyche of prehistoric man cast light on the neurotic behavior patterns of historic man. Conversely, these patterns of neurotic behavior revealed the persistent structure of primitive thought. Frazer and Freud exerted a powerful influence during the early decades of Modernism. Three Modernist masterpieces made deliberate use of materials derived from anthropological and psychoanalytical sources. Picasso's *Les Demoiselles d'Avignon* (1907), Stravinsky's *Le Sacre du Printemps* (1913), and Eliot's *The Waste Land* (1922) evoke a primordial world of blood sacrifice, fertility rites, and slain and risen gods. Picasso's African masks, Stravinsky's pounding rhythms and crashing dissonances, and Eliot's backward journey to the Grail Castle suggest the extent to which primitivism entered the rich and varied context of Modernism. In his notes to *The Waste Land*, Eliot acknowledges his debts to Frazer and Jesse Weston; and in an influential essay

"*Ulysses*, Order, and Myth" (1923), he sees in the "mythical method" a new literary technique: "Instead of narrative method, we may now use the mythical method."

In *A Genealogy of Modernism: A Study of English Literary Doctrine, 1908-1922*, Michael Levenson asks, "But why 'Instead of?' Myth is not ordinarily opposed to narrative . . . " (p. 197). Levenson thus sets forth a penetrating critique of *The Waste Land* — one of the best I have read — which reveals how the poem is a product "of the anthropological habit of mind, if that is broadly conceived, so as to designate the *comparatist* temperament, which retains the widest angle of vision, which refuses to bestow privilege upon any culture or epoch, which regards no human manifestation as too lowly to bear study, which captures the 'primitive' and the 'civilized' in the same glance" (p. 206). For Eliot the mythical method is more than a compositional strategy that evades conventional narrative; it signals the Modernist yearning for new orders, political as well as literary, that might recover an "associated sensibility" and revive the putative European cultural unity that had decayed during the Enlightenment and collapsed during the disastrous nineteenth century. The Modernist concern with myth was essentially an attempt to recover *ways of feeling* that modernity and its urban, technologically dominated culture had lost or suppressed. Ernst Cassirer makes the emphatic assertion that myth "is an offspring of emotion and its emotional background imbues all its productions with its own specific color. Primitive man by no means lacks the ability to grasp the empirical differences of things. But in his conception of nature and life all these differences are obliterated by a stronger feeling: the deep conviction of a fundamental and indelible *solidarity of life* that bridges over the multiplicity and variety of its single forms."[11]

A deep nostalgia colors the Modernist concern with myth. Not surprisingly, it turned out to be a religious quest. Writers as ideologically opposed as D. H. Lawrence and T. S. Eliot searched for the elusive "solidarity of life." Lawrence evoked the blood religion of the Aztecs (*The Plumed Serpent*); and near the end of his life he wrote a blasphemous retelling of the Christ mythos (*The Man Who Died*). Eliot was a God-seeker in the strenuous Jansenist tradition. From the sadomasochism of the unpublished "The Love Song of St. Sebastian," to the crucifixion of Celia Coplestone in *The Cocktail Party*, Eliot's path was that of a man "hungry of an imagined martyrdom."[12]

3. *Return and Politics*

The programs of the various Modernist movements declared their independence from the immediate nineteenth-century past and sought to redefine the substance of tradition. Nietzsche, as the leading propagandist of romantic Hellenism, rejected the "monumental history" of his contemporaries and affirmed an "heroic affinity of the present with an extremity of history": his vision of the primitive Greek world presided over by the figure of Dionysius.[13] Nietzsche is thus "modern" according to the specific meaning Jürgen Habermas assigns to the term: "*Modern* appeared and reappeared exactly during those periods in Europe when the consciousness of a new epoch formed itself through a renewed relationship to the ancients — whenever, moreover, antiquity was considered a model to be recovered through some kind of imitation."[14]

In his *The Tradition of Return: The Implicit History of Modern Literature* Jeffrey Perl reads Modernism in the context of what he names *nostos* ideologies, and the ongoing efforts of Modernist writers to recover a significant and usable past. *Nostos* is Greek for the return home, to one's spiritual origins. Ulysses' painful, much delayed return to Ithaca suggests to Perl a pattern for understanding the dynamics of Modernism; in an age when the typical artist has been a political as well as spiritual exile and has been driven "on literal voyages after the past," Perl asks: "Is modern history, then, the record of our culture's process of return?" (p. 32). Pound loudly announced the Modernist battle cry, "Make it New," and returned to twelfth-century Provence for models of craft and innovation. Eliot, at a crucial moment in his career, proclaimed a new "classicism" that might offer a critique of a society "worm-eaten with Liberalism." Unfortunately, Eliot's "classicism" was heavily influenced by the political program of Charles Maurras and the proto-fascistic *L'Action Française*. Maurras—a vicious anti-Semite and anti-Dreyfusard—was a man with a gift for verbal and physical violence. Early in his years as editor of *The Criterion* Eliot took it upon himself to be Maurras' great disciple and defender—even after the Holy See had placed his books and *L'Action Française* on the Index. [15]

The political connections between Eliot and Maurras and between Pound and Mussolini pose one of the most frequently worried questions asked of Modernism: how do we explain the attraction that fascism and protofascism exerted on European intellectuals of the 20s and 30s? Perl admits, "The question is so complicated that every case presented on every side contains at least a partial truth—and yet there is a sense in which the whole issue (at least as regards Pound) is unnervingly simple" (p. 278). Pound took literally Shelley's notion of the destiny of the modern poet, but refused the role of being merely an *unacknowledged legislator*. He saw the poet's task as nothing less than the renovation of modern society so that optimum conditions for the proper nurture of culture might prevail. Perl argues that Pound's ideas on society and culture were prefigured in the historical work of Jacob Burckhardt and his studies in the Renaissance. It was Burckhardt's notion of "the state as a work of art" which was to have, in Perl's words, "an awful future, one that would culminate in the political career of Ezra Pound and other cultural fascists" (p. 257).

The conventional wisdom on the matter of Pound's fascism tells us that he was genuinely convinced that Mussolini was the Lorenzo de Medici of the twentieth century. (I offer this as explanation, not as justification.) Pound's admiration for Mussolini was based on the belief that poets would play leading roles in the fascist polity, and that the renovation of *Kulchur* was an item of the first priority on the fascist program. But underlying his rhetoric of praise for Mussolini was a pervasive cultural pessimism, shading into nihilism, that had afflicted other European intellectuals at least since the fin-de-siècle. In her comments on the Dreyfus Affair, Hannah Arendt points out that the leading younger anti-Dreyfusards (Barrès, Maurras, and Daudet) "had . . . recently emerged from a ruinous and decadent cult of estheticism [and] saw in the mob a living expression of virile and primitive 'strengths.' It was they and their theories which first identified the mob with the people and converted its leaders into national heroes. It was their philosophy of pessimism and their delight in doom that was the first sign of the imminent collapse of the European intelligentsia."[16]

Walter Benjamin characterizes the fascist aura and its politics of self-destruction in a celebrated *aperçu*: " '*Fiat ars—pereat mundus*' [Let there be art—let the world perish] says fascism, and, as Marinetti admits, expects war to supply the artistic gratification of a sense perception that has been changed by technology. This is evidently the consummation of *'l'art pour art.'* Mankind, which in Homer's time was an object of contemplation for the Olympian gods, now is one for itself. Its self-alienation has reached such a degree that it can experience its own destruction as an aesthetic pleasure of the first order. This is the situation of politics which Fascism is rendering aesthetic. Communism responds by politicizing art."[17] Benjamin's argument directs our way toward an understanding of the impossibly complicated question of Modernism's lurch toward the extreme right. With aphoristic concision Benjamin makes the connections between aestheticism and barbarism, between the revolutionary-reactionary nature of fascist ideology, and its ultimate commitment to self-destruction.

It would, however, be mistaken to insist on any simple connection between an aestheticized politics and the horrors of totalitarianism. Perl cautions that "the modernism/fascism association was not international and at no time involved a necessary correlation" (p. 278). We can only note briefly some glaring contradictions. Both the Nazis and Communists proscribed modernist art and for the same reasons: it expressed "bourgeois decadence"; it used formalist techniques and difficult syntaxes that placed it outside the comprehension of "the people" and the control of their rulers. Most important, as Adorno argues, it expressed and thus exposed the evils of totalitarianism. He speaks here of Schoenberg's atonal and twelvetone work, but what he says is certainly applicable to Picasso's *Guernica* or Mann's *Doktor Faustus*: "The basis of the isolation of radical modern music is not its asocial, but precisely its social substance . . . it points out the ills of society rather than sublimating those ills into a deceptive humanitarianism . . . ."[18]

4. *The Integrity of Modernism*

> But I maintain that each period is immediate vis-à-vis God, and that its value depends not at all on what followed from it, but rather on its own existence, on its own self.
>
> —Leopold von Ranke, 1854

Taken together, these books by Levenson, Perl, and Quinones approach from differing perspectives and with differing thematic linkages and concerns a "discrimination of the modernism."[19] Quinones presents a drawing of boundaries, a canon of major work, and an eloquent hymn of praise to "the enduring longevity of Modernism" (p. 249). He is intent on viewing the work of Lawrence, Mann, Proust, Joyce, and Eliot as products of a central European consciousness: works that not only display richness of language and originality of structure, but also function as critique and prophecy. The Modernists "were committed to depicting the changing truths of their time and experience, but they also had a remarkable sense of history, understood in a critical and comprehensive way" (p. 252).

Levenson's *Genealogy* surveys a narrower field and brings into sharp focus "a specific geographic centre during a confined period" (p. x). He is concerned with the establishment of Modernism as an acknowledged cultural presence on the English literary scene. The struggle for Modernism begins with the formulations of T. E. Hulme during the years 1908-1911; it achieves its particular victory with the publication of *The Waste Land* in 1922, and, in the same year, with Eliot assuming the editorship of the *Criterion*. These two events mark "the institutionalization of the movement, its accession to cultural legitimacy" (p. 213). Levenson's closely written account gives us a large *dramatis personae*, some of whom are quite familiar actors in the play of Modernism: Pound, Hulme, Wyndham Lewis, and Eliot. He also devotes a chapter to the influence of Ford Madox Ford and his contributions to Modernist doctrine and sets him beside Hulme as "an exemplar of the early development of modernism" (p. 48). Ford provides a nexus between the tradition of the highly "conscious" writers of the fin-de-siècle—Flaubert, Conrad, James—and the London avant-garde. Through Hulme, Levenson traces the impact of continental philosophy on the burgeoning Modernism of the pre-World War I period: the currents of influence transmitted through the work of Worringer, Bergson, and Husserl.

Perl projects a different vision of literary history. Unlike Quinones's "mapping," with its detailed and loving attention to Modernist texts, or Levenson's meticulous diachrony, with its orderly sequences and clear *telos*—the ultimate legitimation of Modernism—Perl's concerns are meta-historical. His controlling trope of *return* not only plots the course of modern history or the progress of modern culture: it also functions in a truly polysemous way in a wide range of contexts. Among the *nostos* ideologies are the classical myth of the Golden Age and its Hebraic counterpart with its triadic structure of Eden, Fall, and Redemption. The late psychological writings of Freud, with their darker meditations on the death-instincts, speculate that the organism seeks a *return* to its inorganic state. The figure of return confronts the Modernist vision everywhere, especially if that vision is armed with prior knowledge. As Perl sees it, *return* may be both historical fact and literary fiction: "Like the history of our civilization, from which they sometimes appear to be indistinguishable, the ideologies of return make a compelling story: so compelling, in fact, that the twentieth century may have adjusted its own life to conform with the contours of the narrative. And whether fictitious or factual, spontaneous or artistically arranged, this is an old-fashioned story, one with a moral" (p. 281).

The moral of Perl's story, as well as the testimony of Quinones and Levenson, is that many roads can return us to the Ithaca of history. Modernism was no single event; under its name we can subsume many moments, many movements, and many styles.

It reveals great diversity at crucial points in its development: Proust and Mann, Debussy and Mahler were nearly exact contemporaries. At other points it seems to testify to Ortega's concept of the "compact unity" which every distinct historical epoch discloses.[20] At one great creative moment of Modernism —the period 1905-1914— Schoenberg dismantled tonality, Eliot introduced startling techniques of fragmentation and discontinuity, and Kandinsky painted the first completely non-representational pictures. It is difficult not to attribute these nearly simultaneous shifts in style to the shaping hand of the Time Spirit.

The one indisputible characteristic of Modernism has been its epochal self-consciousness, its inflamed sensitivity to a perhaps only imagined *Zeitgeist*. Whether it was Stendhal labeling *The Red and the Black, A Chronicle of the Nineteenth Century*, or Eliot urging that a poet have a sense of his own age, Modernism has understood itself as inhabiting a specific historical space. Nietzsche may have objected to modernity — its culture, its politics, its feebleness in belief—but he could not avoid composing his polemics in the ironic mode: in what was to become (partially through his own vast influence) the prevailing rhetorical style of Modernism. The integrity of Modernism has been affirmed by its continuing self-reification; we are modern men and women and never cease reminding ourselves of that fact. Modernism developed along with the historicizing of European consciousness. We cannot use a vocabulary that includes such terms as *Renaissance* or *Enlightenment* without acknowledging their historical validity: the complex distinctions and differences they signify. Nor does our understanding of Modernism require less.

Notes

1. René Wellek and Austin Warren, *Theory of Literature*, third edition (New York: Harcourt Brace Jovanovich, 1962), p. 253.

2. See R. G. Collingwood, *The Idea of History* (New York: Oxford Univ. Press, 1956), p. 202.

3. Carl Schorske, *Fin-de-Siècle Vienna* (New York: Alfred A. Knopf, 1980), p. xx.

4. See *The Education of Henry Adams* (New York: The Modern Library, 1931), p. 382.

5. Michel Foucault, *The Archaeology of Knowledge* (New York: Harper & Row), p. 8.

6. Friedrich Nietzsche, *The Gay Science*, trans. Walter Kaufmann (New York: Random House, 1974), p. 307.

7. G.W.F. Hegel, *The Phenomenology of Mind*, trans. J. B. Baillie (New York: Harper & Row, 1967), p. 75.

8. T. W. Adorno, *Prisms*, trans. Samuel and Schierry Weber (London: Neville Spearman, 1967), p. 155.

9. Ortega y Gasset, *The Dehumanization of Art* (Garden City, N.J.: Doubleday Anchor, 1956), p. 4.

10. Adorno, *Prisms*, p. 155.

11. Ernst Cassirer, *An Essay on Man* (New Haven: Yale Univ. Press, 1944), p. 109.

12. See my article, "The Figure of St. Sebastian," *The Southern Review*, 21, 4 (Autumn 1985), 974-84.

13. See Jürgen Habermas, "Modernity versus Post-modernity," *New German Critique*, 22 (1981), p. 5.

14. *Ibid.*

15. Eliot later modified his views on Maurras; see *To Criticize the Critic* (New York: Farrar, Straus & Giroux, 1965), pp. 142-43.

16. Hannah Arendt, *The Origins of Totalitarianism* (New York: Harcourt, Brace and Company, 1951), p. 112.

17. Walter Benjamin, *Illuminations* (New York: Harcourt, Brace & World, 1968), p. 244.

18. T. W. Adorno, *The Philosophy of Modern Music*, trans. Anne G. Mitchell and Wesley V. Blomster (New York: The Seabury Press, 1973), p. 131.

19. I cannot recall who first used the term "discrimination of the modernisms." Those who have used it obviously intended an analogy with A. O. Lovejoy's celebrated essay "On the Discrimination of the Romanticisms." See his *Essays in the History of Ideas* (Baltimore: Johns Hopkins Univ. Press, 1948), pp. 228-53.

20. Ortega y Gasset, *The Dehumanization of Art*, p. 4.

The "Wordsworth Industry" Revisited

John E. Jordan

David McCracken. *Wordsworth and the Lake District: A Guide to the Poems and Their Places.* Oxford, New York: Oxford University Press, 1984. xviii, 300 pp.

Kenneth R. Johnston. *Wordsworth and* The Recluse. New Haven and London: Yale University Press, 1984. xxxii, 397 pp.

James A. W. Heffernan. *The Re-Creation of Landscape: A Study of Wordsworth, Coleridge, Constable, and Turner.* Hanover and London: University Press of New England, 1984. xxii, 256 pp.

One way of thinking about the three works I consider together in this piece is to see them as covering the gamut of the "Wordsworth Industry"—a phrase that Richard Wordsworth has recently refurbished *(The Wordsworth Circle* XIII [Fall 1982], 167). As he well notes, "industry" can be a virtue. And anyone who has studied the poet's onerous manuscripts, full of visions and revisions and multiple repeated efforts, or remembers the leechgatherer in "Resolution and Independence," knows that sometimes Wordsworth both practiced and preached "industry." Of course he also saw a place for "happy idleness" ("A narrow girdle of rough stones and crags," 68). But there is a difference between one's valuing industriousness and one's reaction to having a whole industry built around oneself. At least since Keats complained of dangerous "whims of an Egotist," Wordsworth has been accused of being powerfully self-centered. Accordingly it can be argued that the "Wordsworth Industry" is entirely appropriate to his "egotistical sublime." Modesty was hardly one of his gifts: there are too many stories of his unflattering comments about other writers or of such a remark as his telling Aubrey de Vere, "Indeed I have hardly ever known any one but myself who had a true eye for Nature, one that thoroughly understood her meanings and her teachings"—but even then he went on to note an exception and assure de Vere that Frederick Faber, a young clergyman at Ambleside, "Had not only as good an eye for Nature as I have, but even a better one" (quoted by David McCracken, p. 186). Perhaps, therefore, some qualification of Wordsworth's reputation as an egotist is in order. Note, for example, the alarm he expressed to Sir George Beaumont about the just finished *Prelude*: "a thing unprecedented in Literary history that a man should talk so much about himself" (1 May 1805), his repugnance at the suggestion that his portrait be attached to his published poems ("the notion to me is intolerable" [to George Huntly Gordon, 30 May 1830]), and his insistence that his poems not be published in the chronological order of composition because such an arrangement would place too much emphasis on the author's role. At least, I think, we are entitled to speculate what Wordsworth would have made of all the activity that has clustered around him, centering in what is now called "Cumbria"—from tourists buying pencils stamped "Wordsworth" or throwing coins in Wordsworth "Wishing Wells" and piously pilgrimaging to every spot that can be associated with his life or writings, to scholars assiduously studying every squiggle or meticulously transcribing every misspelling of his often illegible manuscripts. Some years ago I attended a ceremony in Grasmere Church (a building and an institution which the poet revered, but where he rarely attended) when the ancient structure began to tremble. I have lived in California long enough that I recognized an earthquake—and thought apprehensively of Wordsworth's wonderful line: "The earthquake is not satisfied at once" (*The Prelude*, X, 84). But I confess I momentarily considered the possibility that out in the churchyard Wordsworth was turning over in his grave. Although heroic efforts have been made to preserve the amenities of the district (a resident once complained to me that he could not see "Telly" because he was not allowed to show an antenna on his roof), the "Wordsworth Industry" has undoubtedly helped bring the highspeed access roads ("Motorways" they call them

The "Wordsworth Industry" 49

in England) and trailer (caravan) parks—and all that Wordsworth was objecting to in his "On the Projected Kendal and Windermere Railway": "Is there no nook of English ground secure from rash assault?" (*Misc. Sonnets*, XLV, 1-2). We recall also his "Admonition. Intended more particularly for the perusal of those who may have happened to be enamoured of some beautiful place of Retreat, in the Country of the Lakes."

> Well may'st thou halt—and gaze with brightening eye!
> The lovely Cottage in the guardian nook
> Hath stirred thee deeply; with its own dear brook,
> Its own small pasture, almost its own sky!
> But covet not the Abode;—forbear to sigh,
> As many do, repining while they look;
> Intruders—who would tear from Nature's book
> This precious leaf, with harsh impiety.
> Think what the Home must be if it were thine,
> Even thine, though few thy wants!—Roof, window, door,
> The very flowers sacred to the Poor,
> The roses to the porch which they entwine:
> Yea, all, that now enchants thee, from the day
> On which it should be touched, would melt away.
> [*Misc. Sonnets*, II]

Of course Wordsworth himself contributed to such activity. He had been "enamoured of some beautiful place of Retreat" and owned at different times three pieces of land in the Lake District, although he never built on any, never owned his own home in the "Country of the Lakes." Certainly he approved of proper tourists: he was often one, and he obviously valued the professional tourist, the Peddlar, the "Wanderer," his alterego in *The Excursion*. Furthermore, he also wrote a guide to the lakes, published first anonymously in 1810 as an introduction to *Select Views in Cumberland, Westmoreland, and Lancaster* by Rev. Joseph Wilkinson, next attached slightly revised to *The River Duddon Sonnets* in 1820 as *A Topographical Description of the Country of the Lakes in the North of England*, then separately, further revised as *A Description of the Scenery of the Lakes . . .* , then more elaborately as *A Guide Through the*

District of the Lakes in the North of England in 1835, and with accretions and assistance in three more editions before the poet died.

David McCracken's book is in this busy tradition, except that the Lakes have now become important because of Wordsworth's poems: *Wordsworth and the Lake District: A Guide to the Poems and Their Places*. This puts McCracken's work somewhere between the *Guide* and William Knight's *The English Lake District as Interpreted in the Poems of Wordsworth* (1878, 1891). Working on the premise that "no other great poet has influenced our consciousness of an English place as much as Wordsworth has done of the Lake District; no other has written so extensively, perceptively, and fruitfully about a particular landscape; and no other has devoted so much attention to travellers" (p. 2), McCracken goes through the Lake District trying to supply the connections between the poems and the places. His first section, "Poems and Places," follows "The Waggoner and Other Travellers," discusses places having special biographical connections to Wordsworth from Cockermouth to Rydal, goes "Over Kirkstone Pass," "To Llangdale and Beyond" and along the River Duddon. His materials are from the expected places—letters and journals of the Wordsworths, Prefaces, the Fenwick notes and other comments of the poet, and, of course, the poetry. An "Index of Wordsworth's Poems" contains some 145 items, and quoted passages or sometimes whole poems take up about a third of the pages in Part I. Since the criterion for selection is place reference, the poetry is not always of intrinsic worth—what is remarkable is how wide a spectrum appears, from inscriptions to memorable lines from *The Prelude*. The reality of "place" is significantly enhanced by McCracken's inclusion of eighteen nineteenth-century illustrations—much better than the "select views" of the Rev. Joseph Wilkinson. In Part II, entitled "In the Footsteps of Wordsworth (Maps and Guides)," there are seventeen large-scale maps of strategic areas with specific, avuncular "Guides to Places" and traveling/walking directions. All this is very helpfully done. I, for one, am glad to be informed that what some modern Wordsworthians call the "Duck Pond" is properly named "White Moss Tarn."

McCracken's is a good, unpretentious work. He knows the basic items of Wordsworth scholarship—there is a two-page "Select Bibliography"—and, although his aim is to show connections between places and poems, he recognizes and admits, what has been pointed out, that the connections are finally imaginary and that Wordsworth's "eye on the object" is essentially the "inward eye." That "matter-of-factness" which Coleridge complained about in Wordsworth is fundamentally an illusion of verisimilitude, not adherence to actual facts. McCracken ends his section on "Poems and Places" by noting that "Joanna's Rock" is not identifiable: "A friend walking with Wordsworth asked him about the location of Joanna's Rock. They were at that moment walking by Butterlip How, and Wordsworth replied rather casually, 'Any place that will suit; that as well as any other.' But for this poem, no factual place suits very well. Joanna's Rock is the poem, part of an imaginative act which connects people with a landscape" (pp. 193-94). McCracken concludes, more sensibly than might perhaps be expected of the genre: "Hunting Wordsworthian waterfalls and reading Wordsworth's poems are different activities—the first best done in the Lake District, and the second, anywhere. The reading does not require the hunting since the poems are imaginative acts rather than matters of fact to be verified to the physical eye. Still, many have found new pleasures in the places from having known Wordsworth's poems. The connections abide" (p. 196).

If McCracken's book is a journeyman example of the "Wordsworth Industry," Kenneth Johnston's *Wordsworth and The Recluse* is a very sophisticated scholarly exhibit. It also deals with Wordsworth's sense of place, but in the way in which his mind did or did not "find itself at home," noting "the curious fact that almost all major segments of *The Recluse* were undertaken when the Wordsworths had just completed, or were just beginning to contemplate, a move to a new home—and, moreover, that this occurred with each of the residences they occupied from Alfoxden on" (p. 82).

The title of Johnston's book is significant: *Wordsworth and The Recluse.* This is not just a "reading" of *The Recluse,* although it is that; it argues that "Wordsworth *is* 'The Recluse,' " sees his whole poetic career in terms of his struggle to write a great philosophical poem that would be a socio-religious Romantic epic, and in effect provides "notes toward a comprehensive critical biography of Wordsworth" (p. xx). Most of the Wordsworth scholarship of this century divides essentially between that which emphasizes facts—biographical, political, bibliographical, textual—and that which interprets, producing subtle—sometimes arguably oversubtle—"readings." Johnston has a foot in each camp.

Johnston recognizes in his preface the special problem of his work: this is a study which may be considered "in advance of its object, since there is no book entitled *The Recluse* which a reader can pick up and read" (p. xvi). His is in effect an "archaeological project." For of course *The Recluse* was never finished. The King Charles's Head of Wordsworth scholarship has been that Wordsworth had bitten off more than he could chew—or Coleridge had, since the idea seems to owe much to Coleridge's belief that Wordsworth as *spectator ab extra* was capable of a philosophical poem that would "do great good," and Wordsworth was pathetically anxious for Coleridge's assistance: "I would gladly have given 3 fourths of my possessions for your letter on The Recluse" (29 March 1804). Thus the poem could be called by William Minto as early as 1889 "Wordsworth's Great Failure" (*The Nineteenth Century*, September). The poet himself lends support to the "failure" judgment by his straightforward answer to George Ticknor who in 1838 had been set on by Mary to prod William to complete *The Recluse*: "Why did not Gray finish the long poem he began on a similar subject? Because he found he had undertaken something beyond his powers to accomplish. And that is my case" (*Journal*, 9 May 1838). This is essentially the position of Jonathan Wordsworth, who appended to his recent *William Wordsworth: The Borders of Vision* a persuasive analysis of why *The Recluse* did not get written, an epilogue entitled "The Light That Never Was." Johnston's point—an exciting and important one—is that there is more light than has been recognized, and although the philosophical epic was never

The "Wordsworth Industry" 53

finished, enough of it was written that "it is one of his greatest compositional achievements, not his 'great failure' " (p. 62), and it should be read as a great fragment much as we read *The Canterbury Tales, The Faerie Queene, Essay on Man,* and *Don Juan,* seen as "an unresolved and probably unresolvable tension between its subjective, artistic motivations and its objective, social intentions" (p. xiii).

Johnston arrives at his massive reconstructed fragment (some 20,000 lines) by careful analysis of Wordsworth's poetry from 1797 to 1814, more or less accepting the poet's architectural figure of a gothic church of which *The Prelude* is an integral "ante-chapel,"—examining foundations, fragmentary construction and ruins, always trying to understand the interplay between Wordsworth's autobiographical poem "to Coleridge" and his effort to produce the epic of "Man, Nature, and Human Life" Coleridge expected of him. Johnston's procedure is to consider the "First *Recluse,* 1797-1798" ("The Ruined Cottage," "The Old Cumberland Beggar," "The Discharged Veteran," and "A Night Piece") and relate that to "The First Prelude, 1798-1799" (*The Two-Part Prelude*), then follow Wordsworth as he starts over again with "Home at Grasmere" in 1800 and, unable to sustain his paradisical vision, falls back on *The Prelude* of 1805, only to rebound to "Home at Grasmere" of 1806 and then begin anew with *The Recluse* poems of 1808 ("To the Clouds," "The Tuft of Primroses," "St. Paul's") and finally return to *The Excursion.* Johnston sees the process as a fascinating pattern of fragmentation and recoil—three times—as Wordsworth struggled to accomodate his genius to the Human Life theme, being forced to grapple—as did Keats—with the question of the value of poetry.

This is a long book (nearly 400 pages) and it is sometimes indulgently long-winded, supererogatory and repetitious. Still, it covers a lot of ground, dealing with Wordsworth's central work, including not only *The Prelude* and *The Excursion* but also the little discussed "Preface" to the 1815 *Poems* and "Essay, Supplementary to the Preface," and it even adds an epilogue on Coleridge's *Biographia Literaria* as a "privately coded communication" reflecting the *Recluse* ideal. It is a rich book, full of insightful parallels and rhetorical generalizations; I have read it only twice, and feel that I could read it several more times without exhausting it.

And Johnston's book is eminently readable. The first sentence proclaims an exciting style: *"The Recluse was not heralded with trumpets."* There are many more such vigorous passages: "The literary landscape of the time is strewn with huge carcasses of religious, patriotic and scientific poems like so many dinosaurs caught in an evolutionary storm of sensibility"; "He ultimately backs himself into a corner, out of the poem, and breaks it off"; "Wordsworth is also home free compositionally"; "It is hard to imagine the feckless mind-wandering collegian of Book III calming anybody, as he swerves unsteadily between silly social engagements and lonely night walks that made him seem daft." Sometimes this energy gets carried away—a reader who wants a soberer, factual treatment of a part of *The Recluse* might look at Judson Lyon's study of *The Excursion* (which does not appear in Johnston's index). We might question Johnston's "shockingly," "breath-takingly," "sheer paradoxical power"; wonder how helpful it is to talk about the "deep structure" of *The Prelude* and *The Recluse*; suspect that the whole "residential" reading of *The Prelude* gives too much importance to headings Wordsworth attached to certain books. The twentieth-century poet Randall Jarrell remarked, "I know I've so often exaggerated or said things I only half meant in poems, that I don't trust them as truths—except as the way things felt." So probably Wordsworth.

But of course Johnston is talking about "the way things felt" to the poet. He does it ingeniously and honestly. The reader is impressed by Johnston's obvious efforts not to overvalue *The Recluse* he reconstructs, by his frank designation of "soapy exaggeration" (p. 170), "romantically absurd conclusion" (p. 200), "the banality of such phrasing" (p. 222), "illogic dressed up in the guise of logic (circular imagery, circular argument, circular vision)" (p. 226), "murky extravagance" (p. 321). The poet who was notoriously prickly over criticism would wince at some of this, but the man who told Ticknor why he could not finish *The Recluse* ought to applaud it.

The "Wordsworth Industry"   55

The dust cover of *Wordsworth and* The Recluse is appropriately ornamented with a famous example of a gothic architectural ruin identified with Wordsworth, a beautiful watercolor of Tintern Abbey, done by J. M. W. Turner—which leads us to our example of the expansion of the "Wordsworth Industry": James A. W. Heffernan's *The Re-creation of Landscape: A Study of Wordsworth, Coleridge, Constable, and Turner.* Of course Wordsworth is only one of the four subjects of this admirable study, but he looms large; the book is particularly helpful in demonstrating that although Wordsworth repudiated the tyranny of the eye and decided not to call his *Descriptive Sketches* "Picturesque Sketches," he still maintained painterly attitudes—as befit his relationships with Haydon and Beaumont. The rationale of this work's title (which raised the eyebrows of a colleague who saw it on my desk) is that landscape is not a natural but a cultural phenomenon; it cannot be dealt with unmediated; it has already been created jointly by the triangulation of painting, poetry, and gardening; it must therefore be *re-created.* The four men treated were chosen because of the accidents of birth which brought two major English landscape painters and two major poets who wrought verbal landscapes on the scene about the same time at the beginning of the nineteenth century. This is not an influence study; in a brief but solid appendix Heffernan offers reasons for doubting that there was any significant influence between any of the four except, of course, Wordsworth and Coleridge. It is simply a careful discussion of how four English contemporaries—two painters and two writers—came to terms with the implications and limitations of the dominant, evolving *Ut Pictura Poesis* concept, and developed simultaneously a subtly related romantic handling of landscape. The connections suggested between the work of the poets and that of the painters are ingenious and fascinating: e.g., Wordsworth's "spots of time" compared with "temporalized space" in Constable; the "Internalization of Prospect" and relations of verticality to the subjective sublime; the poets' "certain coloring of the imagination" to the painters' atmospheric transformation. Much of this has appeared in articles by Heffernan: the most significant the penetrating analysis of "The Geometry of the Infinite." (The same double mileage is practiced in Johnston's book: it is a common device of academic publishing.)

Of course intrinsic difficulties beset any such interdisciplinary investigation—especially since Heffernan naturally makes detailed comments on paintings the reader does not know well, some of which the reader has probably never seen. Heffernan tries to handle this problem by printing, together in the middle of the book, reproductions of forty-three paintings and engravings. This technique certainly helps, but because of the reduced size (generally two illustrations to a page) and the black and white presentation—particularly unable to do justice to Constable's fresh greens and Turner's fiery lights—it leaves something to be desired.

The predominant note of Heffernan's analysis is a commendable caution; he is well informed (although one is surprised that Hussey's classic *The Picturesque: Studies in a Point of View* appears not to be referenced); he is willing to disagree, respectfully, with Paulson and Kroeber; he seems ever aware of the complexity of his subject (he is, for instance, "skeptical" of the parallels of transformation suggested by Hazlitt's romantic claims for Rembrandt); he notes the often contradictory comments of his subjects, and regularly qualifies his connections. But then he sometimes later acts as if a tenuously put point had been proved—that Constable's 1828 *Dedham Vale* is essentially a reworking of his 1802 *Dedham Vale* and both significantly influenced by Claude Lorraine's *Landscape: Hagar and the Angels* (which seems to give little weight to the passage of time and Constable's realistic impulses); or that the drinking boy in *The Cornfield* is a portrait of the painter's youth, giving the landscape a convenient autobiographical/chronological dimension—*à la* Wordsworth.

In Scott's *Redgauntlet* Alan Fairfort asks Darsie Latimer, "Didst ever see what artists call a Claude Lorraine glass, which spreads its own particular hue over the whole landscape which you see through it?—thou beholdest ordinary events just through such a medium." Claude Lorraine mirrors have gone out of style; indeed part of Heffernan's argument is that Romantics

The "Wordsworth Industry" 57

put some lamp in their mirrors. But a new sort of Lorraine glass has been developed, under the modern metaphor of the "Industry" that surrounds a Blake, Dickens, Shakespeare, Yeats, or Wordsworth, and constitutes a medium to color ordinary events.

Shakespeare and the Stage

Donald Gwynn Watson

Peter Thomson. *Shakespeare's Theatre*. Theater Production Studies, 1. London: Routledge and Kegan Paul, 1983. xiii, 190 pp.

Alan C. Dessen. *Elizabethan Stage Conventions and Modern Interpreters*. Cambridge: Cambridge University Press, 1984. xi, 190 pp.

David Bevington. *Action Is Eloquence: Shakespeare's Language of Gesture*. Cambridge: Harvard University Press, 1984. ix, 227 pp.

John Barton. *Playing Shakespeare*. London: Methuen, 1984. ix, 211 pp.

Philip Brockbank, ed., *Players of Shakespeare*. Cambridge: Cambridge University Press, 1985. xii, 179 pp.

Joseph H. Summers. *Dreams of Love and Power: On Shakespeare's Plays*. Oxford: Clarendon Press, 1984. viii, 161 pp.

Jean E. Howard. *Shakespeare's Art of Orchestration: Stage Technique and Audience Response*. Urbana: University of Illinois Press, 1984. x, 212 pp.

"One grand discovery of the twentieth century is that Shakespeare knew his business as a playwright," writes J. L. Styan in introducing *The Shakespeare Revolution*, his description of the increased reciprocity of influence between "criticism and performance" (his subtitle) in recent decades.[1] Each of the seven books under review here contributes in its own way to our understanding of the theatrical dimensions of the plays and so to this "revolution" in their appreciation *as* plays. If such emphasis upon the dramaturgical artistry and theatrical detail now seems obvious, it is because recent scholars have become more interested in mapping out this vast expanse of inquiry, in healing the breach between text and performance, in seeing drama as incomplete somehow apart from its being "produced." It was not always so.

Perhaps the split between text and theater is inherently potential in the history of drama, although one can find few examples — one thinks of Seneca, for instance — before the Renaissance. As Plautus and Terence became favored authors in the humanist revision of the schools' curricula, as Ben Jonson and others developed a professional disdain for the popular tastes in theater, as playwrights defied the commercial liability of printing their plays — "Reade him, therefore; and againe, and againe," advise Heminge and Condell — the separation of the literary and the theatrical became more likely. Dryden's warning against the ephemerality of the stage's pleasures can serve as a fairly early example of the devaluing of the theater and the privileging of reading:

> In a playhouse, everything contributes to impose upon the judgment: the lights, the scenes, the habits, and above all, the grace of action . . . surprise the audience, and cast a mist upon their understandings; not unlike the cunning of a juggler, who is always staring us in the face, and overwhelming us with gibberish, only that he may gain the opportunity of making the cleaner conveyance of his trick. But these false beauties of the stage are no more lasting than a rainbow; when the actor ceases to shine upon them, when he gilds them no longer with his reflection, they vanish in a twinkling.

For Dryden, "the propriety of thoughts and words, which are the hidden beauties of a play, are but confusedly judged in the vehemence of action."[2] How strange this sounds coming from a successful professional playwright, yet it does describe the critical attitude which would dominate the analysis of drama well into our century: the divorce of the experience of a play from the understanding of a text, of the theatrical from the poetic, of the ephemeral from the permanent, of seeing from reading, of the dramatic from the rhetorical, of the "applause of fools" from the critical judgment. Among other factors, the hierarchy of genres in the eighteenth century, the spectacular and antiquarian productions of the nineteenth, and the rise of the university study of literature in the twentieth helped maintain the separation of text and theater, poet and playwright, in Shakespearean criticism. Even G. Wilson Knight, like Dryden a man of the theater — actor, director, producer, theatergoer — could deny the relevance of his years of experience in doing Shakespeare to his attempts to discover the secrets of the texts,[3] and none of the dominant critical methods of literary study has had much use for or sense of the theater.

In a very real sense, scholars find themselves in the early stages of inventing a criticism of drama — or in the late stages of abandoning the adaptations of methods which have been successfully used to examine lyric, narrative, or other genres. None of these books offers a completely satisfying approach to Shakespeare's plays as plays, but together they do illustrate a wide variety of entrances to the territory of theatrical criticism and an abundance of insights into Shakespeare's uses of the stage. Though the areas of discussion overlap, in general three centers of emphasis can be identified: stage, performance, audience.

The oldest of these is the reconstruction of the physical and historical conditions of the Elizabethan theater: its architecture, its economics, the conventions of staging and acting, professional concerns, aesthetic practice, social custom. What the theaters looked like has been reconstructed in our century from a handful of documents and drawings, and our general sense of the physical characteristics of the Globe (and a few other theatrical spaces) seems fairly certain, though scholars continue to speculate upon and sort through the details.[4] Such scholars as Chambers, Bentley, Hodges, Styan, Beckerman and Wickham have been enormously helpful in restoring to us a sense of Shakespeare as a man of the theater, yet more often than not the plays themselves are fragmented into parts which will demonstrate the particular element of theatrical architecture or of Elizabethan staging, thus subordinating text to the history of theater rather than developing a theater-centered criticism of the text. We should not attribute failure where no such intention exists, but nevertheless these twentieth-century discoveries took some time to be integrated with our interpretive concerns.

Peter Thompson's *Shakespeare's Theatre* appears to be attempting such an integration. Part One surveys what we know about the Globe Theater and Shakespeare's company (the Lord Chamberlain's Servants, later the King's Men) and limits itself to the plays they performed there between 1599 and 1608, the period of the great tragedies. Part Two examines three plays, bringing into his discussions the practical realities of the playhouse: considerations of music, sound effect, costume, staging, and so forth. Sometimes the theatrical elements are forgotten, however, and Thomson presents us with a kind of criticism which remains independent of and uninformed by performance, but most often he is "asking theatrical questions" and investigating "the spirit of the original performance" by examining the necessities of playing in "a theatre in which everything was open and exposed" (p. 108). In his chapter on *Twelfth Night*, he includes a wide variety of topics, from the music to the hand-properties to the fluidity of place; especially suggestive is his analysis of the scenes in which Sebastian magically "untangles" the knots, freeing all from their frustrations and "anguish of rejection" (pp. 101-04). The next chapter, on *Hamlet*, focuses around one carefully considered topic: the play's concern with behavior as acting. The least satisfactory chapter presents us with a scene-by-scene commentary on the special properties and effects needed for the staging of *Macbeth*: the analysis here often gives us less than one could want, becoming too thin when the scene is rich and complex, and more, when Thomson must repeat himself or note what is obvious to anyone with the slightest theatrical sense.

Our awareness of the practical, everyday business of a company of actors is surely enhanced by *Shakespeare's Theatre*. Though the first part adds nothing new to previous research, Thomson synthesizes the historical material judiciously, keeping always at the forefront the problems of "getting on" with the company's

Shakespeare and the Stage 63

business: paying the bills, touring when the plague came to London, pleasing the public, stocking the tiring house with expensive costumes, placating the Master of the Revels, anticipating the taste at Court. His year-by-year survey of the 1599-1608 seasons contains some thought-provoking notions about the plays produced and their connections with contemporary events. Yet there seems too little here that could not be had elsewhere and that we have not long known, and very little in Part Two depends upon Thomson's reinterpretation of the facts about the Globe and the company; the essays on the plays can be read by anyone with a basic knowledge of Elizabethan theater. Thomson's disputing Harbage's estimate of audience size will add little to our sense of the play, nor will our response to his speculation that Shakespeare's writing of tragedies in this period resulted from the company's having some other playwright at work on comedies, the staple diet of London audiences. Who he was is left open, and Thomson's determination to opt for the most practical, financially sound solution is exposed as reverse sentimentality; nevertheless, one can be refreshed by the practical hardheadedness of the stage-hand's view when it comes to such matters. His book is at its best when he applies the common sense of the theater, his knowledge of playhouse practice, and his close attention to presentation and response in all its specificity and variety.[5]

Even more fully aware of the imperfect and scanty evidence about Shakespeare's stage and staging is Alan C. Dessen's *Elizabethan Stage Conventions and Modern Interpreters*. Dessen has read through hundreds of plays in an attempt to "recover the original 'logic' of presentation" (p. 156), mainly because any presentational analysis must "build almost exclusively upon the evidence within the plays themselves" (p. 19). For him many of our problems can be traced to our inheriting the assumptions and logic of realistic fiction and drama, the novelist's characterizations and the proscenium-arch, fourth-wall, darkened-auditorium theater. The stage directions, Dessen argues, most often convincingly, are there, embedded in and inseparable from the dramatic text, and reveal "the full stretch of the dramaturgy" of Shakespeare and his contemporaries (p.

18). No detail is too insignificant for Dessen in its potential for revealing "theatrical technique" and "original staging": "How is Gertrude to be coiffured in the closet scene or at Ophelia's grave? When investigating this rich, complex tragedy, can one dismiss any evidence" (p. 38)?

One, of course, is tempted to answer, "Yes!" But hair, boots, night-gowns are "code-signs" which would have visually told an Elizabethan spectator something (as lamps indicate nighttime) and are key images in signaling "meaningful connections" (pp. 47-49). All the "significant detail" can get more than tedious in its specificity as Dessen turns up stage directions illustrating "as from bed" from dozens of the minor plays of minor writers. Dessen himself is aware of the problem: "How then to use such evidence." No doubt, there may be an "evolving theatrical iconography" in Shakespeare's time, but can we over-intellectualize about the "everpresent metaphoric or symbolic dimension," as Dessen calls it (p. 52)?

Consider, for example, Shakespeare's use of sitting. We have all seen both actors and actresses do it in the theater, but what does it *mean*? Following Castiliogne, Giovanni della Casa, Fabrizio Caroso, and other courtesy book writers translated into English before 1600 describe an entire spectrum of the conventions of politeness. The gentleman should sit with both feet together and flat upon the floor, forward in his seat, with ease and all decorum; similarly, for the women, whose farthingales made sitting difficult, such authors offered instruction in detail (as they did for walking, wearing gloves and hats, even standing). May there not be an entire iconography here which we are missing? After all, our own "readings" of body language are quite developed. Second, what of the practical necessities of staging? If an actor is to sit, he must sit upon something. The instances of a throne center-stage are many in the plays, and, of course, Iago calls for a chair to be brought on for the wounded Cassio in Othello (V.1.82,96). See Henslowe's *Diary* for inventories of stage properties. Third, emblem literature offers us a variety of sitting poses relevant to Death the antic in *Richard II* or "Patience like a monument" in *Twelfth Night*. Further, we might look at sitting in specific scenes. In the first scene in *Hamlet,* Horatio says to Marcellus and Banardo, "Well, *sit* we down, And let us hear Bernardo speak of this" (I.1.34; my italics). Later, after the Ghost enters, they must again be standing, since "Marcellus says, "Good now, *sit* down, and tell me" (70). Again, after the Ghost's re-entrance and the cock's crow, they must be standing, for who can "strike" at a ghost with his "partisan" (140) from a sitting position. Surely, the staging here is loaded with meaning: all this standing and sitting conveys the unease in Denmark, the ups and downs of Elsinore's fate. Or, take the imagery of sitting in the scene of Banquo's ghost. Macbeth opens by asking all to be seated, "You know your own degrees, *sit* down" (III.4.1). After "mingling" with his guests (3), he says "here I'll *sit* i' th' midst" (10), but rises to go speak to a murderer at the door. Upon his return, Lennox asks, "May't please your Highness *sit*" (38), but "The table's full," objects Macbeth, visually circling the table of humanity, replaced by the man he has had murdered who *sits* in his place, keeping him from joining the others. Noticing that Macbeth is "moved," Rosse says, "Gentlemen, *rise*, his Highness is not well" (51), but Lady Macbeth counters, "Pray you keep *seat*" (53, cf. "*Sit*, worthy friends," 52). After the exit of Banquo's ghost, Macbeth is once again calm, "Come, love and health to all, Then I'll *sit* down" (86-87). The re-entrance of the ghost again terrifies Macbeth who in turn puzzles his guests (who must be squirming since Macbeth orders them, "Pray you *sit* still," 107). Finally, they all must stand to leave (see 117-18), not according to their "degrees" but "at once." As in *Hamlet,* sitting illustrates composure, and the ups and downs visible to the viewer's eye are crucial to interpretation as to the response of an audience sitting nervously through these tense scenes.

My digression points to several important general observations. First, in the theater everything is loaded with meaning, including immobility and silence.[6] Second, to see the "everpresent symbolic dimension," we must first *see* the play. With both these points Dessen would agree, and to him and his predecessors we are indebted for our training in reading Shakespeare theatrically and our interest in *all* the details. To change or discard the smallest stage directions, as modern editors as well as modern directors do, is to change the range and possibilities of interpretation. Dessen admits his conservatism, if that is the right word, his allegiance to the "historical camp" of those for whom Shakespeare is *not* our contemporary. His study of the "presentational logic" of dress, "darkness," place, stage violence, and the metaphors of seeing and not seeing often reveals crucial moments in which our own logic of reading and seeing, with its commitment to verisimilitude, continuity, and different theatrical conventions (lighting is the best example), blinds us to the original staging.

Dessen's book, then, affords another example of the historical reuniting of text and theater, and he suggests that "trusting" Shakespeare, as Terry Hands did in producing the Henry VI plays (see pp. 160-61), will help us determine "more fully the terms upon which dramatists, actors, and specators 'agreed to meet' " (p. 11). Such efforts valuably augment the pioneering efforts of M.C. Bradbrook to reconstruct stage conventions by using more thoroughly the plays themselves as evidence. In *Action Is Eloquence*, David Bevington examines a variety of "languages" implicit in stage convention and staging which again are inseparable from the text and the *written* word. Like Dessen, he is attempting to heal the divorce between the literary and theatrical, the permanent and the ephemeral, words and thoughts and their visual embodiment in performance. "Visual interpretation" concerns itself with the languages of hand properties and costume, gesture and expression, theatrical space, and ceremony, each of which is accorded a chapter. These concerns with the visual images complement Dessen's and, Bevington tells us, grew out of an editor's practical problem of dealing with stage directions and business: the groupings, "pictures," and movements communicate, but "for the reader what is happening in the theater" can be overlooked.

Bevington overlooks very little; *Action Is Eloquence* harvests a rich catch of examples from "the unspoken language of the theater" (p. viii), filling his page with the bustling, constantly changing visual activity of theatrical realization. What helps Bevington organize this wealth of detail is a series of valuable contrasts between the fixed certitude of the world of "social

Shakespeare and the Stage

order, hierarchy, and place" and its inverted forms (p. 3), between the dramatic heritages of "a symbolic pageantry of moral example" and of "an illusory mirroring of social manners" (p. 100), between a language of convention, role, gesture, and costume and that of mockery, questioning, and transformation. The first element in the contrast can be established by immediate theatrical shorthand, as Bevington demonstrates fully with the stereotyped gestures of contemporary medical psychology and social manners, the traditions of costume as a register of role and identity, the spatial relationships of theatrical facade and stage grouping, the signifying functions of hand properties, and so forth. Simply identifying the stage conventions, as with Dessen's boots and nightgowns, restores a theatrical dimension to the text, but it also allows us to see the playwright's techniques of separating his characters from the official respectable orthodoxies of their world of appearances. Bevington uses the term "liminality," borrowed from Arnold van Gennep by way of Victor Turner, to describe the instability and ambiguity which result from such losses of certitude. Thus, an "unstructured and undifferentiated" world of "communitas" results, in which the signs of rank and sex are "abandoned," the "kinship system" suspended, social conventions overturned. The play, then, enters a transitional phase, a "rite of passage," necessary for the final denouement in which reaggregation or reintegration redefines the world of social reality. For such a language of the stage Shakespeare "needs two visual vocabularies, one of order and one of holiday release" (p. 5). Bevington demonstrates in a variety of ways how such "contrastive" vocabularies are essential to interpreting the plays' visual images, and he includes the spectator's liminality, his participation in the inversions of a rite of passage, as part of any interpretive approach to theatrical criticism.

My summary does not do justice to the argument in its manifold variations, but should suggest the book's approach to reuniting text and theater. The use of recent anthropological theory should not mislead us, however; Bevington, like Dessen, belongs to the "historical camp" of scholars who seek to determine the original stage conventions. He and Dessen have less sense of the practical necessities of producing a play than does Peter Thomson and a greater concern with interpreting the meanings of a text. In insisting upon the "liminal language" of theatrical inversion, Bevington might have explored more fully the works of Mikhail Bakhtin, Natalie Zemon Davis, Emmanuel Le Roy Ladrurie, Robert Muchembled, Claude Gaignebet, and others who have identified a language of carnival and street festival which includes the kind of counter-ritual, anti-structure, inverted ceremony patterns the anthropologist calls liminal. Though carnivalesque practices were declining in post-Reformation England, May Games and Whitsun Ales are closer to Shakespeare's time and place than the tribes for which Victor Turner developed his theory. And he might also have considered the substantial visual and theatrical element in the omnipresent Ovidian interest in identity, pastoral, and metamorphosis. Shakespeare's visual disordering of appearances "is to a significant degree his own invention" (p. 5), but for his original audience to have been able to *see* it, they must have been familiar with much of its language's grammar.

If both Dessen and Bevington hope to extend the possibilities of a fuller, richer approach to interpretation, the actors, actresses, and occasional directors who contribute to John Barton's and Philip Brockbank's volumes are more concerned with experience than with meaning, yet both scholars and performers surprisingly share many of the same starting points. Barton wants us to ask "How does Shakespeare's text actually *work* (p. 3)?" He and the group from the Royal Shakespeare Company who participated in the freely ranging discussions which comprise *Playing Shakespeare* find that the text is the best director. For them Shakespeare discloses "hidden hints" for staging scenes, speaking the verse, and developing the character; in fact, the insistence upon Shakespeare's "hidden direction" (p. 28) and "acting clues" (p. 32) and their making "friends with the text" (p. 117) is the one theme which recurs throughout. Dessen would heartily approve their trusting Shakespeare, and by doing so they provide us with some unusually precise discoveries and workable distinctions about the text's styles and techniques. For example, Barton asks his company to *scan* the verse to see how it works. Now, scansion seems a very old-fashioned approach to acting, yet a line such as "Once more unto the breach, dear friends, once more," interprets itself once scanned, and the actor will violate the extra strong stresses at his own risk of producing unspeakable nonsense. The actor, unlike the modern interpreter, cannot go against the verse, and, as Ian McKellen concludes, "the verse is there to *help* the actors, and not for the audience to wallow in something vaguely poetic" (p. 45). The discussions pragmatically deal with the contrasts of "heightened and naturalistic verse," with set speeches, soliloquies, silences and pauses, the heroic and rhetorical, the energetic and the ironic. At its most valuable moments, we get as close to the dramatic quality of Shakespeare's poetry in these discussions as in the scholar's inquiries into the logic of presentation. "Playing Shakespeare is at bottom to do with playing with words. . . . If the actor enjoys the word games, the audience will enjoy them too" (p. 117). Can we not assume that this observation also applies to Shakespeare, the King's Men, and the Globe audience?

Playing Shakespeare is an edited and augmented record of televised workshops produced for London Weekend Television in 1984. The videocassettes I have seen of these programs present at times the strange effect of real actors playing real actors rehearsing or performing Shakespearean roles. The "record" in *Playing Shakespeare* often suffers from these origins, as we cannot hear the differences between David Suchet's and Patrick Stewart's Shylocks or Richard Pasco's alternative versions of Orsino, and sometimes the shocks of discovery also appear awkwardly rehearsed in print and the questions or exchanges rhetorical. But the moments of insight are worth all that, for Barton and his actors can tell us how the text works.

Players of Shakespeare complements *Playing Shakespeare* but offers a less coherent approach to uniting text and theater. Philip Brockbank introduces essays by twelve members of the Royal Shakespeare Company, each about a role the essayist has played. The results of this "first of its kind" approach to the analysis of performance are mixed — some essays are more personal than critical — yet again the attention to the text's direction of the acting is fairly consistent. To be sure, some contributors show more concern with the conventions of recent productions or with how someone else has done the role than with analysis, but then, as Brockbank tells us, "The actor feels exposed and vulnerable, both in preparation and performance, feeling that his own personality and human resources are always on the line" (p. 3). Even these concerns can be revealing, for example, Gemma Jones's puzzlement about what to do in the very long interval before Hermione's reappearance in Act V of *The Winter's Tale*: in the study we may be too involved with *meaning* to attend to the *experience* of Hermione's very long absence from the stage. So too does the performer's point of view remind us that every production is an interpretation and none is definitive: Sinead Cusack played Portia for John Barton as a serious Portia, anxious and melancholic, but longs to return to the role lighter, more witty and buoyant (pp. 39-40), and Tony Church played Polonius in 1965 and 1980 as very different characters, but found them both rewarding (pp. 103-14).

Reading about how theater professionals work through a role adds a valuable dimension to our understanding that Shakespeare "knew his business as a playwright." Donald Sinden's remarks about playing Malvolio provide an enlightening approach to the "presentational analysis" that Dessen and Bevington call for. Geoffrey Hutchings asks searching quesstions about Lavatch's relationship with the Countess, and Roger Rees's detective work in discovering the clues in *Cymbeline* about Posthumus' character engages us as narrative as well as helps us with the role's stage history and its problems. In general, this volume may do much to redeem actors from their notoriety as poor analysts of drama. The view from backstage can act as a catalyst or a reminder for the critic and scholar. In the study we might not notice Shakespeare's "special fondness for chief ministers," but Tony Church does because he played Polonius, Gloucester in *Lear,* and York in *Richard II* (p. 114). Michael Pennington's nighttime meditations on Hamlet remind us that the scales need not always be tipped by the weight of meaning; "Sometimes," he says, " it is the theater's job to pass on a riddle, not to solve it" (p. 127).

Shakespeare and the Stage

The first three books are stage-centered criticism, the second two performance-centered. Jean Howard's and Joseph Summers's studies emphasize the audience's response, a consideration by no means neglected by the other scholars nor by the performers but less completely analyzed there. In *Dreams of Love and Power* Summers gives us "readings" of seven plays, essays which "derive from the experience of continually trying to understand with a class what goes on in Shakespeare's plays." These efforts involve a keen appreciation of the literary and emotional power of drama to engage "our own desires, hopes, and fears, both as an audience (however imaginary) and as actors off-stage" (p. vii). Though Summers has no particular theories to argue, in the context of the other books in this review, his may be seen as attempting to restore the balance between meaning and experience, interpretation and response. He is not afraid to be astonished, threatened, or made uncomfortable by the plays and explains why. Both he and Howard are most concerned with how Shakespeare controls those responses, though Summers proceeds more informally, conveying the relaxed atmosphere of a commonsensical chat with bright students: he is informed, intense, but not overpowering nor dogmatic. He likes these plays very much, indeed, and he takes us with him; for example, discussing *A Midsummer's Night's Dream*, he writes of our "astonishment" at its ability to "continually surprise and delight us" and explains that that ability is a result of Shakespeare's "creating a shifting sequence of movements of language, verse, tone, and action, within as well as between scenes": "As we respond to these movements, we are forced repeatedly to shift our perspectives — frequently when we have barely achieved them" (p. 3). Summers's use of the first person plural throughout conveys the value of approaching the plays through our experience of reading them theatrically. Summers never forgets that "we" are responding to a play, though his interest in our response to character and language dominates the analyses, and only occasionally does he become specific about staging and its conventions. The directness of Summers's confrontation of a play's problems or a character's "dreams" produces essays lucid and uncluttered by specialized knowledge, academic jargon, or professional ambition: we seem simply to have here a man reading a dramatic text and sharing his sense of its poetry and theatrical dimension, at times moderately impatient with other critics or trends in updating Shakespeare for the modern stage, but always attending to the action and the characters before him.

Jean Howard's metaphor in the title of her book announces her approach: "As Shakespeare orchestrated plays for performance, he was orchestrating indirectly the responses of an imagined audience" (p. 8), not merely through the language of the printed text but by means of all the aural, visual, and kinetic elements of stagecraft. Her belaboring the metaphor will likely strain most readers' patience, as it spawns tonal diversities, counterpoint, choreography, contrapuntal orchestration, rhythm, and countless repetitions of the musical terms. But beyond the style lie many useful distinctions and observations, none of which seems to rely too heavily on the theoretical studies of "affective" and "reader-response" criticism she cites. Shakespeare "knew his business as a playwright" and wrote cues for our responses. He divides our attention between characters, shifts our perspectives around, places one scene within the context of a larger theatrical sequence, contrasts one speech with another, and so forth. The skill with which Howard unravels the details of a "highly complicated theatrical experience" is often superb, though sometimes she can be quite pedestrian. For example, she uses the "contrapuntal encounter" of Gonzalo and Antonio with Prospero's island to show that "the audience is prevented from passively adopting the perspective of either stage party" (pp. 56-57); the contrast between utopian fantasy and cynical realism needs little clarification and no fancy critical language. What seems more valuable is Howard's sense of Shakespeare's interest in increasing his spectator's self-consciousness about his role as spectator, about his problems with interpreting word and action as perspectives shift and ironies multiply. She wants to oppose thematically oriented, retrospective criticism of Shakespeare, yet writes that Viola "in her selfless service of Orsino finds the proper way to escape passivity and sterile egocentricity without embracing

Toby's hedonistic recklessness" (p. 178). Neither theatrical, presentational, nor "affective," such lapses vitiate the ambitiousness of *Shakespeare's Art of Orchestration*. Nevertheless, her readings of contrasting scenes, of audiences within audiences, of the contours of a sequence of scenes, demand one's attention. For all its failings, Howard's book provides genuine critical dividends; at her best, she *shows* us how to read Shakespeare theatrically when she forgets to *tell* us how and why we should be doing so. Read with Thomson's essay on *Twelfth Night*, her chapter gives us a fine sense of the play as a play; add Sinead Cusack on Portia from *Players of Shakespeare* and Barton, Richard Pasco, and Judi Dench from *Playing Shakespeare*'s "Rehearsing the Text: Orsino and Viola" and create your own mental performance.

Perhaps Dryden was right about the subjectivity of responding to the theater's pleasures, but drama requires theatrical criticism. The variety of ways to remarry the text and the stage suggests that we need not forego those pleasures, even as we "reade him, therefore; and againe, and againe." Each of these seven books is deeply committed to Shakespeare's texts, and each sends us back to the plays to see them afresh. If we have made the "grand discovery . . . that Shakespeare knew his business as a playwright," we have just begun to rethink our interpretive approaches to drama. In the somewhat artificial separation of categories which organize this review, stage, performance, and audience challenge us to further explorations of the discovered territory. Allow me to suggest some possibilities.

The stage-oriented, presentational analysis explored by Dessen, Bevington, and Thomson remains largely within the domain of stage conventions; it helps us to see and hear what readers miss and what our own literary presuppositions, theatrical media, and cultural differences have hidden from us. As aware as they make us of the overlays of meanings from a rich variety of sources of images, they put the history into the text rather than the text into history; that is, the influence of contemporary psychology, pageantry, and emblem and the relevance of other dramatic texts help the reader recover meanings which will lead to a richer, more assured and historical understanding of the play's staging and a more sophisticated interpretation of a passage, scene, or act. The theatricality of Elizabethan culture becomes one more of these important contexts for developing the completeness of our sense of stage conventions. As helpful as is Bevington's examination of the "inversions of ceremony" in *Hamlet* as "signs of disorder," it stops short of connecting the play with the culture and politics of 1600; as shrewd as is Thomson's analysis of the audience's being "pitched" into "watching watchers" and of *Hamlet*'s "preoccupation with theatricality," it has very little to say about the involvement of the real lives of these spectators in a society preoccupied with theatrical politics. The concerns of a recent group of critics with the power, ideology, and subversion dramatized in Shakespeare's texts take interpretation into a historical realm continuous with the play, its conventions, and its visual images. Though this "new historicism" is often guilty of colonizing the text in the interests of new interpretive procedures, the insights it provides into the representations of politics in Shakespeare give us a new sense of Elizabethan theatricality.[7]

Besides seeing dramatic production from the green-room through the perspectives of directors and "players," we may hope for further efforts to exploit the potential value of performance-oriented criticism. No developed sense of what a "criticism of performance" might be yet exists, although surely every production of Shakespeare provides an interpretation of the text. Unlike printed, discursive interpretations, performances must make decisions which preclude other choices and Dryden's leisurely exercise of the critical judgment. Nevertheless, the very nature of theatrical experience offers the excitement and insight that can never be available to the scholar, however active his theatrical imagination and extensive his knowledge of stage conventions. If one's "ideal" performance is made up of these factors along with bits and pieces of actual productions, that does not foreclose the necessity for a criticism of performance which will relate text and performance in a detailed sophistication beyond journalistic description. And even our repertoire of bits and pieces may be augmented by the records of stage history used wisely, though here again the intervention of our own historical biases complicates the task. Along with a criticism of performance, a history of production can illuminate the ways in which the zig-zags of social change color our Shakespeares; Ralph Berry's tracing of post-war productions of *Henry V*, for example, shows us another facet of the text in history as Olivier's patriotic hero becomes Terry Hands's reluctant and morally queasy king.[8]

Audience-centered criticism also might benefit from more attention to the factors which govern interpretive choices: when we think we are finding in the play clues to how to respond, might we not be finding in our responses clues to interpreting the text? In the complexity of reading or theatergoing, the two are often inseparable and form a dialectic which we are too infrequently fully conscious of. Jean Howard's emphasis upon the techniques Shakespeare uses to shape and control audience response often results in persuasive descriptions of the structuring of the play and our experience of its rhythms and meanings. One might object that other possible descriptions of other techniques will suggest other interpretations or that in the linear progression of performance the spectator is only dimly aware of such violations, fulfillments, and deferrals of expectations, but these objections would repeat Dryden's fears of the theater's temporal pleasures and the confusion involved in the "vehemence of action." Again, what seems crucial is not subjectivity but the limitations of only placing the history in the text but not placing the text and its theater in history, whether it is Shakespeare's history or ours. The theater is always marked off as a place we "go to," and apart from the differences in the social and communal nature of the play as event, we must see the element of social practice and cultural conditioning as involved in the dramatic strategies of transgressing this demarcation. How a text establishes and manipulates its relationship to the world its audience has left for a few hours must form part of our consideration of strategy and response. Fortunately, response does depend upon performance and producing Shakespeare's "orchestration," because if it did not, we would only go to the theater to see if the players "got it right" this time; productions are conditioned by what the players choose to emphasize in the over-determined, embarrassingly rich language of the text. Why else would the Royal Shakespeare Company locate its 1985 *Troilus and Cressida* in the midst of the Crimean War? Now, of course, this does not expose the radical subjectivity of audience-centered criticism as an impossible project; instead, it makes it a more complicated and provocative approach.

We may expect the trend toward theatrical criticism of Shakespeare to continue and may anticipate traditional interpretation to be invigorated by the various critical and theoretical formulations now contesting for dominance in literary studies. These seven books richly demonstrate that Shakespeare is and is not our contemporary, that he knew his business as a playwright, and that text and theater are inseparable in dramatic interpretation. Yet we remain with the complex task of unifying stage, performance, and audience response and of seeing the text in history as well as the history in the text.

Notes

1. J. L. Styan, *The Shakespeare Revolution* (Cambridge: Cambridge Univ. Press, 1977), p. 1.

2. "Dedication" of *The Spanish Friar* (1681), in *Of Dramatic Poesy and Other Critical Essays*, ed. George Watson, 2 vols. (London: Everyman's, 1962), I, 274-79.

3. G. Wilson Knight, *The Wheel of Fire* (London: Methuen, 1930), p. vi.

4. See the calculations in John Orwell's *The Quest for Shakespeare's Globe* (Cambridge: Cambridge Univ. Press, 1983), a recent example of reinterpreting the evidence.

5. Some problems arise in Thomson's details; had Shakespeare abandoned acting by 1603 (p. 34) or did he act in Jonson's *Sejanus* in 1603 (p. 72)? Were there "verie great disorders" in the theaters as stated in the Privy Council order of 1597 (p. 4) or were they rare (p. 25)?

6. See Bevington's brief discussion of semiotics (pp. 15-16): "All that is on the stage is a sign." Also, Keir Elam, *The Semiotics of Theatre and Drama* (London: Methuen, 1980) and Alessandro Serpieri, "Reading the Signs: Toward a Semiotics of Shakespearean Drama," *Alternate Shakespeares*, ed. John Drakakis (London: Methuen, 1985), pp. 119-43.

7. The term "new historicism" is Stephen Greenblatt's, from his introduction to *The Power of Forms in the English Renaissance*, ed. Greenblatt (Norman, Oklahoma: Pilgrim Books, 1982). Greenblatt's *Renaissance Self-Fashioning* (Chicago: Univ. of Chicago Press, 1980) was the first important contribution to a "poetics of culture," though his formulations have somewhat changed since. See, for example, "Invisible Bullets: Renaissance Authority and Its Subversion, *Henry IV* and *Henry V*" in Jonathan Dollimore and Alan Sinfield, eds., *Political Shakespeare: New Essays in Cultural Materialism* (Manchester: Manchester Univ. Press, 1985), 18-47. Several other essays in this collection contribute to a new approach to Shakespeare's texts in history, as does Dollimore and Sinfield's essay, "History and Ideology in *Henry V*," in *Alternative Shakespeares*, 206-227. (I have not included these latter two collections in this review, because neither *directly* contributes to our sense of Shakespeare's theater, though both provide essential insights for the development of theatrical criticism.) The various, scattered journal articles by Louis Adrian Montrose are also important; see especially "The Purpose of Playing: Reflections on a Shakespearean Anthropology," *Helios*, 7 (1980), 51-74.

8. Ralph Berry, *Changing Styles in Shakespeare* (London: Allen and Unwin, 1981).

The Stanford *Falesá* and Textual Scholarship

David H. Jackson

Barry Menikoff. *Robert Louis Stevenson and* The Beach of Falesá: *A Study in Victorian Publishing with the Original Text.* Stanford: Stanford University Press, 1984. viii, 199 pp.

Barry Menikoff's *Robert Louis Stevenson and* The Beach of Falesá illustrates many of the ways in which the text of a major work can become corrupted. It also shows how important textual scholarship will eventually be to a just valuation of Stevenson's achievement. Menikoff records the unfortunate publication history of *Falesá* and explains the aesthetic implications of his findings. His book makes an important contribution to the study of Stevenson's reception, his style, and his circle. Menikoff is, however, weak where he might be most convincing: his undertaking is not quite an edition nor is it entirely a critical study employing textual evidence. A more clearly defined purpose would have strengthened this useful piece of scholarship.

Menikoff's foremost achievement is to show how and why Stevenson's novella was corrupted. When Stevenson hit his artistic stride in the 1890s, he found himself separated from his audience by clinging dependents in Samoa and unreliable agents in London. The first group weakened his professional judgment, hurrying him into new writing projects and the premature conclusion of old ones. The second group, headed by his old friend Sidney Colvin, resented and impeded Stevenson's growth toward modern realism. Bowing to these influences, Stevenson allowed corrupt texts of perhaps his finest achievement, *The Beach of Falesá*, to reach serial and book publication.

Falesá (1892) and Stevenson's other Samoan novel, *The Ebb-Tide: A Trio and Quartette* (1894), have in common with *Treasure Island* (1883) an island setting. While Treasure Island is the archetypal charmed island of romance, the islands in the two Samoan novels are microcosms of the modern world, showing in bold relief the hypocrisy and lust for power typical of the fin-de-siécle. Like *Heart of Darkness* (1899), Stevenson's Samoan novels use the frontier setting to highlight the moral corruption of European imperialists. The characters Case in *Falesá* and Attwater in *Ebb-Tide* anticipate Kurtz in that they dominate and exploit native society and discover within themselves a moral savagery that surpasses anything seen in the "natives."

Wiltshire, the protagonist of *Falesá*, comes to the island as the representative of a trading firm dealing in copra and other commodities. He discovers that Falesá's population is under the sway of a rival trader, Case. Wiltshire is paired by Case in a sham marriage with a beautiful young girl, Uma, who is under a taboo. The taboo extends to Wiltshire, who breaks it by destroying the source of Case's power, a devil shrine that Case runs in the woods. Case and Wiltshire engage in hand-to-hand combat in the island forest, and when Case is killed Wiltshire and Uma become the leading figures on Falesá. The focus of the novella is on the moral nature of the European characters, and its prime concern is Wiltshire's growth toward generosity and tolerance. Like Marlowe and Herrick (in *The Ebb-Tide*), Wiltshire has his encounter with a savage mentor, and leaves with heightened powers of moral analysis.

Stevenson's publishers and agents, led by Clement Shorter of the *Illustrated London News* and by Colvin, did what they could to mold *Falesá* to the public's and their own expectations of what a Stevenson book should be. Sweeping changes could not be made to the novel once the manuscript left Stevenson's hands, but innumerable small alterations were made to the holograph text. These variants, as Menikoff shows, dilute Stevenson's attack on imperialist ideology and emphasize *Falesá*'s affinities with Stevenson's earlier romances for boys.

The Stanford Falesá

Stevenson loathed this meddling with his text, and he used strong language to attack it. He referred to *Falesá* as a "tale of mine, the slashed and gaping ruins of which appeared recently in the *Illustrated London News*" (p. 92). Menikoff takes his rhetorical cue from this and similar comments written by Stevenson. The novella, he writes, was "systematically gutted" (p. 59); the textual evidence reveals "a story of systematic abuse by printers and proofreaders" (p. 5); as printed it is "a vulgar and meretricious shadow of itself" (p. 33); and "what got printed was a compromise at best and a mutilation at worst" (p. 5). While Menikoff may overstate the case, he does show how hundreds of accidental and substantive changes significantly blur Stevenson's original intent.

The most famous substantive corruption, mentioned repeatedly in the literature on *Falesá*, is the "marriage certificate" which links Wiltshire with Uma. In Stevenson's manuscript, the wording of the certificate is sexually frank:

> This is to certify that *Uma* daughter of *Favao* of Falesá island of ———, is illegally married to *Mr John Wiltshire* for one night, and Mr John Wiltshire is at liberty to send her to hell the next morning.
>
>   John Blackamoar
>   Chaplain to the Hulks
>
> Extracted from the register
>   by William T. Randall
>   Master Mariner.

Deference to Victorian prudery led Clement K. Shorter, editor of the *Illustrated London News*, to omit the marriage certificate entirely from his serialization of the novella. The first edition (Scribners, 1893) prints the certificate but omits "for one night" and changes "to hell the next morning" to "to send her packing when he pleases." The first English edition (Cassell, 1893) changes "one night" to "one week" and "to hell the next morning" to "to hell when he pleases" (pp. 187-88). Stevenson bitterly opposed these changes.

His intention was again violated in the passage where Wiltshire meets the island missionary, Mr. Tarleton, and crudely identifies himself. In Stevenson's manuscript the episode reads: "I'm no missionary nor missionary lover; I'm no kanaka nor favourer of kanakas: I'm just a trader, I'm a common, low, god-damned white man and British subject, the sort you would like to wipe your boots on. I hope that's plain" (p. 80). No published version prints this passage as Stevenson wrote it. The serialization omits "god-damned" entirely, and the trial issue, which Stevenson had the chance to correct, softens it to "God-d-ned" (p. 81). This is only one example of the profane, off-color language Menikoff sees as "thematically central." Those who prepared Stevenson's later texts for publication tended to delete or tone down this profanity.

Obscenity offended people like Clement Shorter even more than profanity. In an important passage, Wiltshire discusses the obscene speech of his adversary, Case: "When he chose he could blaspheme worse than a Yankee boatswain and talk smut to sicken a kanaka" (p. 74). "Talk smut" was late-century slang for obscene discourse, and the phrase is important to the characterization of Case and to Stevenson's attempt to render faithfully the seedy world of the beachcomber. Shorter changed the phrase to "talk smart," which, as Menikoff points out, "can only [mean] talking smart-ass" (p. 74).

Falesá goes beyond mild obscenity to sexual candor, as in the marriage certificate. When Wiltshire first sees Uma, he notes: "She had been fishing; all she wore was a chemise, and it was wetted through, and a cutty sark at that. She was young and very slender for an island maid with a long face, a high forehead, and a sly, strange, blindish look between a cat's and a baby's" (p. 82). All printed versions change "sly" to "shy" and omit "and a cutty sark" (Scots for saucy wench). The *Illustrated London News* also omits "all she wore was a chemise, and it was wetted through" (p. 82).

Menikoff's discussion of substantive alterations is compelling, but he is even more thorough in his analysis of the changes made to Stevenson's accidentals. His discussion of punctuation, hyphens, spelling and capitalization is precise and fully illustrated. Menikoff shows that Stevenson's fluid and colloquial style, characterized at times by the use of dashes rather than periods, and by phonetic spellings, is part of his realistic purpose in at least two ways: it rounds out our picture of the narrator/ protagonist, and it captures the gritty quality of beach life. In a letter to Colvin, Stevenson stresses the central importance of "the dialects—trader's talk, which is a strange conglomerate of literary expressions and English and American slang, and Beach de Mar, or native English—the very trades and hopes and fears of the characters, [which] are all novel and may be found unwelcome to that great, hulking, bullering whale, the public" (p. 12). At one point in his narrative, for example, Wiltshire quotes Uma: " ' "E le ai!" says she—always used the native when she meant 'no' more than usually strong' " (p. 47). The dash is changed to a period, and the second *she* capitalized— no doubt a more formally correct bit of pointing, but a betrayal of the intended effect of fluidity and colloquialism. In other passages, Stevenson attempts to replicate the sounds of Polynesian speech through altered spelling. As Menikoff, a resident of Hawaii, points out, the correction of Stevenson's "hybiscus" to "hibiscus" loses "the sound [i.e., pronunciation] still heard in the islands today" (p. 53).

Menikoff convincingly argues that these substantive and accidental changes vitiate the artistic purpose of a work meant to depict the corrupt, gritty world on the penumbra of European colonialism. In an important journal letter to Colvin, Stevenson discusses his intent in *Falesá*: "It is the first realistic South Sea story; I mean with real South Sea character and details of life; everybody else who has tried, that I have seen, got carried away by the romance and ended in a kind of sugar candy sham epic, and the whole effect was lost—there was no etching, no human grin, consequently no conviction" (p. 12). Menikoff believes that these corruptions cause a "flattening" of the novel, a deflation of its original intent.

The image is apt. The textual corruptions erode the "subtleties of Stevenson's articles and pronouns, which help to chisel character and distinguish meaning, and which authenticate his style" (p. 72). Hundreds of single-word additions, deletions, and changes flatten the work's realism. Billy Randall, a dissipated Yankee skipper, drunkenly declares: "Never took such thing in my life" when Case accuses him of being inebriated. This reading is revised to the prim "such a thing," thereby effacing one of Stevenson's small but characteristic brush strokes. The "rationale" behind the flattening, Menikoff argues, is to segregate "Wiltshire, and the whites, from the brown people of the island" (p. 71).

Menikoff describes the power of "the distributors of fiction"—in particular the editors of important magazines like the *Illustrated London News*—and touches on their ideological biases and activities. *Falesá* runs very much against the popular imperialist current of the 1890s by showing the moral ambiguity that clouds the border between European and indigenous culture. Case, like Conrad's Kurtz, has become a native devil (*aitu* is the Samoan word) by discovering in his own nature a darker diabolism than that of the natives. But more than Case's villainy, Wiltshire's ambiguous moral stature and identification with Samoans troubled the distributors and many readers of Stevenson's fiction. Stevenson's contemporaries had no easier a time than do we in reconciling the separate yet equal greatness of *Treasure Island* and *The Ebb-Tide*.

Colvin and many others preferred the Stevenson of *Treasure Island* and *Kidnapped*, the brave invalid whose hard-won optimism had made him a sentimental hero and world-wide celebrity. This image of Stevenson sold books, and it also jibed comfortably with the conservative social vision of most of Stevenson's readers.[1] Unfortunately, when Stevenson tired of evading his era's metaphysical dilemmas, not only Colvin but an army of loyal reviewers and readers—readers who had made "R.L.S." the leading British literary celebrity—refused to accept the new body of work. Weakened by poor health and demoralized by a thorny home situation, Stevenson offered little resistance to Colvin.

Colvin was the hub of Stevenson's Anglo-American network of agents and publishers. The evidence of the CEAA/CSE editions, as well as the Oxford scholarly editions currently in progress, suggests that complicated relations with publishers

The Stanford Falesá

were the norm for many Victorian authors. Particularly difficult were the cases of Thomas Hardy, Stephen Crane, the late Stevenson, and others who chose to include "sordidness," "carnality," and other elements associated with French naturalism. The Stevenson of *Falesá, Ebb-Tide,* and *Hermiston* was up against all this but with the further complication of being six thousand miles away. Mail by steamer took a full month each way, so that Stevenson was forced to rely upon his agents. Menikoff gives us Colvin, the literary agent in London, who received and revised manuscripts; Baxter, the business agent in Edinburgh, who negotiated contracts and received royalty payments; Charles Scribner, Stevenson's American publisher; the McClure brothers, Stevenson's American serial publishers; and Clement K. Shorter, editor of the *Illustrated London News.* Menikoff is to be commended highly for not making Colvin the sole villain of the piece, as other Stevenson scholars have often done. Stevenson was himself partly to blame, as were his clamoring relatives. Menikoff analyzes this tangled network in great detail and with considerable lucidity.

Menikoff has done a good job of assembling the materials necessary to produce a scholarly editon of *The Beach of Falesá.* The puzzling thing is that he avoids calling his book an edition and, in fact, seems to distance his work from modern textual scholarship. Scholars have expected an edition of *Falesá* from Menikoff since Roger Swearingen wrote in his important book, *The Prose Writings of Robert Louis Stevenson,* that a "complete critical edition of the manuscript ... is in preparation by Professor Barry Menikoff."[2] At least one early review of Menikoff's book makes the claim that it is an edition.[3] Menikoff calls his work "A Study of Victorian Publishing with the Original Text," yet even this is misleading. The volume is in fact a study of the publishing of only one Victorian novel, and it does not include "the original text" but rather an emended form of it. In short, it *is* an edition, though not a well-executed one.

Menikoff uses terms like "accidentals" and "copy-text," yet implies that he has not undertaken a task of textual scholarship.

Later he scolds Jenni Calder and J. C. Furnas for labeling as "editions" mere published versions of *Falesá* that entailed minimal bibliographical research. Menikoff is surprisingly mild in his rebuke, however: "That Furnas and Calder are not textual scholars is no sin. But they contribute to the easy, uncritical acceptance of a mutilated text" (p. 76). Theological categories aside, Calder's and Furnas' failures are grave indeed. Each should have done additional research into the authority of early texts, research similar to Menikoff's. Given his reluctance to present more of his textual research, Menikoff's exculpation of his predecessors sounds like a plea for mercy on his own behalf.[4]

The fact is that Menikoff has selected an authoritative text of *Falesá* and emended it to reflect what he believes to be the author's intentions. If this is not a scholarly critical edition, then what is? The reader, intrigued by Menikoff's excellent analysis in his textual introduction, feels keenly the lack of textual apparatus—the information that one has come to expect in editions of important works. Had Menikoff published a facsimile or an unemended edition of the manuscript, that would have been one thing; but since he emends his copy-text (without so naming it) with readings from later authoritative texts (the trial issue and the first English edition), he would seem to be obligated to offer full discussion of these changes. He does not do so. The form of the CEAA/CSE editions is not sacrosanct, but this or some other form of textual apparatus should have been adopted. As Menikoff's book stands, the cursory presentation of editorial matters in his "Note on the Text" is inadequate and frustrating.

Menikoff's textual note begins with an ambiguous statement: "The text of *Falesá* is that of the holograph fair-copy manuscript" (p. 111). The manuscript is indeed one of the authoritative surviving texts, but no single text, however authoritative, should be confused with the work (hence the disrepute into which the phrase "definitive text" has fallen). What Menikoff seems to mean is that he has selected Stevenson's holograph in the Huntington Library as his copy-text. But his earlier use of the term *copy-text*, confusing it with *printer's copy*, suggests an unfamiliarity with editorial terms.[5]

The Stanford Falesá

Menikoff's textual note does discuss some of his emendations to Stevenson's manuscript. Concerning Stevenson's corrections to the trial issue Colvin sent him, Menikoff writes that in only eleven cases are these corrections anything but restorations of the original manuscript readings, adding that "in these cases he was working with repunctuated or corrupted sentences, so the holograph punctuation has been retained" (p. 112). Following his own eloquent demonstration of the importance to Stevenson of precise punctuation, this offhand dismissal is unsettling. Readers might at least have been given a list of the cruxes in order to judge the merits of each case and of Menikoff's blanket policy. Stevenson scholars have an additional reason for wanting more information: the importance that a number of standard sources assign to Stevenson's emendations in the trial issue. Swearingen's *Prose Works*, McKay's *Catalogue* of the Beinecke Stevenson collection, and Hill's description of the trial issue copy in which Stevenson made the changes all contradict Menikoff's judgment that these authorial emendations are of little consequence.[6] At the very least it would have been useful to have a list and description of the changes.

The final sentence of Menikoff's textual note is as surprising as the first: "In cases where the manuscript is illegible or unclear, I have followed the Cassell edition" (p. 112). One begins by wondering in what ways the manuscript is illegible and unclear. Are there interlineations or writeovers? Manuscript copy-texts always have unclear words and phrases; however, when this leads to editorial emendation, one needs the information typically included in textual notes so that one can evaluate the editor's judgment. But the key unanswered question in this case is why the first English edition, published by Cassell, has been ceded presumptive authority. Why not the earliest available authoritative text? In the case of *Falesá*, that text is the galley proofs for the *Illustrated London News* text.[7] There might have been good reasons for selecting the Cassell text, but Menikoff's reader is left to guess what they might be.

Not only the textual note but also the earlier, excellent parts of Menikoff's book would have been clearer if Menikoff had begun with a full discussion of the authoritative texts of *Falesá*.

Since he is arguing for a return to the manuscript in a case where the author saw and corrected at least one post-manuscript version of the novel, and where the issue of collaboration should at least be raised, an analysis of the authoritative texts is required. The reader needs first a list of the texts, keyed with abbreviations. References to Swearingen, McKay, auction catalogues, and other readily available sources on the manuscripts and early texts of *Falesá* should also be incorporated in the discussion. The reader can infer what sort of list and analysis are needed from Menikoff's Part I, but Menikoff's exposition in "The Context" would have been easier to follow and evaluate if preceded by this information. I should like to propose the following list, compiled from the mentioned sources and the collections of three libraries: the Bodleian, the British Library, and the Library of Congress.

AUTHORITATIVE TEXTS OF *FALESÁ*

1. **MS.**, Huntington HM2391.

2. **"Galley Proof** [Proof of the edition of *The Beach of Falesá* printed in the *Illustrated London News*, July 2—August 6, 1892]," Beinecke 562, 562A.

3. **ILN**. Serialization of the novel in the *Illustrated London News* under the title of *Uma*. Bodleian N2288b.6.101 (1892).

4. **Copyright Issue**. "Issue for Copyright Purposes." London: Cassell & Company, July 1892. Beinecke 563.

5. **Trial Issue**. THE | BEACH OF FALESÁ | Being the Narrative of a South Sea Trader. | AND | THE BOTTLE IMP. London: Cassell & Company, 1892. Beinecke 564, 565.

6. **A1.** ISLAND NIGHTS' | ENTERTAINMENTS | New York: Charles Scribner's Sons, 1 April 1893. Beinecke 575.

7. **E1.** ISLAND NIGHTS' | ENTERTAINMENTS | CONSISTING OF | THE BEACH OF FALESÁ | THE BOTTLE IMP | THE ISLE OF VOICES. London: Cassell & Company, 8 April 1893.

Although he does not call attention to it, we may infer from Menikoff's discussion in "The Context" that he believes he has

The Stanford Falesá 89

discovered a second stage in the textual transmission, coming before the galley proof. Menikoff deduces the existence of typescripts of Stevenson's *Falesá* manuscript, typescripts made by Robert McClure and sent to Stevenson for his corrections. This indeed would be a momentous discovery—a heretofore unknown layer of authorial revision of a major work of fiction. But since Menikoff's proof is deductive, and draws only on available printed sources, one is entitled to evaluate his reasoning using the same sources. My own conclusion is that in this case a typescript was almost surely not made, although there is no doubt that typescripts of other Stevenson manuscripts were prepared in the 1890's.[8]

Menikoff's argument hinges on an important letter from Stevenson to Colvin (31 January 1892): "I have 58 galleys of the *Wrecker* and 102 of the *Beach of Falesá* to get overhauled somehow or other in time for the mail" (p. 16). Asserting without proof that the *Illustrated London News* galley proofs were "probably set up in May or June 1892" (p. 16), Menikoff concludes that Stevenson must have meant typescript pages rather than galley proofs. This seems extremely unlikely. Stevenson was a seasoned professional; *Falesá* was his ninth novel. His use of technical terms is generally accurate. He knew the difference between typescript and galley proof.

A more likely account of the galleys is offered by a contemporary witness, Stevenson's friend Edmund Gosse. The following note, in Gosse's hand, appears in the second of the Beinecke Library's two copies (562A) of the *Illustrated London News* galleys:

The original MS. of this story was sent from Samoa by the author to Mr. Baxter in November 1891 and passed into the hands of Robert McClure. The latter parted with it to Mr. Clement Shorter, who set it up, exactly as it left the author, in 1892 (January). The author made no alterations, and Mr. S. Colvin made but few. The author refused to let anything be modified, but a great deal was altered, and the following pages contain the sole genuine text of the story. Only one other copy of the first proof is in existence. [*i.e. copy one, described above*]. [McKay, 1, 249.]

If Gosse is correct—and he knew all of the principals involved in the transmission of *Falesá*—then his account explains what surprises Meinkoff: that the galleys "have no corrections by Stevenson at all" (p. 16). Given the pressure Stevenson was under, it is possible he simply did not have time to correct and revise in proof.[9]

I do not mean to belabor the case of the inferred typescripts, but it does illustrate a weakness in Menikoff's book: a paucity of reference to Stevenson scholarship. This weakness is not as important as Menikoff's inadequate textual scholarship, but it does bear mentioning. Swearingen's essential study is never mentioned, and other important sources like the McKay *Catalogue* of the Beinecke Stevenson collection and Shorter's pamphlet are infrequently used. It is not uncommon in critical or textual studies to begin with a list of abbreviations of often-cited standard works. In the case of Stevenson this list would include the Prideaux *Bibliography*, Robert Kiely's bibliographical article in the second edition of the MLA guide to research in Victorian fiction, and J. C. Furnas's biography.[10] None of these is mentioned in Menikoff's book, nor are there comments on the state of Stevenson editing. Some editorial work is being done on Stevenson, albeit not as much as we need. Roger Swearingen recently discovered and published an unknown work, "An Old Song"; David Mann and William Hardesty have been at work on an edition of *Treasure Island*; Ernest Mehew (not Mayhew, as Kiely erroneously has it in the MLA *Guide*) is preparing an edition of the letters for Yale; and I am assembling a critical edition of *The Ebb-Tide*.[11] The general scholar coming to Menikoff's book would never know that a Stevenson revival is under way, and that many scholars are discovering ways of discussing Stevenson's stubborn refusal to be anything less than a major presence in late-nineteenth-century fiction.

Menikoff's book suggests the direction in which Stevenson scholarship should be moving. At its best, his intermingling of textual, biographical, and aesthetic criticism is skillfully done. The book is an important contribution to late Victorian studies. Yet this very good book would have been an excellent one had

Menikoff provided more of the textual information modern scholarship has led us to expect.

Notes

1. As I point out in a forthcoming article (*"Treasure Island* as a Victorian Adults' Novel," *Children's Literature Quarterly*), *Treasure Island* allays fin-de-siècle bourgeois anxieties by celebrating a hierarchical vision of eighteenth-century social order. Stevenson's wide readership responded to this vision. Other and generally smaller groups of readers welcomed the more forward-looking social vision of Emile Zola and his English and American followers.

2. Roger G. Swearingen, *The Prose Writings of Robert Louis Stevenson* (Hamden: Archon Books, 1980), p. 153.

3. Brian Morton, "Restoring the Text," rev. of *Robert Louis Stevenson and* The Beach of Falesá, *Times Higher Education Supplement*, 1 March 1985, p. 19.

4. Jenni Calder, ed., *The Strange Case of Dr. Jekyll and Mr. Hyde and Other Stories* by Robert Louis Stevenson (New York: Viking Penguin, 1979); J. C. Furnas, ed., *The Beach of Falesá* by Robert Louis Stevenson (New York: Heritage Press, 1956).

5. Discussing the earlier post-manuscript forms of *Falesá*, Menikoff comments on "how many 'texts' were serving as 'copy-texts' " (p. 20).

6. Swearingen, p. 153; George L. McKay, *A Catalogue of a Collection of Writings by and about Robert Louis Stevenson Formed by Edwin J. Beinecke*, 6 vols. (New Haven: Yale Univ. Press, 1951-64), 1, 251; Walter M. Hill, *Unique; or a Description of Proof Copy of* The Beach of Falesá *Containing over 100 Manuscript Changes* (Chicago: n.p., 1914).

7. The galley proofs were "set . . . up, exactly as it [i.e., the manuscript left the author" (Clement Shorter, quoted in McKay, 1, 249).

8. Research for my edition of *The Ebb-Tide*, for example, shows that heretofore unremarked typescripts were almost certainly made from the holograph of that novel. In an unpublished letter to Baxter (Beinecke 4252), Colvin urges that "a copy ought to be set up in type or typewriting *at once*, both because of the risk of loss and in order that I may revise it before it is printed, even in serial form." Less than a week later Colvin writes Baxter once again: "Thanks for yours of this morning—I think your clause about revision provides all that is necessary" (Beinecke 4254).

9. Other tangential evidence suggests that Stevenson did in fact review the galley proofs. Gosse's explanation is supported by Clement Shorter, who confirms that Stevenson was "correcting proof sheets" in late January, 1892. Clement K. Shorter, *Letters to an Editor* (privately published, 1914), p. 111.

10. W. F. Prideaux, *A Bibliography of the Works of Robert Louis Stevenson* (1917; rpt. New York: Burt Franklin, 1968); Robert Kiely, "Robert Louis Stevenson," in George H. Ford, ed., *Victorian Fiction: A Second Guide to Research* (New York: Modern Language Association, 1979); J. C. Furnas, *Voyage to Windward: The Life of Robert Louis Stevenson* (New York: William Sloan, 1951).

11. Roger G. Swearingen, ed., *An Old Song & Edifying Letters of the Rutherford Family* by Robert Louis Stevenson (Hamden: Archon Books, 1982).

Ben Jonson, Realist

Alastair Fowler

Anne Barton. *Ben Jonson, Dramatist.* Cambridge: Cambridge University Press, 1984. xiv, 370 pp.

Most students of Renaissance drama will by now be familiar with the argument of this important book. *Ben Jonson, Dramatist* has a corrective thesis: it strives, successfully, to overturn the common view of Jonson as a rigid classicist, by showing how deeply he was involved with Elizabethan irregularity and the romantic grotesque, and how much he remained throughout his life ambivalent towards classicism. Barton does not deny the greatness of the Jacobean comedies supporting Jonson's current reputation; but she exposes how unclassical these are, and traces their connections through the development of his art, backwards with the comical satires and forwards with the Caroline comedies (*The New Inn, A Tale of a Tub,* and *The Sad Shepherd*), which are commonly dismissed as symptoms of decline, but to which she—almost for the first time—pays the respect of serious treatment. She has no difficulty in establishing that Jonson is far from classical in his early plays, and that even in *Sejanus* and *Catiline* he deliberately avoids the correct tragedy of elevation—preferring a grim comedy of grotesque indignity. For the pupil of William Camden, classicism was a means to explain rejection of the styles of his contemporaries, and to define his own artistic vision.

But the importance of *Ben Jonson, Dramatist* is not to be reduced to that of an extractable thesis. Barton has achieved nothing less than a new characterization of Jonson's drama in relation to that of his contemporaries. And it is one that brings him into focus sharply, both as dramatist and as man. The two at times coincide; as in the bereaved Jonson's almost obsessive interest in father-son relations. (Virtually all the

Spanish Tragedy additions, here plausibly attributed to Jonson, evince this preoccupation.) His character emerges with special distinctness from a series of contrasts with Shakespeare, against whom Barton paces him throughout. Thus Jonson's return to Henry Porter's style of Elizabethan comedy in *A Tale of a Tub* is likened to Shakespeare's return to romantic drama in *The Winter's Tale*. Or, their minor characters are compared or contrasted—as Bobadilla with Ancient Pistoll, but also with Falstaff. Such comparisons can be to Jonson's advantage, since his characterization sometimes aspires to greater subtlety, with motivation (as in life) only obscurely glimpsed:

The apparent simplicity of characterization in Jonson's mature comedies is deceptive. His imaginary people are far less self-aware than most of Shakespeare's. They do not fully understand, let alone find themselves able to articulate, why they act as they do. Shakespeare works through a kind of super-realism, allowing characters insight into their own motives, and an ability to externalize complex states of mind—Angel's response to Isabella, or Shylock's to the Christians—rarely met with in life as it is. Jonson's method is different, and in many ways truer to normal experience. Important facts . . . must be deduced from . . . behaviour as a whole, not from anything they say about themselves or each other. It is a technique dependent upon inference and suggestion, rather than Shakespearean revelation. [p. 108]

But such effects are not absent from Shakespeare's work. Barton's generalizations about Jonson's great competitor occasionally seem a little broad; on page 138, for example, she implies that in *The Taming of the Shrew* Katherina is initially happy with her lot.

Barton's brilliant opening chapter states the theme of Jonson's ambivalent relation to the work of his contemporaries and immediate predecessors. However much he cherished ancient models, he was bound to respect the unclassical achievements of Sidney and Spenser and Shakespeare and Donne. He wished to "sing high and aloofe," and found his way by reacting against the comic practices and conventions of his time. Nevertheless, he was himself a brilliant practitioner of these conventions.

Throughout his life he continued to work out his Elizabethan involvements. This is an important insight of Barton's—even if her subsequent Elizabethan chapters are a little lacking in penetration (apparently because she finds non-naturalistic dramatic modes less congenial or more difficult to approach). Surprisingly, she refers only once to the author of *Jonson and Elizabethan Comedy* (and then misspells his name). This is a pity, since Beaurline has interesting things to say about Jonson's passion for particulars—a topic Barton engages with more than once. For Jonson discovered his own style of realism in large part through rejecting 1580s generality.

As a chronicler of Jonson's dramatic career—and especially as a military historian of the poetomachia—Barton makes an invaluable contribution. Her inwardness with Jacobean stage history is such that she is able to treat the milieu as an organic situation, attending omnisciently to appropriate details of theater companies, rival dramatists, plays, poems, patrons and personalities: all seem at her prompting, to cue as she decides. Perhaps, though, she takes the war of the theaters a shade too seriously, so that she misses nuances of some of the friendly insults. On questions of authorship she is admirably cautious. Unlike most historians of Renaissance literature, she understands the extent to which skills of *imitatio* allowed authors to simulate one another's style. And on the strange history of the reception of Jonson's plays, *Ben Jonson, Dramatist* has several new points to make. It offers penetrating (although sometimes debatable) suggestions, for example, as to why certain individual plays appealed to the Restoration theater. Was *Epicoene* valued because of its "readiness to dismiss the old"?

On matters of genre and of period style, Barton's performance is a little less even. Quite often she writes of Jonson's style as if he created it *ex nihilo*. For instance, it is odd that the author of *Shakespeare and the Idea of the Play* should discuss the dramatist roles of Sejanus and Tiberius, or Fitzdottrel's intention in *The Devil Is an Ass* to go to see *The Devil Is an Ass*, or the same play's references to the actor Robinson purely in Jonsonian terms, without any mention of Shakespeare or Marston or Webster or the other mannerist writers, with whom such self-referring effects were as common as alienation is with the School of Brecht. (Of course, differences between the mannerists are as noticeable as similarities: Shakespeare's dramatist figures tend to gesture towards the divine artist, where Jonson's illuminate types of human experience.) Again, what Barton describes as a purely Jonsonian rhetorical style—full of low and gritty particularity—was in fact a period phenomenon: the emergent epigrammatic style of the seventeenth century—a style certainly based in part on Jonson's own achievement, but depending also on other late Elizabethans like Nashe and Donne. Similarly, the urban localization of Jonsonian comedy has a generic dimension; it was a central feature, indeed, of citizen comedy. Jonson was certainly a main undertaker of this genre. Nevertheless, it developed a powerful corporate momentum—as witness the fact that Jonson in revising *Every Man in His Humour* felt it necessary to replace Florentine locations with London ones, in accordance with what had become a convention.

Barton might be faulted for a certain tangentiality, so far as the great Jacobean comedies are concerned; for however effective she is at describing the single impression of *Volpone* or the chaotic transmorality of *Bartholomew Fair*, she hardly aims at criticism that could stand on its own as a complete and adequate account. She prefers to focus on a few aspects on which she can make original contributions—such as the moral relation of characters to dramatist, or the method whereby they are named. But this plan can be defended, in that it makes for maximum interest to Jonsonians, besides enabling her to trace the sequence of the *oeuvre* more precisely. This can be very telling, as with a theme like betrayal of trust. Moreover, Jonson's naming, at least, proves to be an element fundamental to his art, justifying Barton's "Names: the Chapter Interloping," the finest onomastic study I have come across anywhere in dramatic criticism. Jonson came to share William Camden's complex position on naming—essentialism much modified by scepticism and historical analysis; and he used names in increasingly subtle ways after *Every Man Out of His Humour* (1599), the first play he considered deeply from this point of view. In *Volpone* (1606), for example, Volpone and Mosca are aware of the meaning of the other characters' bird names—Corvino, Corbaccio, Pol and the rest—whereas the gulls themselves have no comparable understanding. In *Bartholomew Fair* (1614) charactonyms or definitive names are avoided, while allusive, deliberately unapt names such as Argalus and Palemon imply shrewd criticism of their bearers. Barton's judgment in these matters is generally reliable; although she seems to me to go wrong in contrasting the Jonson-Camden position on names with that of Spenser, whose unapt and multifaceted names she overlooks. Even with Jonson's own names, she occasionally rests too easily content with a single explanation. Surely "Ursula," the name of the cook and bawd in *Bartholomew Fair*, not only means "little bear" but also implies its avatar, the unchaste Callisto, besides alluding, with satiric incongruity, to the saint who went to her martyrdom accompanied by 11,000 virgins. And the odd name "Wittipol," besides being "Witty Poll," can hardly have failed to carry an obscure suggestion of "Wittol."

A remarkable feature of Jonson's *oeuvre*, which Barton has occasion to stress time and again, is its avoidance of Elizabethan romantic plots—avoidance, indeed, of any continuous story-line. What can have motivated this extraordinary rejection of the conventional methods of his contemporaries? It was not simply the negative response of the classicist: as Barton amply demonstrates, Jonson was anything but automatic in his classicism. The dominating motive can only have been realism. Realism appears throughout his work in countless guises, from the "random quality" of *The Case is Altered* to the unschematic naturalism of parts of *Bartholomew Fair*. Barton characterizes this well. Nevertheless, the full ramifications of Jonson's realism are not to be tracked without a broader cast than she cares to make. One has to recall that realism was relatively new in the late sixteenth century, not only in drama, but in literature generally. Its tentative beginnings had been intermittent, or limited to short passages occurring, sometimes quite awkwardly to our eyes, in the midst of writing in other modes (usually allegorical or satiric). Full length fictional models were lacking.

Indeed, the very conception of continuous realism had yet to be imagined. It was thus inevitable that Jonson should present realistic imitation of nature not in the form of whole plays, but of discontinuous scenes.

From this point of view, Jonson's practice of breaking up narrative and multiplying plot lines (as in *The Alchemist*) can be recognized as a strategy of emergent realism—however distancing, paradoxically, it may now appear. Similarly with the satiric Theophrastian portraits that swarm so oppressively in his early comedies. Barton is severe on these "undramatic" elements: she thinks they must have "dismayed the original actors" and may have been cut in performance. But this is to assume a naturalistic standard of acting, in a way that may be unjust: "characters" seem to have been a voguish form of state-of-the-art realism, taken up by other dramatists, and only conspicuous in Jonson because of his innovative extremity. Barton's approach is perhaps a little too closely text-oriented, so that she finds some difficulty in imagining non-naturalistic stage action. Business was not necessarily motivated in Jonson's time: a Theophrastian portrait would offer excellent opportunities to a good Elizabethan actor.

Ben Jonson, Dramatist is a subtle, if occasionally an oversubtle, study. It has a few disproportions, such as overemphasis of naming, and underemphasis of Jonson's masque *oeuvre*—which is only brought to bear effectively with *A Staple of News* and *A Tale of a Tub*. And it has the unusual, almost laudable, fault of trying to justify too many of Jonson's oddities; so that he is almost denied the license of deficiencies and blunders. Nevertheless, this is the best account I know of the development of the dramatist's art. It traces the growth of Jonson's partial and reactive classicism; his increasing turn to unclassical material, or traditional forms; his appropriation of the morality inheritance; his personal involvement in themes of trust and paternity; and his participation in the nostalgic cult of Elizabeth—assembling all these into a coherent and judicious synthesis. How many dramatists could successfully have been taken as the subject of a study so complex and subtle as this? On the late plays—these disgracefully neglected works—

it excells all its predecessors. Indeed, there it sets Jonson criticism a new standard of penetration, and perhaps will precipitate the general revaluation long overdue.

"No Such Scarecrows in Your Father's Time": A New Tennyson Bibliography[1]

P. G. Scott

Kirk H. Beetz. *Tennyson, A Bibliography, 1827-1982*. Scarecrow Author Bibliographies No. 68. Metuchen, N.J. and London: The Scarecrow Press, 1984. vi, 528 pp.

Tennyson was, I think, the first poet to attack bibliographers by name. He distrusted critics, but it was, specifically, bibliographers that he abhorred, because scholars such as Churton Collins (a "louse upon the locks of literature") kept digging up all the early poems and discarded variants Tennyson hoped were long forgotten. What he would have thought about this book, and its five-hundred-page listing, not of forgotten poems but of forgotten critics, defies my imagination. He might even have relished its ironies, or recalled his notebook jotting of 1833, that in this imperfect world "seldom comes the poet . . . / And the Critic's rarer still." Rarest of all, we might add, is a really good bibliographer.

Kirk Beetz's new *Tennyson, A Bibliography* is essentially a minimally verified, sparsely annotated cumulation of the entries on Tennyson from previous bibliographies and from the better-known book-length studies of Tennyson's reputation. It is arranged chronologically year by year with separate alphabetical sequences under each year for book (and book sections), dissertations, and periodical articles. It does not offer any systematic coverage of non-English language criticism, though it includes foreign entries from previous bibliographies. In accordance with the general style of the Scarecrow series, it provides a very simple sketch of the major scholarly and critical sources (pp. 1-9), and there are quite substantial author and subject indexes (pp. 479-528).

It is a depressing work to read—all those endless lists of books, dissertations, and articles (over 5000 entries in all), most of which will never have been read or even looked at by modern Tennysonians (nor, apparently, by the bibliographer himself). The book's usefulness, in fact, lies not in bibliographical diligence or editorial accuracy or in the discovery of new materials, but simply in the convenience of having the separate sources conflated into one volume. Its derivativeness, indeed, is among the reasons it is worth extended examination, for a conflation like this reveals the widely differing degrees of bibliographical control we have over different periods and critical sub-genres in the literary tradition.

The task of tracking down Tennyson criticism differs greatly from period to period. Not only does the existing bibliographical guidance vary in its accuracy and completeness, but the actual scale of the task varies too, as also do the conventional definitions of what constitutes an item of "Tennyson criticism" and what constitutes a form of publication worth checking. Broadly speaking, for the early phase of Tennyson's career, previous scholars have tried to locate every comment on the poet, from newspapers as well as from the more manageable reviews and magazines. For the later nineteenth century, with the increased number of literary and general weeklies, there remains a bibliographical tradition of covering non-scholarly comment and sources, but it is much more selective by genre, with little attempt to cover even the better newspapers, while in the twentieth century, with the growth of discipline-specific or professional bibliographies, there has been a concentration of bibliographical effort on academic and quasi-academic journals and books, with only patchy coverage even of literary magazines, and a virtual abandonment of coverage for more popular or ephemeral comment. It is bibliographical convention as well as convenience, for instance, that includes the reviews from New York evening papers in the early Victorian period, but does not list the hundred or so American newspaper reviews of Sir Charles Tennyson's landmark biography in the mid-twentieth century. It is convention, too, that records comment within books more fully from the early period than from the modern one,

A New Tennyson Bibliography

and that includes comment published in print-form but not that broadcast over radio or television or circulated on audio-cassette.

The common observation on a bibliography of this kind is that it "shows the changing nature of Tennyson criticism over the last one hundred and fifty years"; it does do that, but only after such criticism has already been sieved through changing definitions of what is worth listing. Existing sources list very different kinds of "Tennyson criticism" in, say, the eighteen-forties, the nineteen-tens, and the nineteen-seventies, and the differences reflect change not only in the actual criticism being written and published, but also in what bibliographers choose to count as recordable. Beetz, as an extremely derivative bibliographer, mirrors the selectivity and the gradual professionalization, not just of criticism itself, but of bibliographical focus, built into the sources on which he relies.

For the first thirty years of Tennyson's career, the bibliographical groundwork was laid early, because of a long-running debate about whether and how Tennyson was affected by the few famous hostile reviews. Lounsbury's extraordinarily detailed study of the early life (1915, item 2797) was followed by Helen Pearce's 1930 Berkeley dissertation (item 3124) and Muriel Bowden's book on Tennyson's French reception the same year (item 3101). The two landmark studies are by John Olin Eidson on the American reception to 1858 (*Tennyson in America*, 1943, item 3328) and by E. F. Shannon on the British reception to 1850 (*Tennyson and the Reviewers*, 1952, item 3496, supplemented for the years up to 1855 by Shannon's articles on the reception of the Wellington Ode, 1960, item 3716, and *Maud*, 1953, item 3539). The subsequent anthologies of early criticism by J. D. Jump (item 4013) and Isobel Armstrong (item 4333) both have useful interpretative introductions, but neither Jump nor Armstrong collected any early reviews previously unknown.

For the earlier years, therefore, Beetz has been able to put together quite a respectable looking list simply by collating existing previous work. I made a quick check of the entries from 1834 through 1843 (items 33-89) and found only one that did not derive from the text or bibliographies in Shannon, Eidson or Bowden (in his "Note on Sources," p. vi, Beetz litotically acknowledges finding Eidson and Shannon "particularly helpful"). The single exception (item 81, referenced without page number) is taken, with acknowledgment, from W. D. Templeman's 1963 article on the reputation of "Locksley Hall" (item 3843). One giveaway to Beetz's method is that where (as frequently happens) Eidson or Bowden do not give a volume or page numbers, Beetz too omits the information (e.g., item 56 from Bowden, p. 13). Beetz's annotation frequently draws on the discussions and extracts given in his three major sources; indeed, I didn't pick up any direct quotation from the sources being annotated that wasn't in Shannon, Eidson or Bowden, or from items available in Jump's Critical Heritage volume.

However, the recycling is by no means complete; Beetz's guidelines mean that he does not always include important incidental criticism uncovered by these earlier scholars, such as "Christopher North's" later discussions of Tennyson in *Blackwood's* (February 1836, May 1836, and April 1839, all discussed by Shannon on pp. 26-27) or the items from *Revue des Deux Mondes*, 1841 and *Revue Britanniques*, October 1842 (noted in Bowden on pp. 12-14). Even within Beetz's general guidelines, coverage is sometimes spotty: a few of the early American reviews from Eidson seem simply to have got lost, such as the second reviews from the *Evening Post* (July 12, 1842, in Eidson p. 161) and the *New World* (July 23, 1842, in Eidson, p. 169). Nor does Beetz always include the reprint information Eidson provided, such as reprintings of the *Evening Post* review of July 8, 1842 (item 59) in the *New York Daily Tribune* of July 12 and *Weekly Tribune* of July 16. Since microfilm files are more readily available for the *Tribune* than for the *Post*, this kind of omission is important.

There are several snarl-ups or inconsistencies in the choice of entry date and reprint information for reprinted periodical items. For example, W. E. Aytoun's parodies of Tennyson (items 85 and 86) are listed under their original 1843 periodical appearance, but cross-referenced only to a worthless reprinting in the 1890 New York edition of Bon Gaultier, while Aytoun and Theodore Martin's parody of "Locksley Hall" — "The Lay of the Lovelorn" — is entered under the first book edition of Bon Gaultier in 1845 (item 99), without any entry for its periodical appearance (in *Tait's Edinburgh Magazine,* December 1842, pp. 801-02), or for the 1890 reprint. "The Lay of the Lovelorn" gets another entry (item 644, from the eleventh edition, 1870), but with no cross-referencing from either end.[2] One curious error that I noted was the duplication between items 65 and 74, where a single review from *Graham's Magazine* is attributed, with different annotation, both to Rufus Griswold and Edgar Allan Poe, exactly the kind of mistake that in other bibliographers Beetz himself castigates as "astonishingly egregious" (item 4016; cf. other duplicate entries at 4115 and 4397, 4197 and 4268, and 4206 and 4222).

How comprehensive were the scholarly predecessors on whom Beetz relies for these early years? It's easier to answer for his American source than for the others. A good cross-check can be made from Daniel Wells's *Literary Index to American Magazines, 1815-1865,* put out by Beetz's own publisher a few years ago, which gives a second listing over the period of Eidson's book. From such a check, Eidson (and therefore Beetz) comes out surprisingly well. Eidson's list was restricted to whole items substantially about Tennyson, and the extra items I noticed in Wells were all short news notices or mentions within a longer article: for instance, under 1850, Beetz has the *In Memoriam* review from *Literary World* (item 226; volume 7, pp. 30-31), but not the two other briefer items from the same periodical (vol. 6, p. 622, and vol. 7, p. 436). Wells also indexes American periodical reprintings of Tennyson poems or extracts, something outside Eidson's (or Beetz's) scope, yet significant in the growth of his reputation.

Wells's entries suggest some weakness in Beetz's annotation, for Beetz's item 504 (from *North American Review* for January 1860) is glossed simply as "Review of *Idylls,* 1859," while Wells indexes some of it as being a discussion of Tennyson's *Maud.* Similarly, Beetz's item 299 (from *Graham's Magazine* for September 1853) is glossed as "Review of *The Princess* (fifth edition). Praises the poem," while Wells indexes it as a review of the new Ticknor *Poems*; here, Beetz's entry seems to be based on a misreading of Eidson, who on p. 177 lists the review as of *Poems*, but on p. 72 cites it as including rare early American comment on Tennyson's revisions to *The Princess*, first reprinted in America in the Ticknor collection. There is no modern scholarly subject index for British literary periodicals equivalent to Wells, so it is impractical to make any equivalent cross-check on Beetz's Shannon-derived British coverage. I find it impressive how durable the pioneer studies of Tennyson's reception have proved to be over the years, but I have a lingering feeling of the inherent probability that some scholar, somewhere, has recorded additional early Tennyson reviews in the thirty-odd years since Eidson and Shannon, even if Beetz did not set out to find any for himself.[3]

Up to the 1850s, then, Beetz's bibliography may be taken as a handy, if neither new nor error-free, reference tool, because he was working from good sources. After 1858, however, his task was much more difficult, because guidance from previous scholars is less reliable and less complete. The result is an instant drop in the annual total of items Beetz can list, even though there can have been no such drop in actual published comment. For the later 1840s and early 1850s, he records an average of thirty items a year, but for the early 1860s, which saw the publication of one of Tennyson's best-selling volumes (*Enoch Arden, Etc.*, 1864), he provides an annual average of just over eleven items. The major loss is in detailed coverage of newspaper reviewing, though there are also many periodical omissions. For this period, Beetz is primarily dependent on the 1936 Tennyson bibliography by Theodore G. Ehrsam, Robert H. Deily and Robert G. Smith (item 3241; noted as "particularly helpful" on p. vi, where it is misreferenced as item 2756). Because Beetz is arranged year by year, while most of Ehrsam, Deily and Smith's items are arranged partly by author and partly by the title under review, it is difficult to check the degree of Beetz's reliance on the Ehrsam list, and its supplement by Joseph G. Fucilla (1939, item 3280, for which Beetz gives wrong page numbers), but it is certainly extensive, if not total.

What can be said with confidence is that Beetz's list is very incomplete. In my Tennyson Society monograph on *Enoch Arden* (1970, item 4219, which Beetz annotates as "useful"), I cited sixteen reviews from 1864-1865; Beetz's listing includes only eight of the sixteen, omitting the reviews in such important organs as *The Times, Saturday Review, Guardian,* and *Illustrated Times,* as well as the four essays from the *British Controversialist* debating the poem's morality (these last had also been included in Sir Charles Tennyson and Christine Fall's 1967 bibliography, item 4016, which Beetz decries as "sloppily, almost casually, put together"). The 1860s are, of course, also too late for Beetz to get Eidson's help on American reviews, and there's an additional review of *Enoch Arden* listed in Wells (in *Knickerbocker,* 65, 282-89).

Nor has Beetz done very much with the reduced number of items he has collected. One of the major achievements of recent scholarship in nineteenth-century British bibliography has been the *Wellesley Index*, with three volumes out and a fourth near publication. *Wellesley* allows author-identification for a substantial number of fortnightly, monthly and quarterly reviews, but Beetz appears not to have used it routinely. I noticed on pages 64-66 alone items left without author identification from the *Dublin Review, Fraser's,* the *National Review,* and the *Westminster,* all *Wellesley* periodicals (items 529, by A. K. H. Boyd; 546, by C. W. Russell; 552, by Walter Bagehot; and 558, by Sheldon Amos—this last item following Ehrsam *et al.* in giving the wrong page numbers).

The 1864 entries also include another of Beetz's duplications, with Bagehot's famous essay on the "Pure, the Ornate and the Grotesque" styles once being correctly attributed and once entered without its title as an anonymous review. The two entries (items 537 and 552) share the same date and page references to the *National Review* of November 1864, but get different volume numbers by using respectively the continuous and new series systems, and both give (completely different) notes of subsequent reprintings; neither, however, mentions the obvious modern reprinting in St. John-Stevas's *Collected Works of Walter Bagehot* (1965), II, 321-66. Item 567, in the next year, is a two-part reprinting of the same Bagehot essay (unattributed) in the *Eclectic Magazine*, but receives no cross-reference to either of the previous entries; indeed, this 1865 entry derives in every particular, including its erroneous title, from Ehrsam, Deily and Smith. The duplicate 1864 entries get differing annotations, too, once as simply "Review of *Enoch Arden*" (item 552), and once as "Longwinded essay on the nature of literary art, much of which is illustrated by Tennyson and 'Enoch Arden' " (item 537). If this is the treatment given to one of the most famous critical essays of the period, what must we expect for more ordinary entries? But of the thirty-six entries (including duplicates) from 1864-1865, only seven get any annotation (other than "Review of ————," easily derived from Ehrsam's arrangement); three of those annotations are of French items discussed in Bowden, while two others are of items reprinted in Jump's Critical Heritage. The apparently learned note for a German source (item 563) comes from Ehrsam *et al.* (p. 351). In short, for Tennyson's later years, Beetz has not gone beyond the most convenient of sources, and as a consequence this section of his bibliography is the weakest in coverage. However full oldfashioned author bibliographies like Ehrsam, Deily and Smith's might seem, they are nowhere near complete, and researchers into the reception of Tennyson's later work cannot rely on them alone (nor, therefore, on Beetz).

By the closing years of the century, the problem gets worse. The continuing expansion of the weekly and daily press, and the growth of book-chat papers such as those edited by Robertson Nicoll, enormously increase the scale of the bibliographer's task. Indeed, the early 1890s were peak years for publication about Tennyson, with Beetz recording seventy-odd items annually, a rate not surpassed till the early 1970s. *The* peak was 1892, the year of Tennyson's death; he published two volumes that year, and had a play produced, so the combined effect of book reviews, theater reviews, obituaries, memorial tributes, and retrospective assessments pushes Beetz's annual total up to 266. Since much of the material from that age of the cheap press and the literary tidbit is now by almost any criterion worthless, doing 1892 is a prospect to daunt any Tennyson bibliographer, but it is precisely for such periods that one most relies on a bibliography to do the sifting, annotation, and indexing that help locate the intelligent comment and first-hand information among the reams of empty chatter. I checked a single opening (Jacobs to *Literary World*, pp. 148-49), which lists twenty entries. Of these, seventeen were in Ehrsam, Deily and Smith, and two more in Fucilla's 1939 supplement.

More dismaying than the derivativeness, therefore, is the paucity of Beetz's annotation; nineteen of the twenty items receive no annotation not derived from Ehrsam *et al.*, with even Lionel Johnson's long *Academy* piece on *The Death of Oenone* going undescribed. There is no note, for instance, that Joseph Jacob's article (item 1507) was included in his book on *In Memoriam* (item 1397). The single "annotated" item is James Knowles's *Nineteenth Century* poem about Tennyson's funeral, which (on Beetz's usual pattern for poetic tributes) is reprinted in full. One is grateful for such reprintings (the material is not easily available elsewhere), but one is tempted to ask if the value of this late-Victorian section of Beetz's bibliography could not have been achieved almost as well simply by producing a slim edition of poems about Tennyson. Nine of the sixteen memorial poems Beetz reprints come from a single issue of the *Nineteenth Century*, and three more from a single issue of the New York *Critic*.

Even the books and book chapters get short shrift in the way of annotation, for of the twenty-four book items listed for 1892, only one gets more than a line of annotation (Anne Thackeray Ritchie's memoirs, for which Beetz gives thirty-one lines of direct quotation), and seventeen get no annotation at all. What annotations there are do not offer much: Eugene Parsons's *Tennyson's Life and Poetry: and Mistakes about Tennyson* (1892) is said to be "Of interest to the specialist in Tennyson because it discusses mistakes about Tennyson made by other critics." I had never imagined the mistakes of the title were Parsons's own (and there ought, too, to have been some cross-reference to Parsons's *Dial* article the same year [item 1572], titled "Mistakes about Tennyson," and some note that the book was issued in an enlarged form the following year). I should have liked to know *something* about William Greswell's

Tennyson and Our Imperial Heritage or Jacobs's book (which four periodicals thought worth a review), but neither they nor William M. MacPhail's lecture on the *Idylls* get any annotation from Beetz; he doesn't even record how many pages they have. In short, Beetz's coverage of the early 1890s, which would raise real problems of scale and treatment for any bibliographer, is simply shoddy.[4]

It is tempting to believe that bibliographical control significantly improves once one enters the twentieth century. However, such is not the case. Certainly the general periodical indexes proliferate, and expand in the range of weekly and monthly material they cover, and Ehrsam, Deily and Smith made good use of the general indexes. But most newspaper material simply drops from view — there are several boxes of press-cuttings in the Tennyson Research Centre at Lincoln about the Eversley edition and Hallam Tennyson's *Tennyson and His Friends* (1911), but such material is unrepresented here, as it would be in almost any conceivable Tennyson bibliography; the point, of course, is that precisely the same kind of material gets scrupulous listing in the 1850s. Assuming, however, that one accepts the conventional constraints on what material is to be covered, the problem for the early twentieth century is not in accumulating material year by year, but in reconciling the various sources and spotting partial or belated entries that require back-up research. My notes on Beetz's book for this period consist very largely of references to omissions, and queries, and puzzled attempts to work out why Beetz made the snarl-ups he did.

I looked first at the thirty-three entries for 1914 (items 2756-2789). Item 2756, on Baker's *Concordance*, does not sort out the publication history for the various supplements, nor note that the 1966 reprint was from the British publishers Routledge and Kegan Paul, not just from Barnes and Noble. Item 2761 omits not just the dates of Oxford's various printings for A. M. D. Hughes's edition, but also the 1968 reprint (Bath: Cedric Chivers "at the request of the Library Association"). The list of 1914 books and book chapters could usefully have included the expanded edition of Morton Luce's handbook (here only

A New Tennyson Bibliography

under 1895, item 1872), Hugh Marwick's introductory essay to his edition of *Enoch Arden* (Clarendon Press), Edward Parrott's essay from *The Pageant of English Literature* (Thomas Nelson), Stanley Schell's essay on *The Princess* published with a dramatization (New York: E. S. Werner) and Amos Russel Wells's comment on Tennyson in his *Treasury of Hymns* (United Society of Christian Endeavor, 1914, reprinted 1945). Two items entered only under their American publication in 1915 should be here under their 1914 British appearance: W. Forbes Gray's *Poets Laureate of England* (item 2795), and Arthur Turnbull's *Life and Writings* (item 2799, which also fails to note the 1977 Folcroft reprinting). The book section should also, for consistency, have included the published editions of Josef Bausenwein's Heidelberg dissertation (item 2769), published at Wurzburg, and of Leonie Villard's Paris one (item 2772), published by Mulcey at St. Etienne, 1914; other published dissertations get duplicate entries in the book section.

Among the periodical entries, item 2776 from the *Dial* is given neither annotation nor title (it should read "Moody and Yeats on Tennyson"). Items 2774, 2783 and 2785 are all comments on the same disputed phrase, yet none of them gets any annotation to indicate which poem the phrase comes from ("Alexander"). Neither the annotation for Baker nor the periodical list includes A. H. Johnson's "Concordances to Tennyson" (*Times Literary Supplement*, July 30, 1914). The title of item 2775 should read "a study in," not "a study of." Beetz annotates item 2787, from the November New York edition of *The Bookman*, "First publication of a poem by Tennyson," without noting that it also appeared in the British edition of October 13, 1914, or that it was actually first published under a different title, "The Pennywise," in 1852 and in 1884-85, or that it was included in a volume of *Tennyson's Patriotic Poems* (1914), through which, presumably, the *Bookman* picked it up (cf. Ricks's edition, *The Poems of Tennyson*, pp. 994-96). A reader working from less-than-perfect library resources might have liked to know whether Henry Lucy's "personal notes" on Tennyson (item 2778), from the *Nation*, were the same as those in his *Memoirs* (1916, not included here). In summary, for 1914 alone, Beetz has at least ten omissions and eight entries that are in some way defective.

During the period between the two World Wars, the low-point in Tennysonian interest, the annual number of titles gradually slipped from twenty-odd in the early 1920s to a mere ten or twelve during the later thirties. With the start-up of the MHRA's *Annual Bibliography* just after the Great War, and the annual Victorian Bibliography in *Modern Philology* in the early thirties, bibliographical control, at least of academic items, substantially improves, even though the MLA list isn't much help before the 1940s. Beetz reproduces these professional sources faithfully, and it is convenient to have this material gathered in one listing, though he seldom seems to fill in article titles or other publishing information not in the source bibliographies. It would perhaps be uncharitable to overemphasize Beetz's omissions here, for it is the nature of his bibliographical sources that leads to his consistent omission of locally published or non-academic material. All the same, these *are* consistent omissions. I checked 1924, for instance, and the list lacks the quite useful illustrated article from *Morton's Lincolnshire Almanack* on the house in Westgate, Louth, where Tennyson lived while attending Louth Grammar School. This pattern holds, for later omissions include A. E. Smith's *Tennyson and His Age* (South Ormsby: the Rectory, 1951); the first two of J. M. Gray's five preliminary pamphlets for his study of the *Idylls* (Lincoln: Keyworth and Fry, 1973); and the anonymous *A Guide to Tennyson's Lincolnshire: the Poet's Years in and around Somersby* (Skegness, 1973). About a dozen of Sir Charles Tennyson's earlier or more popular writings about his grandfather also are omitted, unnecessarily in view of Lionel Madden's excellent bibliography of Sir Charles (rather oddly included here as item 4415, but apparently not much utilized). I noticed for instance the omission of Sir Charles's 1933 pamphlet *The Story of Farringford and Tennyson*, and the much expanded version *Farringford, Home of Alfred, Lord Tennyson* (Lincoln: the Tennyson Society, 1976); the first publication of his important biographical research ("The Tennyson Family: Unpublished Facts Revealed," *Louth Times*, June 8 and June

15, 1935, incomplete in Madden); his war-time article on "Tennyson's England" (*Geographical Magazine*, July 1941); and his lecture on *Tennyson and "Locksley Hall"*, printed for the fledgling Tennyson Society in 1961.[5] Nor, of course, would Beetz or his bibliographical sources stoop to the much more popular material on Tennyson published from time to time in the local magazine *Lincolnshire Life*, to which Sir Charles was a regular contributor. I have a note for instance of a piece on "Tennyson country—the making of a film," in November 1981, that documents an otherwise unrecorded aspect of Tennyson's reputation.[6]

Nor is it just local sources that are neglected: both the popular piece "Tennyson at Home" (in *Hobbies*, New York, for February 1950) and Hallam Tennyson's note about his radio production of *Harold* (in *Radio Times*, October 10, 1966) are also left out. Academic items published in non-academic forums are particularly vulnerable to this kind of bibliographical amnesia; for instance, Frank McManus's two-part essay on Tennyson's religion is omitted, because it appeared in *Open Door*, an Open University religious society's newsletter (December 1976 and March 1977), while I. A. Copley's article "Tennyson and the Composers," which drew on unpublished letters, is left out because it appeared in *Musical Opinion* (September 1978). What these omissions suggest is that the "improved" bibliographical control provided by the professionalization of twentieth-century scholarship has been accomplished in part by a progressive tightening on the criteria for bibliographical notice.

By the middle of the century Beetz's omissions of normal critical materials from standard-literature sources become far fewer, but omissions there still are. Under 1940, for instance, Beetz lists seventeen items, yet I noticed no mention of the original *Cambridge Bibliography* entry; nor of the comment on Tennyson and John Wilson Croker in Myron Brightfield's book; nor of Ifor Evans's *Tradition and Romanticism*; nor of Myra E. Hull's essay on the Merman lover from the O'Leary-Whitcomb *festschrift*; nor of G. G. Loane's third *Notes and Queries* note (November 16, 1940, p. 359); nor of W. Mansford's essay in *Poetry Review*; nor of Emery Neff's *A Revolution in*

European Poetry (which the *Victorian Bibliography* annotated as containing "arresting passages" on Tennyson); nor of George Schuster's *English Ode* (which discusses Tennyson on pages 276-97). With eight omissions Beetz has a coverage ratio of 68%, about what one expects from the annual bibliographies, but a retrospective bibliography like Beetz's ought to score better.

And a retrospective bibliography ought to do better, too, in synthesizing and filling out the entries it cumulates. Item 3288, for instance, lists Walter de la Mare's *Pleasures and Speculations* (1940), without adding the page references for the Tennyson essay, or following up on the *Victorian Bibliography* annotation that it had first appeared in the *TLS*. The 1942 *TLS* article on "Tennyson's Mystic Imperialism," here listed without an author, could easily have been identified and cross-referenced to Wilson Knight's *Neglected Powers* (item 4279, 1971), if Beetz had verified the 1971 entry. The 1944 entry for Auden's introductory essay (item 3345, first published in New York) gives no cross-reference to the British publication (Phoenix House, 1946, not noted in Beetz), nor to the formal reprint in Auden's *Forewords and Afterwords* (1973); Beetz also misses at least two reviews, by Francis Golffing in *Poetry* and by Lloyd Frankenberg in *Commonweal*. The 1944 periodical entry for Cleanth Brooks's famous "Tears, Idle Tears" essay (item 3350) does not give Brooks's original title, "The New Criticism: a brief for the defense," but the later book-form title instead. The entry for George Ford's 1944 book, *Keats and the Victorians* (item 3346), gives no page references for the Tennyson section and omits any reference to the 1962 reprint; it also omits the publication series and volume number (Yale Studies in English, volume 101) needed for location in many libraries.

By now, the nature of Beetz's bibliographical research should be clear, and I hardly need to say that my listing of omissions and errors is a selective one. I've checked in detail only a few sample years, and I have included here only the more easily communicated and less disputable flaws. Almost any year or any page raises some query for the moderately informed user, and I forbear from dragging through the 1960s and 1970s error by error. Items from the *Tennyson Research Bulletin* get particularly uneven coverage in Beetz, because they have never been fully or consistently covered in MLA or the Annual Bibliography of English Language and Literature. But I would have expected any moderately committed Tennyson bibliographer to sit down with the back-files and make a list for himself. Examples of what Beetz misses include John Pfordresher's description of an unrecorded *Idylls* manuscript (*TRB*, 2:5 [1976], 203-04) and J. M. Gray's "Literary Echoes in 'Guinevere,' 21-52" (*TRB*, 3:2 [1978], 75-76), which discusses previously unnoticed echoes from Milton, Spenser, Chaucer and Shakespeare. An item like T. H. Warren's "Tennyson and Dante," here given under 1970 because of a Kennikat reprint (item 4221), receives no cross-reference to the original periodical article of 1904 (item 2381) or the first book publication in 1909 (item 2545). Item 4119 has no reference for the reprinting of Robert Stange's essay in H. J. Dyos and Michael Wolff's seminal collection on the Victorian city. Gordon Ray's separately published Sedgwick Lecture, *Tennyson Reads* Maud (Vancouver, B. C., 1968), is only entered under its 1972 reprint in the Marshall memorial volume (item 4341). Owen Dudley Edwards's important essay on Tennyson and Ireland (from *New Edinburgh Review*, 1977) is simply missing, as is Leonee Ormond's monograph on Tennyson and Woolner (Tennyson Society, 1981). Item 4602 lists without annotation a 1974 article that reprinted an interesting provincial Victorian essay (from the *Central Literary Magazine*, Birmingham, October 1888), but there is no entry for this under 1888, presumably because Beetz never looked at the 1974 item himself. Substantial British dissertations, such as those by well-known Tennyson scholars like J. M. Gray, Isobel Armstrong, James Sait, and Aidan Day, are missing from the dissertation sections, as is Christopher Kent's 1971 dissertation on the *Idylls* and the periodical press. Item 3458 is by Canon Adam Fox, not Adam Cox, and item 5048 by Sally Minogue, not Minoque. It seems a bit over-refined to add that Michael Trevanion (item 4126) is a pseudonym for the British bibliographer Simon Nowell-Smith, for it is one of the few corrections that Beetz couldn't easily have made for himself, if he had taken a bit more trouble.

I had not expected to have to give this book so critical a review. Very few bibliographies are flawless, and I fully recognize the inevitability of some error creeping into so large a number of bibliographical entries. I knew, too, that Beetz was not inexperienced as a secondary bibliographer; he has previously published in the same Scarecrow series volumes on Ruskin (1976), Wilkie Collins (1978), and Swinburne (1982). His Tennyson bibliography has been commended in the library selection journals as "an essential acquisition" (*Choice*) and, more guardedly, "useful to serious students of Tennyson" (*Reference Books Bulletin*). It is the most comprehensive bibliography of Tennyson ever attempted, and the only one to cumulate the enormous academic output of the late 1960s and the 1970s. Experienced Tennyson scholars will undoubtedly find its author-index a very handy desk-reference tool for locating items they already know. The sources on which it draws, at least for its first four decades and its last four, ensure that it includes a great deal of the more valuable material. And it is handsomely produced, by comparison with the bibliographies of pre-word-processing days. Even as I started to examine the book, and recognized Beetz's heavy reliance on standard sources, what chiefly interested me was the unevenness of our bibliographical control over different periods, rather than the minutiae of Beetz's particular errors or omissions. But it is impossible to ignore or to fail to report the fact that this book's flaws lie thick as dust in vacant chambers. Perhaps one romanticizes the accuracy and industry of earlier scholars, but one is tempted to say, with Renard in *Queen Mary*, there were "no such scarecrows in your father's time."

Notes

1. My work on the Tennyson bibliography has been supported in part by a grant from the University of South Carolina Research and Productive Scholarship Fund.

2. Aytoun and Martin get good treatment by comparison with other parodists: on pp. 247-49, Beetz follows his source in entering under their 1913 reprint in Walter Jerrold's *Century of Parody and Imitation*, without any reference to their original dates of appearance, nine parodies by such easily-bibliographed authors as C. S. Calverley, Lewis Carroll, and D. G.

A New Tennyson Bibliography

Rossetti. In a chronologically arranged bibliography, this constitutes a crucial distortion of the historical record.

3. A further cross-reference, to Nelson F. Adkins's *Index to Early American Periodicals to 1850* (Readex, 1964), confirms the feeling: Adkins has an additional entry for 1848, from *Hogg's Weekly Instructor*, reprinted in *Eclectic Magazine*, 13 (May 1848), 289-95, and he also has an additional reprinting for item 255, in *North American Miscellany and Dollar Magazine*, 2 (May 17, 1851), 126-31.

4. Beetz follows Ehrsam *et al.* in omitting A. T. Lyttelton's 1893 essay in the *Church Quarterly Review*, and when he records, as they do, the 1904 reprinting (item 2355), he follows them not only in getting Lyttelton's book title wrong, but in misspelling his name. And Beetz follows Jump's *Critical Heritage* volume (and the Ehrsam entry) in giving W. E. Henley's essay under the 1908 reprint in his two-volume *Views and Reviews* (item 2489), without making any cross-reference or entry for the 1890 one-volume reprint (mentioned in Jump's headnote), let alone the original appearance in the *Scots Observer*.

5. Incidentally, Madden's bibliography provides author identification for a couple of items that are anonymous in Beetz: item 2752, from *The Spectator*, 1913, and item 3282, from *Poetry Review*, 1939, are both by Sir Charles Tennyson.

6. One should, I think, forgive the omission of Laurence Elvin's "From Rags to Riches: the Story of 'The Beggar Maid,' " *Fireside Magazine, the Monthly Journal of the Forget-Me-Not Club of Lincoln*, 10 (August 1973), 11-15, though Elvin advances a real-life source for the poem not recorded in Ricks's edition.

Authorial Revision

James McLaverty

Hershel Parker. *Flawed Texts and Verbal Icons: Literary Authority in American Fiction.* Evanston, Illinois: Northwestern University Press, 1984. xix, 249 pp.

Hershel Parker's book has such splendid aims, and he displays so much energy, learning, and humor in prosecuting them, that I wish I could agree with more of his arguments. In a relatively short volume he sets about two tasks which have long demanded the attention of an experienced and humane textual critic. The first is to combat the isolation of textual criticism within Anglo-American letters; when Parker says that literary critics and theorists of all persuasions have taken no notice of the processes which lie behind the text they read and have treated it as a given, he is largely right; and he is bold enough to set about showing how this sort of evidence might be used. The second task is that of confronting the problems posed for editors by authorial revision. Here Parker has the advantage of reflecting on the vast amount of information uncovered by the Center for Editions of American Authors and its successor, the Center for Scholarly Editions, and if he has not come through the civil wars generated by those projects unscathed (only Saint Catherine of Alexandria or G. Thomas Tanselle could do that), he is able to present the reader with a fascinating array of authorial reconstructions, tinkerings, and botchings. His examples of authorial ineptitude may not be the final nails in the coffin of the "final intention" school of editing, but they are at least going to take a good deal of explaining away. The subject of the book, therefore, and the link between the two tasks undertaken, is the creative process. Parker discusses psychological theories of creativity (or, at least, one of them), and he examines not so much what publishers, compositors, and house-correctors do to texts, as what authors themselves do to them. He analyzes the revisions of *Tender Is the Night, Pudd'nhead Wilson, The Red Badge of Courage,* and Mailer's *An American Dream*; he discusses the literary criticism of Henry James's rewritings of his novels; and he surveys the development of literary theory from Wimsatt and Beardsley's "The Intentional Fallacy" to the present day. All this is perhaps too much for anyone to chew, and the diffuseness of the book's ambition poses problems for writer and reader alike.

A serious difficulty with this work lies in knowing precisely what claims it is making. The position is complicated because the first chapter began as a response to, and partial endorsement of, an essay by Steven Knapp and Walter Benn Michaels, "Against Theory," in *Critical Inquiry,* 8 (Summer 1982), 723-42. Knapp and Michaels argue specifically against any form of prescriptivism; they say that theory is quite useless because the issues it discusses are not real; theory cannot tell us how to interpret; it has no consequences. Parker's emphasis is quite different: he applauds Knapp and Michaels for "admitting the existence of the author and welcoming him back from . . . banishment" and he talks about the lessons to be "learned from 'particular texts' " (p. 2); he discusses the founding of a new "biographico-textico-aesthetico 'movement' " (p. 241) (he cannot find an adequate name for it) with revolutionary implications for the whole range of textual scholarship; and he calls his surveys of the last three decades of scholarship "detailing the waste of human effort in editing, criticism, and theory" (p. 239). Parker is not, then, against theory: he only agrees with Knapp and Michaels in so far as they seem to afford some support to E. D. Hirsch and P. D. Juhl (in fact they afford none; their "author" might be the Muses); his statement on theory at the start of the concluding chapter is a flat contradiction of the Knapp and Michaels thesis: "An incorrigible empiricist, I bow to the power of theory. It was, after all, theory, however simplified, which led to the habit of ignoring biographical-textual evidence and its implications, the condition which has warranted my writing this book" (p. 213). Hirsch, on this account, simply did not go far enough; with Parker's evidence,

Authorial Revision

he could still triumph (pp. 221-24). Parker sees his arguments, therefore, as something more than elements in a rhetorical strategy; he aims to make a contribution to the theory of literature and editing. But what he really offers, I believe, are useful generalizations, generalizations which he itches to press too far.[1]

Parker writes a good deal about the "creative process": proper attention to, and respect for, the creative process is at the heart of his recommendations; only by studying the creative process can we determine the authority of the author's textual decisions (pp. 49-51). This line of investigation leads to the conclusion that "because the creative process is by nature determinate, revising authors very often betray or otherwise blur their original achievements in ways they seldom intend and seldom become aware of" (p. ix). If I do not emerge from reading this book sharing Parker's unfavorable view of authorial revision, a major reason is that I am unhappy with the approach to the creative process he adopts—it is generally much too unreflectingly asocial and romantic. I am even unhappy about how it is decided what counts as a creative process. One would expect Parker, being, as he claims, an empiricist, to use "creative process" in one of two ways: either for (1) an activity which produces a complete work of literature (for literature is being discussed); or (2) a period of continuous activity which goes towards, or is intended to go towards, producing a complete work of literature (it might be thinking or writing; the work might be finished or not). What is dangerous is any wavering between the two so that all instances of (2) are treated as failures to achieve (1). I suspect Parker falls into this trap when, in the chapter on the "Determinacy of the Creative Process," he tells us that "distractions may come on such a grand scale that the book may be the result of more than one creative process, one or more of which may never have been completed, or that a book will be the result of an incomplete creative process" (p. 28). The second clause looks like a muddle between (1) and (2) (why otherwise should the remark be worth making at all?), while the final possibility presented makes no sense unless Parker is either postulating some sort of thing (a creative process) which is independent of what authors actually do, or using the phrase evaluatively, to mean "good creative process"—so that "incomplete" means "bad."[2] Parker claims that his view of the creative process derives from the writings of John Dewey and Albert Rothenberg, but their work does not lead to these conclusions; it does not have the sort of authority he claims for it and the view of revision it presents is quite different from his.

Parker quotes the same phrase or two from Dewey several times. Dewey says in *Art as Experience* (London: George Allen & Unwin, 1934) that the "artist is controlled in the process of his work by his grasp of the connection between what he has already done and what he is to do next" and that he (or the writing as Parker has it on p. 23) must "at each point retain and sum up what has gone before as a whole and with reference to a whole to come"; otherwise there will be "no consistency and no security in his successive acts" (*Art as Experience*, pp. 45 and 56). But this is not, as Parker implies, some disinterested account of the creative process which will allow us to know a proper one when we see one and spot an incomplete one; it is part of an argument that the artist is worth as much as the scientist—the artist is important because of his command of relations and because of the combination of doing and undergoing in his work. Dewey is not writing about the creative process so much as about what you need to do to get a good unified work (that is, remember what your aims are and what you've already written). Moreover, Dewey thinks revision is a good thing: "Writer, composer of music, sculptor, or painter can retrace during the process of production, what they have previously done. When it is not satisfactory in the undergoing or perceptual phase of experience, they can to some degree start afresh. This retracing is not readily accomplished in the case of architecture—which is perhaps one reason why there are so many ugly buildings" (*Art as Experience*, pp. 51-52). Nor is Rothenberg any greater help to Parker in his pursuit of the evils of revision. It is true that Rothenberg writes of the arousal that accompanies composition, but Parker's resulting jibe at Greg, "all empirical evidence should tell us that Greg is wrong, that in any mature human being, writers included, a state of indefinitely sustained arousal toward one object is unnatural" (p. 35), misses its mark because all Greg's theory of copy-text plus Rothenberg requires is that the author should be aroused by the same "object" twice. Parker emphasizes Rothenberg's view that deletions can "represent attempts to conceal unacceptable thoughts" (p. 189), but he does not refer to the psychologist's conclusions about an unnamed major American poet, "a subject of mine," and his poem "In Monument Valley": "he also, like O'Neill, embodied his deeper, more unconscious preoccupations in the final product. The result is that the final product is far better than the initial formulation; it is an achievement of something new—not only the description of the author's actual experience—and valuable. The process of revision shows us how this achievement came about" (*The Emerging Goddess* [Chicago: Univ. of Chicago Press, 1979], p. 99). Of course, it is still open to Parker to argue that revision after a lapse of time is likely to produce poor results, but I see no support for him in the work of Dewey or Rothenberg.

Parker admits at some points in his discussion that an artist may leave a work and then return to it successfully (for example, Hemingway, p. 33), but the discussions of particular works that make up the body of this book proceed on the assumption that creativity should be continuous. A quotation from the discussion of Mark Twain will help:

Never during the composition of this big manuscript which contained what we know as *Pudd'nhead Wilson* and what we know as *Those Extraordinary Twins* (as well as many passages not ultimately used in either of these books) did a single, coherent creative process culminate in the completion of anything like a unified work of art. Months after completing this long manuscript . . . Mark Twain salvaged roughly half of it as *Pudd'nhead Wilson*, a text riddled with incoherencies that critics have rarely noticed. And Mark Twain's work in salvaging this material did not spring from a renewal of the creative process, as the grossness of surviving anomalies show, but from a hardheaded merchandiser's hasty scrutiny of unsold goods. [p. 28]

In addition to the inadequately supported assumption about good creative processes and the value-laden character assessment, there is an incipiently dangerous circularity here. The first manuscript work is not unified; therefore, the creative process is not coherent. *Pudd'nhead Wilson* is not coherent; therefore, the creative process was not renewed. But how do we know the versions are not coherent—critics have not noticed? By looking at the creative process. The status of the evidence is surely only muddled by use of terms like "coherent" to describe the creative process. The final test is critical analysis of the work; if the work is unified and coherent (questions of accidental coherence are discussed later), the process which has produced it will have been a good one. Evidence of messy creative processes can only help us to read more carefully, suspicious that the conventions of modern critical reading may have blinded us to the true nature of the text; investigation of the development of the text is preparation for good critical reading, just as reading an author's other works is.

Parker's discussion of the creative process, therefore, tells us less than he imagines. Unless there is a general rule for all authors, or for a particular author, or unless we can hope through further research to establish one—for example, "all good works must be written within six months by an author working continuously in isolation" (note that if you leave out "good", you get nonsense)—examination of the process behind a work will be no more than vaguely suggestive of its quality. The point is worth emphasizing because behind Parker's remarks lies a typical textual-bibliographical mistake about induction, a mistake one would think too obvious to mention were it not so common. If Parker flirts with this error, it is because he is still bound by the practices of the paternal figure he is rebelling against; for nothing is more striking about this book than the Bowersian plethora of examples leading so often to a few pages of sketched-in theory which is undermined by an exaggerated respect for these same examples. The weakness of the form of argument can be illustrated by noting Parker's use of the word "apt." He writes about our realizing "that the creative process, like any other process, has bounds, beyond which no author, however fine a craftsman, is apt to intervene with impunity" (p. 51). The sentence seems to be heading towards a firm

Authorial Revision

conclusion, perhaps "no author . . . is able to go," but its author suddenly (and to his credit) seems to lose confidence and adds not only a "with impunity" (some are stupid enough to cross the boundary and spoil the work) but also an "apt" (some authors get away with it); so there really are no boundaries after all. The same word is used to dodge the theoretical issue elsewhere: "What are the aesthetic consequences apt to be when an author excises passages just before publication or in post-publication revision?" (p. 78). "No one asked how successful an author is apt to be when he tries to give a different cast to a novel by making his ending more explicit or how successful James (and any other author) is apt to be when he attempts to alter any one aspect of a work without revising the rest" (pp. 105-06). The reason no one asks these probability questions is because a sensible answer would depend on (a) more information and (b) more accumulated value judgements than anyone could hope to have; sometimes Parker so loads the questions that common sense will think it has a ready answer, but common sense will be wrong. I am left with the conclusion that Parker uses "apt" to dodge questions about the number of instances needed for a satisfactory generalization and about the status such a generalization would have. Induction is useful for filling in some gap in our knowledge which matters to us. If all the swans I have seen are white and I am told a swan is coming around the corner (perhaps I am painting and want to know which tube to squeeze so I can capture the newcomer), it will be right to assume the swan will be white; it probably will be white. However, if a black swan comes around the corner, the previously established probability will not make it either (a) white or (b) not a swan. The reason for this is that sound induction depends on using all known examples and this will be one of them; the evidence before me is as good as the evidence which led to the generalization. Just as Bowers defended his theory of copytext (before the William James heresy) by treating rules of thumb as laws, so Parker constantly edges towards claiming a law-generating capacity for his examples—hence "apt." But they can have no such authority over the particular case.

The second major strand in Parker's argument about authorial practice is based on a sopisticated argument about intention. Parker's work depends, understandably, on the basis laid by E. D. Hirsch and P. D. Juhl; all valid meaning, Parker claims, is authorial meaning (p. ix), and the arguments which go to support this position go unstated and unanalyzed—rightly; no one can do everything. But what is missing is this area is any clear account of the contribution Parker believes himself to be making to the intentionalist/anti-intentionalist debate. He does say that his is the first book "directly to challenge the textual ideology explicit in W. K. Wimsatt, Jr.'s note on his title to *The Verbal Icon*" (p. xvi) and there is a general assumption that he has something important to say in this context. Unfortunately, in so far as we are thinking about an independent contribution, I think that is not so. Parker could mount an attack on New Criticism in two ways: by demonstrating that New Critics (either consciously or unconsciously) really want the author's text and that this entails an interest in authorial intention (this would be the Juhl approach); or by recommending the author's text on ethical grounds (the Hirsch approach).[3] He does neither; the textual position he advocates follows *from* the arguments of Juhl and Hirsch; it does not lead to them or add to their persuasiveness. The intentionalist critic will be troubled by Parker's demonstration that *Pudd'nhead Wilson* is incoherent and that Mark Twain did not intend some of it, but why should the recalcitrant New Critic or structuralist be disturbed? He or she can respond by saying (a) your evidence on coherence is irrelevant because the test of coherence is reading; or (b) the best interpretation is the one which provides most coherence and complexity—and I judge the best text on the same basis; or (c) I am interested in the study of reading practice; any text provoking interesting responses will do for me; or (d) your evidence simply shows that your beliefs about authorship are false; there are no authors in your sense. I suspect these responses seem so extraordinary to Parker that he has not been willing to consider them. Although he suggests the opposite, all his arguments are directed at those who already respect authorial authority.

In this area, where he is arguing with theorists like Hirsch

Authorial Revision

and Michael Hancher, Parker has an important contribution to make. The basic question he raises is neatly formulated in a quotation from Hirsch: "With a revised text, composed over a long period of time (*Faust*, for example), how are we to construe the unrevised portions? Should we assume that they still mean what they meant originally or that they took on a new meaning when the rest of the text was altered or expanded?" (p. 2). Parker's answer is roughly this: except in very rare cases (Parker does not seem to know of any) where the author's creative effort in revising has been sufficiently intense, the unrevised portions will mean what they originally meant; if the old meaning and the new meaning conflict, the text will be incoherent; if the author has allowed changes to be made without considering their implications, the result will be meaningless (pp. 3-4; 11-12). The conclusions about incoherence and meaninglessness are, I believe, correct, and Parker has made an important contribution to scholarship by calling attention to them, but the underlying arguments about intention are seriously wrong and could have a significantly distorting effect on textual scholarship. Parker argues that intentionality or meaning cannot be poured into the work at the last minute; they must be "built into the text at the moment each part is written" (p. 3); intention has to be "built in, piece by piece, during the process of composition, rather than being bestowed retroactively, like a blessing" (p. 22). Later in the book Parker expresses his view with one of the *num* questions he is so fond of: "Can a writer infuse intentionality into a passage or a chapter or a group of chapters by an act of will, or of wishing, after the passage is composed? or can he do so by a new placement of passages?" (pp. 142-43). If Parker is mistaken here, and I believe he is, it is because he has been led astray by his choice of metaphors. Intentionality is not "built" into action or things, or "infused" into them; it is a matter of relation to a person, a relation we generally recognize through conventions. According to John Searle, whom Parker cites with approval, Intentionality (of which intention in the ordinary sense is a part, like desire or belief) "is that property of many mental states and events by which they are directed at or about or of objects and states of affairs in the world" (*Intentionality* [Cambridge: Cambridge Univ. Press, 1983], p. 1). "Directedness" may itself be a metaphor, but it has the virtue of being a helpful one. Searle himself asks the question, "What does his [the speaker's or writer's] intention add to that physical event [utterance or inscription] that makes that physical event a case of the speaker's meaning something by it?" (*Intentionality*, p. 161). And his answer is that the appropriate act "is performed with the intention that the utterance itself has conditions of satisfaction." For example, if I believe that it is raining, my belief is correct if it is raining; if I say "It is raining," my statement is correct if it is raining. In uttering I intend the same condition of satisfaction to apply to the utterance.[4] This explains why (in an example popular with Hirsch, Juhl, and Knapp and Michaels) if the words (if they would be words) of "A slumber did my spirit seal" were typed out by a monkey or created by rock erosion, they would not mean anything. Parker's building metaphor ought to work in the opposite direction from these accounts (of which he approves), because it suggests that any identical "building" would have the same meaning. (Of the infusion metaphor I can make nothing at all; it has a whiff of theology about it.) But if intention is a matter of relationship, there must be a possibility that the appropriate relationship can be created later than the first point of creation; I hope to show that that is so.

We don't make up the language which conveys our intentions as we go along; most of the time we are using it secondhand, but it nonetheless (or, perhaps, therefore) expresses our intentions. To take an example. I am very anxious to edit some volumes in the Northwestern/Newberry Melville. I write to Professor Parker urging on him my view that these volumes should be based on the last edition issued in the author's lifetime. I suggest he hand over all volumes for which he has any responsibility to me, and I conclude, "I look forward to your reply; tread softly because you tread on my dreams." Professor Parker will not, as his argument would lead us to suppose, believe on the basis of my final injunction that I am writing him a love letter; he will believe that I am frightfully keen

Authorial Revision

on editing these volumes and have bound up much of my imaginative life in the project. In appropriating Yeats's line I have given it new meaning; it is no longer about love and the power of a loved one, it is about editing and the power of a general editor. Professor Parker will remember the original Yeats line, but that creates no problem: he is aware of two different utterances (and intentions and meanings) which he relates in recognizing that I care for the editing as Yeats cared for Maud Gonne. Writers are appropriating others' phrases in this way all the time, and in so doing they are bestowing new intentionality on them; this is not strictly retroactive because it does not change the meaning of the earlier utterance, but it changes the meaning of that set of words for the new utterance. Eliot discusses the process at some length in "The Use of Poetry and the Use of Criticism" ("Those are pearls that were his eyes")—and if Eliot and I can both do it, the question of intensity seems not to arise. If a writer can bestow new intentions on another's phrases, he must surely be able to do it with his own. A simple speech-act example may be of some service. I am a Colonel sitting quietly in the Mess sipping my Perrier water, and Private Smith is behaving in a drunken and disorderly way (there is only one Mess in this advanced regiment). I say, "Oh leave the Mess and go home, Smith," and when Smith looks bewildered and about to argue, I say, "And that's an order." I appropriate my earlier locution (in an act of suggesting or advising) and make it into an order by bestowing a new intention on it. We all know the same sort of thing happens in our own humble compositions: an example which illustrated this argument finally illustrates that; a section which led here finally leads there. When authors improve their work in the same way, when George Eliot combines two previously separate stories to produce *Middlemarch* or Pope adds the Sylphs to the already published and highly successful *Rape of the Lock*, they are not doing something extraordinary but something well within the logic of ordinary speech acts.

Parker, contrary to his arguments about intention, allows that there may be some examples of successful revision but he insists that the new versions can only be successful if they are recreated, if they are completely thought through afresh; only then can they be fully intended. He gives a very telling example of a case where he believes the author has failed to do this and the result is an unintended meaning—and, since all valid meaning is author-intended meaning, therefore, strictly meaningless. In *Pudd'nhead Wilson* in a passage before Mark Twain decided to make Tom of mixed race, Tom snatches his hand away from Wilson, the finger-printer, afraid he will be revealed as a thief. Parker suggests that the passage in the revised version would be taken to mean that Tom is afraid his racial origin will be discovered; not a meaning that was ever intended. Accepting for the sake of argument that Parker's interpretation of the passage in the new context is likely, we are confronted with a problem: what available biographical evidence could help us decide whether or not the new meaning was intended? It is so difficult to establish a negative, that Parker understandably equates intending the meaning with complete recreation, starting afresh; there might be enough biographical evidence to show there was no time for that. But do you have to create something in an intense way to bestow a meaning? I think not. When we are trying to decide what Mark Twain's attitude to the new text was, we are probably faced with two shades of meaning for "intention." The first would apply if Mark Twain had considered deleting the passage, suddenly seen the new meaning, liked it, and decided to retain it; Parker would accept that as intending a new meaning, I think; it involves a clear action, or deliberate refraining from action. The second would apply if Twain had simply noticed the new reading and left the passage standing. This too should count as an intended meaning (though it would be very difficult for biographical evidence to show it had or had not taken place) because, as we have seen, intending a meaning and creating its mode of expression are not the same thing—otherwise there would be no intentional formal prayer or oaths. The arguments in Parker's thesis which seem to move together, therefore, soon split apart: a concern for intentionality does not take us along the same path as a concern for a unified creative process; we can even intend meanings whose form of expression we have not created ourselves.

In the rather odd sense which Parker uses the word, therefore, Mark Twain *could* be said to have conferred a meaning retroactively (I am not saying he did); the episode could have been intended to mean something the second time which it was not the first. The possibility depends upon the same form of words having different meanings in different utterances, just as "He licked him" might. For this reason I think Parker's criticism of Michael Hancher misplaced. Parker criticizes Hancher for defining active intentions as those which "characterize the actions that the author, at the time he finishes his text, understands himself to be performing in that text" on the grounds that the intentions must be active throughout the process of composition (p. 22). But Hancher is looking for an utterance. It is utterances, not processes, that have meanings, and the moment the text is uttered is either when the writer lays down his pen and says "That's it" (an utterance ready for its readers) or when he publishes the work (issues it to the readers). The latter is James Thorpe's view, frequently ridiculed by Parker, but never, as far as I can see, adequately criticized. Meaning is essentially social, even though we can mean something without conveying it to a hearer or reader. The text is not taken to mean piece by piece (sentence by sentence, or word by word) because the pieces are not complete utterances and the items will only convey their proper meaning in a complete structure, which will be the utterance; until the structure is complete, their meanings are not clear ("Wait till I've finished!"). As Parker himself wisely observes, each sentence is composed with some end in mind. What he seems unable to accept is that when the end is reached it may modify what has gone before or that the writer may modify the same material in a new utterance. Of course, if the author is unaware of the way in which the earlier text is modified by later decisions, the result will be incoherence or the opening of the text to the discovery of unintended "meanings." This does not make revision a bad thing: the first version of *Pudd'nhead Wilson*, which includes *Those Extrordinary Twins*, is even more incoherent than the revision; neither version of *An American*

Dream gets Rojack's acquistion of a full professorship squared with the date of his marriage, but the second one could have done, especially if Mailer had had Professor Parker's help. Once we accept that an author can mean something muddled and incoherent, a lot of problems, including some of those about revision, disappear. When Parker says intentionalists should recognize muddle and incompetence more often, I suspect he is right.

In so far as Parker's book is designed as a contribution to editorial and critical theory, therefore, its lines of argument are mistaken. It is not possible to identify a normative creative process with which we can compare a particular creative process and draw conclusions about the work; it is possible to change the meaning of passages by intending them to mean something different from what they first meant, and authors may legitimately and successfully intend them in a minimal way. What we are left with is the possibility of making certain sorts of evaluations and using the evidence of textual development to support them. The evaluations, and here lies a main strength of the book, are of a sort which is not permitted by New Criticism and is unacceptable in academic criticism generally: this work is not coherent; these elements are contradictory; the relation between this section and that has not been worked out. New Critics have always sought unity and have chiefly triumphed in finding it where it is not readily apparent. The ideal text for New Criticism to operate on is not one mainfestly unified, but one offering the critic some resistance. Perhaps the roots of this approach lie in the secularization of the sacred. The inspired utterance, be it the gift of the Holy Spirit or the Muse, will have a unity and truth beyond ordinary human understanding (as will that which is colored by the sacred light of the poetic imagination); a priesthood finds its role in revealing that unity and truth to others. But Parker's accounts of the process of composition, or, to be precise, his account of the texts that represent different stages in composition, tell another tale. When the early, manuscript version of *Maggie* is compared with the first edition, Parker argues, it is clear that the intelligible order of the original has been disrupted for no discernible rational purpose; the text which underlies *Pudd'nhead Wilson* contains contradictions which have not been resolved in the published books; the *Red Badge of Courage* manuscript version contains clear, ironic judgements which have been obscured in the revisions for the first edition. The strength of these evaluations is that they are based not just on one text, but on two or more; texts so related that they clarify the realm of possibilities open to the writer and his decisions among these possibilities—closing some down, opening others up. The judgements of a critic using this material should be sounder because they are based on more (and relevant) information; it should be possible for such a critic to construct a genetic account of the work which will serve in some ways as an explanation. The covincingness of any genetic explanation is nevertheless dependent on the interpretations and evaluations which underlie it, and Donald Pizer is right in saying that Parker's preference for the first version of *The Red Badge of Courage* is based upon a critical evaluation which he must try to persuade others to accept; it does not spring ready-made out of the evidence. But, since evaluation is not the simple and stark matter we sometimes pretend, those basing their position on a genetic explanation of the text are in a position of advantage, and their opponents (over *Pudd'nhead Wilson*, for example) will have a responsibility to provide a plausible alternative explanation—or reject talk of the author altogether.

Parker's own evaluations are generally less persuasive than his central act of drawing our attention to the new field of evidence would lead us to hope. The subtle discussion of the late changes in *Tender Is the Night*, drawn from an article published in 1975, sets a standard which is not maintained elsewhere. The basic weaknesses in the critical stance Parker adopts are to overvalue information and explicitness and to place too much stress on sequence. Parker's criticisms often remind the reader of A. C. Bradley: did Lady Macbeth have any children or not? why doesn't the news account at the end of *Billy Budd* mention Vere's death? how did Huck Finn know that the Ohio and Mississippi do not like to mix? One of the forces directing the New Critics was the need to acknowledge that texts could have an imaginative unity which transcended such details. Their discussions of image, symbol, and theme in Shakespeare (a critical practice Parker has some fun with) served Shakespeare better than the strictures of Rymer or the investigations of Bradley in his most nitpicking mood. Parker, in one of the book's most useful sections, draws attention to psychological research which explains why the New Critics were on good ground; but he misapplies the information. Quoting the work of Ralph W. Rader (who draws on that of James J. Gibson), Parker explains that the mind is a "meaning-seeking faculty"; it "scans and interprets it [an utterance] so as to discover that meaning which renders the whole coherent and significant, to the exclusion of partial and incomplete meanings" (pp. 144-45). It is this tendency of the mind, Parker argues, that impels some readers—chiefly New Critics—to celebrate a "faked" novel like *Pudd'nhead Wilson*. But the reports of the psychologists suggest that this activity goes on all the time; it is not just something New Critics perform on difficult texts. On the one hand, readers do not find all texts complete and coherent; the coherence-seeking faculty can be defeated by poor writing and the reader left dissatisfied. On the other hand, even the greatest writers must make some positive use of this tendency or capacity in readers to complete, to actively participate in constructing the work, or much of their writing would seem redundant. Even that most directive of novelists, George Eliot, knew that for the creation of a full fictional world she needed the cooperation of her readers: "Reader! *did* you ever taste such a cup of tea as Miss Gibbs is this moment handing to Mr. Pilgrim?" she asks nervously in *Amos Barton*, acknowledging the need for the reader to supplement what she suggests. When Conrad deliberately disarranges his historical narrative and filters it carefully through incompetent narrators in *Nostromo*, he is merely forcing this practice of cooperation as one might a plant in a greenhouse. Very often, therefore, a novelist will want to withdraw information and make his or her work less explicit. Parker may have difficulty in accepting this practice because it runs counter to the general movement in any composition, which must be from a relatively indeterminate general project, through choices and exclusions, to the particular achieved work; but the work of the psychologists explains why the author may wish to re-open his text and create space for the reader's imaginative powers to function. Parker's discussion of Mailer's *An American Dream* does not treat this possibility with the respect it deserves. Noting the deletion of a reference to "the controlled murder which rested in the eyes of this detective [Roberts]," Parker goes on to claim: "This deletion leaves Roberts's behavior the next day inexplicable, when after learning that he must free Rojack he looks as if he will attack him with the telephone receiver then seizes his own jaw 'in a grip which must have been equal to pressing a button in the machinery of himself for it served to return his control' " (p.198). But if the deleted phrase explained Roberts's behavior, it cannot be inexplicable in the revised version, merely unexplained. Nor do I believe the episode poses intractable problems of interpretation for the reader. Parker is effectively insisting on the writer's doing all the reader's work for him, when the writer may legitimately be trying to engage the reader more actively in the text. I accept a distinction Parker makes, with the help of Albert Rothenberg, between ambiguity and confusion, but that leaves untouched a whole range of suggestions, implications, hints and guesses, which may enter into the relations between writer and reader.

To illustrate the disproportionate emphasis on sequence, one example, from a footnote, will suffice. In defending the Pennsylvania *Sister Carrie* Parker remarks that "Worrying about endings is often unprofitable because they are frequently more contingent than the rest of the novel and in any case are connected to the rest of the text only at one side" (pp. 6-7). This is completely at odds with the oft-quoted extracts from Dewey in which the writer must always be in contact with the whole which is to come. In the sort of unified work Parker and most of us admire, the end is present in the beginning, and the beginning in the end; no sophisticated work is purely sequential and no good ending contingent or connected only at the side.

The other important achievement of this book may be dealt

with more briefly. It is to leave the reader puzzled as to why anyone should insist that in editing a work the editor must follow the author's final intentions for his text. I have yet to see a plausible argument for this view; it is, as Parker suggests, a form of Platonizing. Parker demonstrates that revision can come from conflicting intentions or from the vaguest of intentions (Fitzgerald), and I think he succeeds in showing that authors sometimes spoil their work. I have only two reservations: Parker kowtows too much to the scientism which originally barred value judgements in editing, and tries to substitute a psychologism of his own; and he needs to develop a theory of utterance to conform with his emphasis on authorial intention. Questions of utterance aside, I can see no reason why an older man (be it one day older) should be given any authority over his younger self.

Parker's assault on the citadels of the New Criticism (with its obsession with demonstrating unity and complexity) and the Greg-Bowers theory of copy-text (with its reverence of final intentions) deserves the widest possible attention because it is based on new forms of evidence. If his theoretical attacks often misfire, it is because he has not been willing to cast aside some of the attitudes implicit in the positions he attacks. The most important of these is focused in the use of religious ideas and vocabulary in talking about art. Noticing that works of art lack the sacred unity they are supposed to possess, Parker merely moves the sacredness back a stage to the creative process, where intention can be infused like sanctifying grace. "For Hemingway, the rare 'belle epoque,' the mood in which body, soul, and circumstances conspired to produce great writing, was to be cherished as something very like a divine gift of grace" (p. 27). Although, we are told, the creative process is not magical (p. 162), we are to approach it "in reverence, not with impudent knowingness" (p. 51). Once we recognize the integrity of the creative process, "we can cheerfully give up the superstition that the author is infallible and that the literary work is necessarily a perfect verbal icon" (p. 51). But we achieve nothing if we replace one superstition by another; the wholeness we find in literature is surely the result of cooperation, not a divine

Authorial Revision

creative process. Professor Parker knows this in his own case; true, he is writing a work of criticism and theory, not fiction, but he believes his arguments apply to Dewey (p. 77), so why not to himself? This book, celebrating the integrity and determinacy of the creative process, is made up from revisions of previously published essays: parts of Chapter 1, Chapter 2, Chapter 5, and Chapter 7 have been published before, and "a few other passages are also recycled from reviews and essays" (pp. xviii). Moreover, Professor Parker has been engaged in the sort of activity American textual critics generally disapprove of when they catch their authors at it: he has been talking to other people, and admits to being influenced by them. He has had practical help with the ending from Gerald Graff and he has reordered a chapter at the suggestion of Laurence Buell. I have not undertaken a collation of the different texts to establish a Parker-style view of the new text's coherence but, barring a few repetitions and a wavering as to whether Wimsatt and Beardsley are being attacked, it seems a pretty good job to me. I suspect Parker is quite wrong about the determinacy of the creative process and that a little introspection might have served him better than a reverent reading of John Dewey. He quotes a moving passage from Melville which implies not so much, as Parker suggests, that once a work is complete the artist can safely put it out of mind; but that the artist is never satisfied that it is complete; he can only avert his gaze and let it rest.

I am glad you like that affair of mine [*Mardi*]. But is seems so long now since I wrote it, & my mood has so changed, that I dread to look into it, & have purposely abstained from doing so since I thanked God it was off my hands.—Would that a man could do something & then say—It is finished.—not that one thing only, but all other—that he has reached his utermost, & can never exceed it. But live & push—tho' we put one leg forward ten miles—its no reason the other must lag behind—no *that* must again distance the other—& so we go till we get the cramp & die. [p. 35]

"And every attempt," says Eliot, "Is a wholly new start, and a different kind of failure." In drawing our attention to these truths about authorship, and in challenging our assumptions about literary texts, Parker earns our gratitude.

Notes

1. The *Critical Inquiry* debates about pragmatism are to be published by the University of Chicago Press in *Against Theory: Literary Studies and the New Pragmatism*. The replies to Knapp and Michaels, including Parker's, appeared in *Critical Inquiry*, 9 (June 1983), and further contributions to the debate appeared in 11 (March 1985). I have drawn on Stanley Fish's contribution to this later number, "Consequences" (pp. 433-58, especially 434-35 and 442) in discussing the sort of claims Parker is making. It will be apparent that, like Parker, I believe in theory which generates principled activity and that I write as an intentionalist. I am grateful to Charles Swann, David Amigoni, and Colin Cruise for discussing these and other issues with me.

2. It might make sense to talk of an incomplete creative process if the author abandoned his manuscript or dropped dead in the middle of a sentence; but we would then talk of the work as incomplete. My opposition is to arguments that the work is not finished when the author has decided it is.

3. P. D. Juhl, *Interpretation* (Princeton: Princeton Univ. Press, 1980); E. D. Hirsch, *Validity in Interpretation* (New Haven: Yale Univ. Press, 1967) and *The Aims of Interpretation* (Chicago: Univ. of Chicago Press, 1976).

4. There are serious problems in applying this account to fictions, where sentences precisely do not have these conditions of satisfaction: the novelist says "It was raining" without making any claims about the weather. I do not think the difficulties are resolved by Juhl (*Interpretation*, pp. 153-95) and Searle does not attempt to resolve them in "The Logical Status of Fictional Discourse" in *Expression and Meaning* (Cambridge: Cambridge Univ. Press, 1979), pp. 58-75. I suspect many of the problems discussed under the heading of authorial intention are properly questions of fictionality. Parker's case, of course, depends on some such account as Searle's being applicable to fictions.

Homophobia in English Culture

Seymour Kleinberg

Louis Crompton. *Byron and Greek Love: Homophobia in 19th-Century England*. Berkeley: University of California Press, 1985. xiii, 419 pp.

Eve Kosofsky Sedgwick. *Between Men: English Literature and Male Homosocial Desire*. New York: Columbia University Press, 1985. x, 244 pp.

The love that dared not speak its name, the sin so unmentionable it was referred to by its Latin alias, *peccatum mutum*, has recently provoked a considerable scholarly utterance. Much of what is new is barely more than a variety of gossip, but there is also now in print a small shelf of books on homosexuality that has permantly altered our sense of what it is, what it was, and why it has evoked such fear and loathing.[1]

Both Louis Crompton and Eve Kosovksy Sedwick have written ambitious books about homosexuality and its connection to English culture, particularly the literature of the nineteenth century. Crompton's study is primarily social history while Sedgwick's is an example of recent trends in academic literary criticism. Crompton calls himself a gay activist, but he is a traditional scholar, conservative in his methodology and his academic values. Sedgwick is polemical and claims her point of view results from a reconciliation of Marxist and radical feminist ideas (as well as a good deal of French psychoanalytic assumption).

Crompton takes a controversial subject, Byron's rumored homosexuality, and presents his conclusions, steadily, reasonably, and with so much scholarly support that no one can again dismiss, suppress, or distort the importance of loving men in Byron's life and work. Sedgwick brings considerable intelligence to the very complicated subject she calls "male homosocial desire," but her attempt to use Marx, Freud, feminism, and the latest in French thought is unwieldy.

Crompton has his polemical moments, but even then his tone is mild and his explanations so detailed that the reader is left without a demur. For example, he explains his use of the terms "Greek love," "homosexual," and "gay," so that even when he uses the latter two, he is not anachronistic. Crompton uses "Greek love" when he writes from Byron's point of view and "homosexual" when he writes from his own; he uses "gay" when he relates his subject to contemporary sexual politics. Crompton concludes that Byron was really bisexual, and that sexual desire for young men and for women were equally powerful at different times in his life. But that is an equivocal use of the term "bisexual," which some people regard as meaningless anyway. Most authorities agree that bisexuality, defined as an equal attraction to either sex at any time, is quite rare. In modern life, it is presumed that the *majority* of homosexual men and lesbians are probably leading heterosexual lives as well as closeted homosexual ones, or that they have experienced both lives, but no one claims that they are bisexual. Crompton's acceptance of the term as if it were one commonly agreed upon has its ironic side. So much evidence has come to light about the private lives of public figures — everyone seems to have kept a diary, letters were never burnt no matter how compromising, even casual scribbles were preserved for posterity — that Crompton can be quite conservative in his interpretations and in his selection of evidence. Thus he says that Harold Bloom's reading of Byron as "basically" homosexual amounts to an iconoclastic overcompensation, a response to the evasions and prudery of Byron's biographers. However, Crompton is certain about the kind of homosexual Byron was: he preferred adolescent boys.

Crompton's first task regarding Byron is to address the question of evidence, particularly when it is located in the effusive language of affection used by upper class men to express a highly idealized view of friendship. That rhetoric has a long tradition beginning in England in the sixteenth century;

Shakespeare's sonnets are its most famous example. It ends with the Wilde trials of the late nineteenth century; after the scandal, the expression of such sentiments was completely suspect, and, indeed, the entire language of sentimental love came to be regarded as duplicitous. This language of intense emotional intimacy between men has confused or embarrassed, sometimes affronted, social historians. Recently the trend has been to compensate by claiming that all such effusions are erotic in character and therefore homosexual in nature, using or rather abusing Freud's idea of "homosexual."[2] Crompton is concerned with distinguishing between sentimental and erotic language when it is offered as evidence about sexuality. "How," he asks, "in reading the poems or letters or fiction of the past, are we to distinguish between romantic friendship and homosexual love? Both may speak with intense devotion, both reflect strong passion. Can we ever be sure the feeling has or has not an erotic side to it?" (p. 72). Byron himself distinguished between "romantic friendship," and "love, violent though *pure*." That's interesting but not clear; what would for Byron constitute impure love? Sexual consummation or merely self-consciousness? One would have thought that "pure" and "violent" were very apt descriptions of the infatuations rife in nineteenth century British public schools.[3] Shelley was quite clear about the possible relationship of the two types of feelings. He said one might precede or even create the other: intense Platonic friendship may engender sensuality if infatuation persists.[4]

Crompton is aware of these psychological ambiguities, but he is not interested in them. Generally, he is not interested in psychological issues, and when he offers an explanation of Byron's motives, he hedges, or he becomes commonplace, or, most often, he relies on the ideas of three Byron scholars to whom he is heavily indebted.[5] Nor is Crompton particularly interested in literary matters. The subtitle of his book identifies his true subject: the emotional climate of Georgian England regarding sexual deviance. Besides Byron, Crompton has another protagonist, the authentic center of the book, Jeremy Bentham. Bentham's efforts to give England a rational and humane criminal code were radical and at least a century ahead of his time. Those efforts and the subsequent struggle to decriminalize homosexuality in England are the subjects that really interest Crompton.

For reasons not yet entirely clear, England remained vehemently homophobic while continental Europe grew, if not tolerant, at least more discreet about sodomy. The Napoleonic code inaugurated important legal reforms, among which was less regulation of private sexual conduct. There was also a traditional tolerance about some forms of male homosexuality; pederasty, for example, was largely ignored in Mediterranean countries, especially if the adult party was upper class and generous. Crompton speculates that British homophobia was fed by a national desire to distinguish British culture from the continent's, especially from Napoleon and French culture and from Catholic sensibility in general. Throughout Byron's lifetime England remained the most dangerous place in Europe for homosexuals. Class privilege was no real protection. William Beckford, one of the richest men in the country, was driven into exile after his homosexuality was made public. His wealth gave him the option of exile over the pillory or prison or even execution, but those too poor to flee usually suffered one of those fates.

Crompton is sure that because of the Beckford scandal, no Englishman, even one who had discovered himself world famous overnight, would be bold enough to confess homosexual passion. Byron, therefore, changed the gender of the dead beloved in his "Thyrza" poems, which were a lament for John Edleston.[6] Byron's understandable prudence makes Bentham's boldness in championing the rights of homosexuals appear all the more singular — especially so since no one has claimed that Bentham himself was homosexual. Bentham's arguments in his various notes and essays on homosexual acts and the British penal code are cogent, precocious, and unprecedented. Even before Malthus' essay on population in 1798, which Bentham used to argue that homosexuality was a natural antidote to overpopulation, he was already championing sexual pleasure as a matter of taste. In his unemotional philosophic voice, Bentham dispensed with all the unquestioned fears about homosexuality in his time, and indeed in ours. In fact, there isn't very much that gay liberationists have added to his arguments in the last fifteen years.

Bentham's views, temperament, and achievements are deeply engaging and sympathetic to the scholar and political activist in Crompton. The virtue of his book is to have brought Bentham forward without slighting Byron. We recover some important truths here about both these men and about the special anxieties of Georgian England.

Eve Kosovksy Sedgwick is concerned with large relationships, particularly the effect of abstract social forces upon individual lives as they are illustrated by literature, mostly the novel up to the mid-nineteenth century. She argues that "homosexual" is too narrow a term to encompass the complexities of intense male bonding, and prefers "homosocial desire," which would include that special fraternal world so typical of patriarchical society: "To put it in twentieth-century American terms, the fact that what goes on at football games, in fraternities, at the Bohemian Grove, and at climactic moments in war novels can look, with only a slight shift of optic, quite startlingly 'homosexual' " (p. 89). Sedgwick is interested in homophobia as "a *necessary* consequence of such patriarchical institutions as heterosexual marriage" (p. 3). She puts questions about female bonding and lesbianism outside her province. Her interest is in the effect of male bonding upon the lives of women, in how men's relationships with each other reflect their sexism and misogyny. In a dense introduction she offers her political credentials: she is a radical feminist sympathetic to Marxist thought, and she has also assimilated "French" feminism — deconstructive, Lacanian feminism—to her own radical feminism.

Sedgwick has chosen her readings to illustrate a "basic paradigm of male traffic in women" (p. 16), the recurrence of a triangle among two men and a woman in which the manifest competition disguises the men's own suppressed erotic bond. Such readings, requiring an analysis of the unconscious motives of literary characters, will naturally be heavily indebted to

Freudian thought. To her credit, Sedgwick's ambition is very high: nothing less than intellectual originality and excellence of an order that would have real influence on her readers; in short, to make a mark on human thought. But the ambition is too high for this book; her materials will not bear the weight. And the book fails for another, less admirable reason. The striving for depth, to be at the cutting edge of intellectual culture, creates or provokes a style of writing that is often unclear, sometimes pretentious, and frequently irritating. One grows dismayed to see the author's intelligence sabotaged by a rhetoric that one can only call bad writing. That Sedgwick uses such a style is not just a blunder, a point I will return to later.

Sedgwick's idea of her audience is unclear to me. She repeatedly defines her terms to set the matter straight, but often the definition leaves the reader with less confidence than before. When she uses a term like "homosocial desire," of course she tells us what she means by "homosocial," though I do not think it more than a fancy version of "male bonding." When she tells us what she means by "desire," which I thought I understood, it turns out I was wrong. Homosocial desire is "a kind of oxymoron . . . a neologism . . . intended to mark both discriminations and paradoxes." She continues, "The word 'desire' rather than 'love' . . . is used . . . to name a structure; in this study, a series of arguments about the structural permutations of social impulses fuels the critical dialect. For the most part, I will be using 'desire' in a way analogous to the psychoanalytic use of 'libido' " (pp. 1-2). She says she is using her term as analysts use "libido," but that her term is deeper, broader, more complex. Perhaps so, since current psychoanalytic thought has discarded the term "libido" as hopelessly vague and over-generalized. Speaking of the effect of industrialism on the family, she talks of using "linguistic metaphor . . . not because I mean to suggest that the ideological realm was the theater in which it was mainly enacted" (p. 136). But Sedgwick does not mean she is using linguistics as a metaphor, only that she is going to use a metaphor. What is the purpose of the adjective? It stops and puzzles the reader. Her use of the adjective is meaningless. It chills whatever rapport exists between reader and writer, and it recalls too many other examples of the same sort. Instead of an invitation to enter into intellectual discourse, the reader is shut out. Instead of feeling that one is being educated, one feels talked at, lectured to, reminded that he or she does not know, is uninformed, is intellectually inferior. We are all back in the classroom with a very self-absorbed professor. The bad writing is not just incompetence; it seems to indicate a kind of perverse vanity.

I think I understand why Sedgwick feels she needs rhetorical enlargement. In her best chapter, on *Our Mutual Friend*, she illustrates her thesis perfectly and also gives us the most simply written chapter in the book. Here in Dickens' darkest novel, she finds a proper illustration of feminist, Marxist, and psychoanalytic analyses. Her prose has authority and quietude, her thought flows with rich reference to eighteenth-century literature, to Tennyson, to earlier Dickens. Here the scholarly support is never ornamental. She shows how this novel embodies the social anxieties and sexual disarray of mid-nineteenth-century England.

In contrast to the style she uses when she generalizes, full of intellectual portent, when she has insight, her prose is cogent, her desire to speak to the reader clear. Here, for example: "Perhaps it would be more precise, then, to say that *Our Mutual Friend* is the only English novel that everyone *says* is about excrement in order that they may *forget* that it is about anality. For the Freudian insights, elided in the critics' moralistic yoking of filth and lucre, are erotic ones. They are insights into pleasures, desires, bonds, and forms of eros that have to do with the anus. And it is precisely the repression of these pleasures and desires that, in Freud, turns feces into filth and gold" (p. 164). She is also excellent when discussing the history of homosexual roles or types in England. She thinks the homosexual aristocrat—High Church, effeminate, a connoisseur, aesthetically enthralled to Catholic Europe (e.g., Lord Alfred Douglas) — can be seen from the early seventeenth century until the late nineteenth century. She notes that such men had stronger bonds to heterosexual rakes and dandies of their own class than to either working class homosexuals or middle class ones like Edward Carpenter. She notes that aristocratic sensibility survived intact into modern England where it played a devious and interesting role in the stories of sex, class, and espionage in establishment politics that we have been treated to since Maclean and Burgess defected. At the same time, "there seems to have been considerable tacit, and in many respects conservative male homosexual influence over English high culture" (p. 94). In England, the stereotype of the apolitical aesthete, the culturally conservative homosexual, served as a foolproof cover for espionage. In America, the same type became the model of gay sensibility for middle-class homosexuals (until gay liberation offered them alternatives). Sedgwick makes her remarks in passing in her chapter on Gothic novels, but her intelligence is much more evident in these remarks than in most of her discussion of the fiction.

The bad writing in this book is symptomatic of what it means everywhere, especially in academic work: the failure to think through what one wants to say or the absence of anything serious to say to begin with. The inflated prose attempts to distract the reader from the thin content. In recent years the influence of French intellectualism in academia has been devastating. It has provided men and women, forced to publish, with new occasions for restating old observations. Given the notorious taste of the French for convoluted prose, the worst writing has been accepted as fashionable. Of course structuralism, French psychoanalysis, Foucault have inspired some demanding and interesting work here, but most of the inspiration has produced novelties to answer the demands of a profession troubled and confused by its loss of power and prestige in the last two decades. What is so special about this latest pedantry? There have always been those who admire mandarin discourse. But even the narrowest scholarship expressed in the dryest prose (held up to generations of graduate students as models of professional propriety) had the integrity of seriousness. The scholarly subject may have been small, but it was about something, even about literature sometimes. This new work is frequently full of nothing so much as self-admiration.

Well, what is the harm of such discourse among those who

Homophobia in English Culture

enjoy speaking to each other in the most arcane of languages, who admire exclusivity and endorse the values of the coterie? Given the nature of vices in the academy these days, it is by no means the worst or the most dangerous. But to claim one is a feminist, or a Marxist, and to take seriously those ideas, is certainly to take on the responsibility of proper address. Neither of these schools of thought are interested in speaking to privileged minorities; both of them are intensely social, political in origin and purpose, and hostile by their natures to elitism as a value. Professor Sedgwick believes herself to be a radical feminist, but in my view she has not written a book which fulfills that claim.

Notes

1. A flyer from A Different Light Bookstore with branches in Los Angeles and New York lists over 300 *new* titles for the first half of 1985.

2. Freud's idea that all "affective relations" between men or between women are homosexual in character is literal but hardly clear, nor did he mean by "homosexual" much more than "same sex." The psychoanalytic reading of "homosexuality" is very different from the meaning of the term as it is used by everyone else. Freud tried not to be pejorative; he thought he was classifying sexual feelings according to the object of emotions. He also said that all categories of feeling were universal and natural, as it was natural — in the course of things — that homosexual desires be suppressed in favor of adult heterosexuality.

3. Crompton cites Disraeli's *Coningsby* as an example of unselfconsciousness (p. 75): "At school, friendship is a passion. It entrances the being, it tears the soul. All loves of after-life can never bring its rapture, or its wretchedness; no bliss so absorbing, no pangs of jealousy or despair so crushing or so keen! What tenderness and what devotion; what illimitable confidence; infinite revelations of inmost thoughts; what ecstatic present and romantic future; what bitter estrangements and what melting reconciliations; what scenes of wild recrimination, agitating explanations, passionate correspondence; what insane sensitiveness, and what frantic sensibility; what earthquakes of the heart and whirlwinds of the soul are confined in that simple phrase, a schoolboy's friendship" (London: Longmans, Green & Co., 1877, Book I, pp. 43-44).

4. Crompton cites Shelley's comparatively sophisticated view from his "An Essay on Friendship."

5. Crompton acknowledges that he is deeply indebted to G. Wilson Knight's *Lord Byron's Marriage* (1957), Doris Langley Moore's *The Late Lord Byron* (1961, rev. 1977) and her *Lord Byron: Accounts Rendered* (1974), and Leslie Marchand's edition of *Byron's Letters and Journals*, 13 vols. (1973-1982) as well as his three-volume *Byron: A Biography* (1957).

6. John Edleston died young of tuberculosis. Byron was fifteen when he met him at Cambridge where Edleston was a choirboy.

Authorship in America during the Progressive Period

James L. W. West III

Christopher P. Wilson. *The Labor of Words: Literary Professionalism in the Progressive Era.* Athens: University of Georgia Press, 1985. xx, 240 pp.

Christopher P. Wilson's book is a study of the American author and the literary marketplace during the Progressive Era, from 1885 until approximately 1915. Wilson examines the period during which the United States publishing industry made the transition from a conservative, late-nineteenth-century style to a mass-market-oriented, twentieth-century approach. Of special concern to him are the long-range effects of this transition. He believes that the weakening and ultimate failure of Naturalistic writing in America can be attributed, in part, to pressures of literary commercialism. He also believes that the Progressive period marks the beginning of the media-dominated Information Age in which we now live.

Wilson is the first literary historian since William Charvat to publish a significant study of professional authorship in America. Charvat, it must be remembered, did his groundbreaking work as long ago as the 1950s and 1960s.[1] The literary marketplace has been an unpopular subject for study since then, partly because fashions have changed, but also because the materials one must use are so recalcitrant. House histories and memoirs exist in abundance, but they are nearly all written from the publisher's viewpoint and are usually cursory and anecdotal. Typically they concentrate on the publisher's memorable coups, list his bestsellers, and recount his relationships with the literati of his day. In most of these volumes there is little information about the actual workings of the publishing trade. For such data, one must search through house archives, if they survive, and one must read trade journals of the period. Information is also available in the papers of individual authors. Particularly useful is the author who was with a single publisher over a long term. Wilson has done these kinds of research: he has read widely in nineteenth- and twentieth-century booktrade periodicals, and he has worked with authors' and publishers' papers at Princeton, Columbia, Harvard, the Lilly, the Beinecke, and the New York Public Library.

Many books which treat publishing history and literary authorship are damaged by too narrow a focus, by an inability on the part of the author to go beyond personalities, gossip, or the simple recounting of facts (interesting as they may be) to the larger implications of the subject. This is unfortunate, because publishers are crucial figures in any literary period, and they deserve serious and extended study. Publishers reflect the cultural currents of their times and, simultaneously, influence the direction of those currents. They are intellectual arbiters and gatekeepers, but only the most sophisticated of them seem aware of this fact. William Jovanovich, himself a publisher, described the affliction accurately: "Of publishers," he wrote, "it may be said that like the English as a race they are incapable of philosophy. They deal in particulars and adhere easily to Sydney Smith's dictum that one should take short views, hope for the best, and trust God."[2] Most historians of authorship and publishing suffer from the same malady, especially if they themselves have had careers in some phase of the book business. No charge of narrowness can be brought against Wilson, however. He has thought long and seriously about the implications of what he has discovered, and he has explained those implications carefully. In fact, if there is a fault with his book it is that some passages are overly dense with abstract language and broad statement. One is occasionally left dizzy by the theorizing and speculation.

Wilson's method of organization, by contrast, is one of the strong points of his study. In his introduction, entitled "The Divine Literatus," he sets forth his major ideas and lays out his strategy of attack. The initial three chapters follow; they deal respectively with broad changes in the newspaper, magazine, and book publishing industries during the Progressive Era. The final four chapters treat individually the careers of four prominent writers of the period — Jack London, Upton Sinclair, David Graham Phillips, and Lincoln Steffens. An epilogue, entitled "The Legacy of Literary Professionalism," takes the discussion forward into the present time and reiterates Wilson's view that many features of our current literary scene have their roots in the period he has examined.

The newspaper, magazine, and book publishing industries all changed in similar ways during the late nineteenth and early twentieth centuries. The old, relaxed style of newspaper reporting described by H. L. Mencken and Theodore Dreiser in their memoirs gave way to a new professionalism, a vocationalism, that traditional newspapermen found unattractive. The camaraderie of the news rooms at Charles Anderson Dana's *New York Sun* was replaced by the more highly organized and efficient atmosphere at the Pulitzer and Hearst papers. Reporting became a career, not an occupation in and out of which one drifted. Aimless newsgathering was not encouraged; "beats" were assigned and news began to be managed. Many national stories were now syndicated, and municipal news came under the control of editors fully aware of the political power and cultural influence of the press. Individual initiative among reporters was not as highly valued as corporate loyalty. The paradox, according to Wilson, was that the reporter, now with his own by-line and public identity, had much greater visibility and influence than he had enjoyed in earlier decades, but he had lost his autonomy, his freedom to give play to his own newsgathering instincts. Wilson writes: "Rather than a sphere of philosophical or leisurely reflection, reporting had become a pressurized and unstable world; rather than an objective social laboratory, reporters now witnessed events in which their own presence and craft were implicated: events that were preplanned, promoted, or, in extreme cases, even fabricated" (p. 39).

Something similar happened in the magazine industry. New developments in printing technology had made it possible for periodical publishers to reach huge audiences of middle-class readers and to provide them with an attractively designed product for a nickel or a dime. (Revenues came chiefly from advertising fees rather than from newsstand sales.) In the magazine world especially, the creative process was reversed. Rather than depending on contributor initiative, editors of the Progressive Era themselves became the originators of ideas which were assigned to teams of staff writers or to dependable freelances. Not only the subject of the article but its thrust, its message, its organization, and even its style were dictated ahead of time by the editor. Inspiration was relocated in his office. "In particular," writes Wilson, "the promotional spirit encouraged greater emphasis on advance ideas: creating a public need and then filling it with a designed product. This anticipatory role influenced the entire process of magazine production. As editing became an energized, inventive business role, a trio of related strategies became essential to efficient, top-down organization: bidding for writers, article commissioning, and, finally, the formation of internal writing staffs" (p. 50). All this was a far cry from the days when editors at *Scribner's* and the *Century* would sift through the past month's contributions and choose a balanced, well-rounded array of items for an upcoming issue, rather as one would dress a shop window or plan a restaurant menu.

Book publishers were slower to change, but eventually they too altered their way of doing business. A powerful impetus to do so was the passage of an international copyright law by Congress in 1891. International copyright was designed ostensibly to promote the free interchange of books and ideas between the United States and other countries, especially Great Britain. In practice, Wilson believes, it worked to strengthen established American publishers like the Putnams, Scribners, Appletons, and Harpers because it cut off the supply of uncopyrighted British material on which manufacturers of cheap reprints had battened for years. These lower orders in the publishing industry had survived chiefly by underselling, and their activities had made price maintenance impossible for bigger, more respectable trade houses. Now the price-cutters were starved out of the market; most of them perished in the depression of 1893-97. Because valuable copyrights from England were now safe, American book publishers could indulge in the unfamiliar luxury of long-term planning.

New strength on the part of these publishers brought about more hierarchy and division of responsibility within their houses. The editor emerged as the most powerful figure in the typical trade firm; he drew his power from above and below, and he came to function as an extension of his publisher's mind and style. In book publishing as in magazine publishing, the editor—the quintessential middle manager—became the source of ideas within the operation. He conceived books and assigned them to writers, and he pursued authors whose writings would be valuable properties on the backlist. The editor also began to take an active part in shaping and revising the manuscripts that came to him, exercising powers which formerly would have been considered excessive and unwarranted. The author gained a wider audience and stronger influence by signing on with such an editor, but according to Wilson he lost much of his artistic freedom.

The authors treated in the last four chapters of Wilson's book played out their careers against this commercial background. All of them served apprenticeships by writing for newspapers or magazines, or, in the case of Upton Sinclair, by pounding out dime novels for Street and Smith. All of these authors, and especially London, adopted workmanlike attitudes toward writing, exchanging ease and inspiration for self-discipline and "dig." All became famous—Phillips and Steffens for their work as muckrakers—and all were extraordinarily prolific. Each man eventually felt trapped by his success, however, and lapsed into self-imitation for a time; each subsequently believed himself compromised by the marketplace and became disillusioned. Each had achieved early success by rejecting the image of the author as Romantic dreamer, dabbler, dilletante; but ironically each retreated in his middle years to something very like that idealized conception of authorship, an imagined territory free from the pressures of commercialism.

The changes in the literary marketplace during the Progressive period helped foster a new kind of writing in America: realistic, political, masculine, democratic in spirit—Naturalistic, in short. Pure style was now seen as a weakness typical of the effete, feminized, elitist writers of the previous era. The new writing, vigorous and fresh at first, was a welcome development; but as Wilson recognizes, a plain, direct style can be mimicked easily and turned to the service of political and moneyed interests. (One is reminded of certain clichés of Modernism which lately have been picked up by Madison Avenue.) Too, once a writer has sold his work on the marketplace, he has little control over how it will be merchandised or interpreted. Two examples are mentioned in this book—Lincoln Steffens' wrangles with S. S. McClure over the management of the *Shame of the Cities* series and Upton Sinclair's disappointment over the fact that *The Jungle* was seen, not as a depiction of the working man's plight, but as an exposé of the Chicago meatpacking industry.

The Labor of Words is an excellent performance, and there is little about which a reviewer can complain. Two shortcomings: Wilson does not emphasize strongly enough the role of the literary agent in the transformation of the book and magazine industries, nor does he consider the possibility that some of the new developments in publishing style were borrowed from the British literary marketplace, where they had already been tested. But it would have been difficult for Wilson to have pursued either angle, since there is no book-length study of the rise of the literary agent in America, nor is there an examination of cross-influences between the British and American publishing industries after 1840. Wilson's book may well stimulate such research.

There is, perhaps, one other weakness. Wilson seems to share with many historians of the publishing industry a tendency to view, with some nostalgia, the generation just previous to the one he is studying. This kind of thinking is endemic to people in the publishing business, and historians of the booktrade seem to acquire it from them by osmosis. The previous generation is always seen as more genteel and leisurely than the one which followed; earlier publishers and editors, unlike their successors, were men of large spirit who issued important books with no thought of the balance sheet. This backward-looking mind set is so typical of people in the book industry that one wonders whether it is not a necessary part of their vocational equipment. Perhaps publishers and editors must hold in mind imaginary models from earlier generations; perhaps they must feel their contemporaries to be degraded in order to fight against their own commercializing tendencies.

Publishers during the Progressive Era, especially Walter Hines Page and Henry Holt, thought in precisely this way. Literary publishing in America for them had become overly commercialized, and they stated their misgivings about the situation zealously and prophetically. It would probably have surprised them to know that their predecessors—men like George Palmer Putnam, Daniel Appleton, and Charles Scribner—believed with equal certainty that their own times had become much too commercialized. Their golden age had occurred in London during the late eighteenth and early nineteenth centuries; but the British publishers of that era themselves looked back to their own idealized earlier time, before labor problems had come to be so large a factor in the book trade.

My own belief is that a historian of the publishing industry ought to cultivate an objective and independent attitude and should have a sense of the commercializing tendencies common to all periods of booktrade history. It is true, for example, that such modern developments as conglomerate ownership, book "packaging," and the blockbuster mentality appear to have developed from conditions present in American publishing during the Progressive Era, but these same conditions can be observed in virtually all historical periods. They are present in the British booktrade as early as 1725. Commercial tendencies in publishing are not necessarily bad. Writers have always had to adjust or compromise, in one fashion or another, if they have meant to reach audiences of significant size. And economically successful writers have always come to feel, in their middle years, a sense of regret at having allowed themselves to be influenced by the marketplace. This variety of regret comes as naturally to authors as veneration of previous generations does to publishers. The role of the historian who studies authorship and publishing is not to adopt the thinking of his subjects, but objectively to describe their behavior as they walk the line between commerce and art.

But this is a small complaint, perhaps not wholly justified, for Wilson appears to recognize the dangers of retrospective nostalgia and to guard against them.[3] In the end one must be pleased that his book—serious, scholarly, thoughtful—has been written and published. Wilson cuts across disciplines in ways that most American literary scholars are unprepared to do, and he treats authors who have been neglected because they have not exhibited the modern critic's shopping list of desirable characteristics—alienation, isolation, sexual unhappiness, religious skepticism. This book is also a healthy sign that young scholars of Wilson's generation can do first-rate historical and archival research and, one hopes, be fully rewarded for it. The historically uninformed critic soon reaches the end of what he can say about individual works of literature and must take up, as his subject, the critical act itself. His writing becomes incestuous, narcissistic, and inaccessible: it stimulates no further thinking or research. Books like *The Labor of Words*, by contrast, open up new areas for study and stimulate other scholars to examine authorship and literature in fresh and useful ways.

Notes

1. William Charvat, *Literary Publishing in America, 1790-1850* (Philadelphia: Univ. of Pennsylvania Press, 1959); *The Profession of Authorship in America, 1800-1870* (Columbus: Ohio State Univ. Press, 1968).

2. William Jovanovich, *Now, Barabbas* (New York: Harper and Row, 1964), pp. 7-8.

3. On page xv of his preface, Wilson writes: "That I offer an often-pessimistic assessment of the naturalists' legacy should not be interpreted as expressing a preference for their Victorian predecessors—nor, let it be said, for the antimimetic creeds of our own time. When at all possible I have tried to take these writers on their own terms, to evaluate them by the goals they set for themselves—and, finally, to take their own disillusionment seriously."

Samuel Johnson's Enthusiasm for History

James L. Battersby

John A. Vance. *Samuel Johnson and the Sense of History.* Athens: University of Georgia Press, 1984. xi; 206 pp.

In advertisements and on the book jacket, Donald Greene, who has spent some considerable part of his academic career alerting readers to the importance and subtlety of Johnson's thinking about politics and English history, recommends Vance's work to the public in very strong terms: "An excellent work, it knocks on the head an old and influential legend about Johnson. Required reading for anyone seriously interested in Johnson and eighteenth-century intellectual history." Such praise from such a writer is no common occurrence, and from him to whom such praise is given much is expected. Unfortunately, between Green's praise and Vance's book there is a space that all outdoors cannot fill up. If Homer can nod occasionally, then I suppose Greene can be allowed to doze once in a while. Whatever may have induced Greene to praise and the University of Georgia Press to publish this book, it must now, alas, make its way in the world on the strength of its intrinsic merit.

On its own, the book is in no condition to support praise half as generous as Greene's. Indeed, if "jejunity" were an acceptable word, then Vance's book would provide at once an appropriate occasion for its application and a fully satisfactory illustration of its meaning. Nothing displeases Johnsonians more and displeases them longer than unjust representations of Johnson's thought, and of unjust representations few are extended over more topics or sustained at greater length than Vance's. More exactly, where Vance is just, he is never new, and where new, never just. And if we owe "regard to the plight of a young student of Johnson, there is yet more respect to be paid to the complexity and integrity of Johnson's thought."[1] I take the liberty of using "we," because I am convinced that every reader who puts aside external considerations, every disinterested reader, will feel that in rushing to judgment Vance has missed opportunities to carry his project to excellence and to make his commentary answerable to Johnson's views, as the following discussion will, I think, make clear.

The "legend" that Vance wishes to "knock on the head" is the one, largely originating with Macaulay, which asserts that Johnson had little regard for history or history writing. Despite advances in scholarship and a profound reappraisal in our century of Johnson's writings, even many modern commentators, Vance asserts, still "fail to appreciate how large a role history played in Johnson's thinking and writing" (p. 2). Thus, Vance's purpose is "to demonstrate that history was one of Johnson's major interests, that he was well versed in historical works, that his mind was ripe with historical analogues and personalities, that he was desirous of employing them in his writings, that he wrote often in the historical vein, that he was cognizant of current historical theory and articulate on what made for good history, and that he was one of the best historical minds of the eighteenth century" (p. 3). In stating his purpose in the introduction, Vance also outlines the topical structure of his book: the order of his topics, as of his chapters, follows the order of these relative clauses.

Chapter 1, "Learning about the Past: The Development of Johnson's Historical Sense," is designed to establish Johnson's familiarity with historical works and his developing interest in history by means of a chronological review of significant facts relative to the making of his "historical sense." The chapter as a whole is meant to refute the "monolithic fallacy," which assumes that "Johnson burst forth on the scene with a strong historical sense" (p. 3). (The heretics responsible for this fallacy are never specified; more important, since Vance's whole project has its basis in the assumption of a general failure to recognize in Johnson "a strong historical sense," it is difficult to imagine just who these monolithites are. Certainly, one cannot express the fallacy and deny to Johnson a strong historical sense.) Having demonstrated in Johnson a knowledge of history, Vance in Chapter 2, entitled "Looking at the Past: Personalities and Events," focuses on "Johnson's use [of] and delight in history's famous names," giving special attention to his remarks on the monarchs from Elizabeth to Anne, and to "his response to the most memorable event in his recent memory: the English Civil War" of the seventeenth century (p. 31). (Some readers with a knack for chronology may wonder how the war, as distinct from accounts and the still visible effects of it, could have been a part of Johnson's memory.)

Chapter 3, "Observing the Visual Record of History: Johnson and Antiquarianism," explores, as its title suggests, Johnson's attitudes toward and involvement in various antiquarian projects. Here Vance attempts to show that Johnson's approval of them was "tentative"; "he appears torn between the undaunted critic and the timid friend of all learning" (p. 82). In his fourth and fifth chapters, "Johnson as Historian: Looking at Literature, Lives, and the Law" and "Johnson as Historian: Looking at the Modern World," Vance concentrates on the "large role history played in his compositions," on works or parts of works in which Johnson assumes "the mantle of the historian," as he does, for example, in his reviews of "historical" books, his historical asides in the early biographies, his historical contributions to Chambers' Vinerian law lectures, and his political/historical essays of the 1750s and 1770s.

The sixth chapter, "Thinking about the Philosophy and Presentation of History: Johnson on Historiography and the Historians," is "theoretical"; it is here that Vance gives expression to his sense of the intellectual nature and quality of Johnson's thinking about history and explores what Johnson has in common with those writers (principally Bolingbroke, Hume, Gibbon, and Robertson) who were articulating the most advanced views on history at that crucial moment in time when historiography was moving from its "infancy" to "adulthood," when "humanistic" emphases were yielding to "Rationalist" or "scientific" ones. Finally, in Chapter 7, "The Significance of History: Conclusions," Vance briefly sets forth his sense of Johnson's sense of history, concluding the whole with a speculation on the *personal motive* behind Johnson's lifelong interest in history; i.e., Johnson looked to history for evidences of permanence ("religion, with its prospect of eternal life, rarely comforted him"), believing that the "only way men and women could feel reconciled to the inevitability of their own ends" was through the discovery of "things that would last" (p. 178). (Whatever charm these sentiments might have for some readers, Johnson would undoubtedly find in them something bordering on the sacreligious.)

Admittedly, this brief overview presents no clear outline of a coherent argument, no clear account of a regular concatenation of propositions coming to culmination in a compelling proof; but to overcome these defects in my summary I would require from Vance a different book. As it stands, the book has no developing argument. Even though Vance insists that his work is arranged "thematically," he everywhere confuses themes with topics, and instead of expressing a series of theses, he simply examines various works and issues with an eye open to signs of what is invariably and vaguely referred to as Johnson's "historical sense." In conception and execution the book is, I think, massively flawed. At every point, Vance diminishes as he seeks to raise Johnson's stature as a historian by trivializing Johnson's views and by working at a level of discourse that even the most agile limbo dancer could not get under. To speak thus harshly has the appearance of persiflage gone bad. Something must be done to justify the severity of these charges.

In an effort to gratify the not perfectly compatible interests of economy and justice, I shall in what follows comment briefly on the project as a whole and then on salient aspects of the respective chapters, devoting most space to Chapter 6, in which we find Vance working at full stretch to delineate the theoretical bases of Johnson's conception of the nature and importance of history.

The amount of pressure against which one is pushing is certainly one indication of the importance of a topic, and we can legitimately ask what Vance is pushing against—a body of received opinion, the force of a problem that resists solution, or both? If the question is whether most Johnsonians today suppose, with Macaulay, that Johnson thought the study of history worthless, then Vance is pushing his way through an open door, as he is if the question is whether Johnsonians believe that Johnson thought little about history or that he had very little knowledge of historical writing. Since the appearance of W. R. Keast's seminal essay, "Johnson and Intellectual History," in 1959 and of Donald Greene's *The Politics of Samuel Johnson* in 1960, since, indeed, scholars began looking seriously at the range of Johnson's writings, no one (except perhaps an occasional oddball, who hopes to derive eminence from the heresies of paradox) has assumed that Johnson treated the study of history with contempt. And no one more than casually familiar with Johnson's works and life is unaware of the diversity of his historical reading and writing. Wimsatt, it is true, has said that Johnson "disdained history," and Krutch has argued that "history was meaningful [to him] only if it was social history or the biography of historical persons and he had little use for any other kind." Moreover, Butt and Carnall have noted that "he professed to 'hate historic talk,'" while also admitting that "there is more to Johnson's view of history than this.... Undoubtedly he felt impatience with history as it was fashionably understood."[2] Each of these critics, however, is emphasizing only that kind of history that Johnson actively and persistently disliked.

A substantial portion of Vance's book is given over to the mere documentation of Johnson's reading and writing in the "historical vein." For this sort of thing to be useful, one would have to suppose what Fancy herself dare not imagine, that those who took the trouble to read this book would not know that Johnson was born in Lichfield, a town with a history, that he worked on the Harleian Collection, had many historical works in his library, alluded to history frequently in his essays, poems, and biographies, wrote Parliamentary debates, reviewed historical works, knew familiarly many who had historical or antiquarian interests, planned a history of the revival of learning, and much else that Vance is at pains to disclose. No crowd has gathered at the docks waiting for Vance's shipment of information. To the extent that his project is concerned with flattening a dead legend, his efforts are wasted. Vance labors to prove what nobody denies and, in the service of the "real" Johnson, uses a battering ram to knock over a cardboard cutout of Johnson unsteadily erected by Macaulay. A figure so natively disposed to supineness is ill-equipped to resist even the Johnsonian's yeoman.

The real pressure on Vance comes from the broader problem he sets for himself: to prove that "history was one of Johnson's major interests," as evidenced by its prominence in his thinking and practice. With the exception of a few articles (Keast's, and Godfrey Davies's "Dr. Johnson on History") and scattered remarks in biographies and critical studies, there has been very little discussion of Johnson's views on history and almost no detailed analysis of his historical writing.[3] In prospect, then, given the general recognition of Johnson's interest in and knowledge of history, Vance's book happily arrives with something necessary to our understanding of Johnson. The pressure on Vance is to illuminate more clearly and precisely what has heretofore been seen only obscurely or imperfectly. Here is a real project that, if completed successfully, would not only command attention but evoke applause. But Vance no sooner announces his project than he restricts its significance by saying that he will look at Johnson's "writings and philosophy from a strictly historical angle" and, hence, "avoid delving too deeply into his theories on politics, biography, travel, and literature, even though history often crosses through and joins with these . . . interests" (p. 3).

Leaving to one side the issue of what Vance might mean by Johnson's theories on politics, etc., we can see that at the outset he has made impossible a discussion of Johnson's views on history in relation to his general principles of reasoning, to his characteristic habits of mind, to those questions and assumptions that regularly inform his inquiries, or to the general ends of his writing (i.e., to make life more endurable or enjoyable). Because of this decision, Vance is obliged to focus on "historical" doctrines, statements, and ideas isolated from the larger intellectual framework governing their meaning and significance. What this focus produces, in the place of analysis, is a form of historical sightseeing, which highlights either the particular statement or the persistence of some few opinions over several texts. No text in which historical views are expressed (or in which the history of a time, event, or condition is deliberately explored) is examined by Vance in terms of its peculiar occasion, aim, or method; nor are the constituent statements of any text seen in relation to Johnson's broader interests and concerns. As a result, in spite of the extensive documentation of historical commentary in Johnson's writings, the reader who silently weighs this accumulated evidence against Johnson's production as a whole is forced to conclude that history was not one of Johnson's *major* interests, though it is certainly a topic to which he regularly turned. (A simple review of the table of contents of any anthology of Johnson's writings or of the topics addressed in the periodical papers will confirm this point.)

This conclusion is unfortunate, because in a real sense history (or a kind of historical thinking) can be said to be essential and central, as Keast noted long ago,[4] to Johnson's approach to criticism and morality (of which history is, for Johnson, a branch). To Johnson, all knowledge is valuable, but that knowledge is most valuable which is most useful. And since all knowledge not based on demonstration is comparative, the product of comparison informed by prior experience and learning, we are historians (as well as moralists) by nature, and chemists, dancers, mathematicians, or gardeners by chance. As Imlac says in Chapter 30 of *Rasselas*, "To judge rightly of the present, we must oppose it to the past; . . . to know anything we must know its effects" (and then reason back from them to the instruments by which they were produced or to the motives, desires, fears, or hopes which made them possible); "to see men we must see their works, that we may learn what reason has dictated, or passion incited, and find what are the most powerful motives of action." The habits and principles of mind briefly sketched here operate everywhere in Johnson's writings, as he reasons from known effects to causes or consequences on the basis of a general probability founded on that experience by which "we gain more principles of reasoning" and form "a wider basis of analogy."[5] They are exhibited in "Observations on the Present State of Affairs," in which Johnson attempts "to shew by what causes every event was produced, and in what effects it is likely to terminate"; in "An Introduction to the Political State of Great Britain," the principal aim of which is to explain "some of the causes of our [i.e., England's] present weakness"; in the "Preface to Shakespeare," where Johnson says that "there is always a silent reference from human works to human abilities, and as the enquiry, how far man may extend his designs, or how high he may rate his native force, is of far greater dignity than in what rank we shall place any particular performance, curiosity is always busy to discover the instruments, as well as to survey the workmanship, to know how much is to be ascribed to original powers, and how much to casual and adventitious help"; in *Rambler* 83, in which we learn that it is "always advantageous to know how far the human powers have proceeded, and how much experience has found to be within the reach of diligence"; and throughout the *Journey to the Western Islands*. Moreover, it is clear that what Johnson dislikes about most histories is what he dislikes about most biographies—a concentration, in history, on "rapid narratives involving a thousand fortunes in the business of a day" and, in biography, on great, public events, those "performances and incidents which produce vulgar greatness." Just as, according to Johnson, most people do not know how to take a walk (i.e., know how to derive either pleasure or benefit from the scene before them), so most people do not know what to notice about historical events or persons. What Johnson is always doing, whatever his ostensible subject, is teaching us how to observe with a "philosophical eye," to think with a philosophical mind, in short, to reason from this to that, so that in the end we can better enjoy or better endure this conditional and probationary existence. Vance knows that *causation* is a matter of interest to Johnson, but he does not seem to know how to describe what exactly it entails for him or how it connects with his characteristic habits of mind. Consequently, the book which deals with the large role history played in Johnson's thought is yet to be written.

With the preceding as preamble, we can now begin a more detailed, though very selective, examination of the peculiar infelicities of Vance's study, giving special attention to the principal features of each chapter. The reader should know that almost every page contains something that rubs the grain in the painful way and that throughout Vance's text the term "historical sense" has the following broad meaning: "Johnson's *perception* of history influenced and exemplified by a knowledge of, interest in, or *enthusiasm* for historical facts, *personalities*, events, and causation and by an *intuitive* understanding of the importance of history to modern life" (p. 4, my emphases). (This term is a beast of many burdens, at whose loaded back Vance points whenever explanation or analysis is called for.) In the first chapter, which is "chronological" rather than "thematic," Vance hopes to show how Johnson's "historical sense" developed over time, as he learned progressively more about history and engaged himself in a succession of historical tasks or addressed himself periodically to historical issues. Working from an anorexic evidentiary base, Vance must frequently let idle speculation supply the deficiencies in our knowledge. For example, since Vance will later make much of Johnson's occasional remarks on Elizabeth I and the English Civil War, he can imagine that "even before he began reading on his own, [he] *must have* listened to stories of medieval England, the reign of Elizabeth, and the English Civil War told by the *elder sages* of Lichfield" (p. 8, my emphases). Later, as a schoolboy, Johnson must have sought occasional relief in historical writings from the rigors of scholarship: "a diversion from this concentrated study *was likely* a historical work or two in addition to the chivalrous romances he always loved. One *can picture young Sam* retiring from the labors of translation and seeking refuge in the medieval panorama depicted in a work like Holinshed's *Chronicles*" (p. 9, my emphases). Throughout the chapter we find a rich assortment of such *must haves* and *was likelys*, few of which, I suppose, are utterly preposterous, though each tells us less about Johnson's developing "historical sense" than about the level of subtlety at which our writer is content to work.

A couple of additional instances will have to serve for many.

After working on the Harleian collection, Johnson, we are assured, "never again could . . . view government, the church, society, or the weaknesses of human beings from the narrow perspective of one who sees all achievements and failures as indigenous to the world of the present" (p. 20). That Johnson ever held or ever was in danger of holding such a view may surprise some readers, as will the information that the many historical works in Johnson's library were not there as "shelf dressing." No, he was "probably familiar with most of the books in his library" (p. 7). "To Johnson, as to most of us, *displaying books in his personal library was tantamount to wearing his mind on his sleeve*" (p. 8, my emphases). I will forbear commentary on the diction here and only wonder, without enlightenment from the author, what exactly such a diverse collection of works governed by a multiplicity of principles and aims can tell us about Johnson's mind. (Something may be learned from the titles, surely, but every inference from them would involve a dangerous leap of conjecture.)

At various points, Vance refers to a *stage* or a *major stage* in Johnson's development, but nowhere are we given to know what exactly characterized the stage, what principles, opinions, views distinguished it. We hear of a *mature stage* late in Johnson's life, but how it differed in any particular way from a less mature stage of thinking we are not informed. At the very end of the book, Vance says that over time "Johnson refined his historical sense rather than altered the impressions he developed in the 1740s and 1750s" (p. 177), but the reader will scrutinize the text in vain to discover on what evidence this judgment is based or in what particular ways Johnson progressively refined his views. Aside from informing the reader that Johnson did not think the present was unrelated to the past, this chapter, when it is not flatly asserting something about *stages* or hopping about jerkily in the open field of idle speculation, simply recapitulates those facts, and *only those facts*, with which all Vance's readers are familiar. Such facts are necessary and useful only to the extent that they illuminate in discernible ways genuine development in Johnson's views, but they do not do so here. The chapter is rich in common knowledge and trite reflections and fails to demonstrate any clear line of development in Johnson's "historical sense," to elucidate a peculiarly Johnsonian perspective on the events of the past, to delineate the particular set of attitudes or assumptions that Johnson brought to the study of history, or to define the special demands he made of good historical writing.

Vance's focus in the second chapter is on "Johnson's use [of] and *delight in* history's famous names and on his response to . . . the English Civil War" (p. 31, my emphases). For the most part, Vance is concerned with Johnson's scattered remarks on English monarchs from Elizabeth to Anne and on the Civil War, but before getting to these, he comments on "historical" references in, among other works, *London*, *The Vanity of Human Wishes*, and *Adventurer* 99. In this section, Vance introduces the distinctions—"romantic" and "objective"—that will dominate his discussion of Johnson the historian until Chapter 6 (where in an effort to find analytic terms sufficient to the "theoretical" complexity of his topic he presents additional terms, no less meaningless than these) and begins his exploration of the "skeptical nature of Johnson's historical sense." Briefly, in *London* and *Vanity* Johnson subordinates the historian to the moralist and presents "romanticized" history, though the portraits in the *Vanity* are "more truthful" and objective. "For literary purposes he saw nothing wrong in emphasizing only positive aspects of a monarch's personality or reign"; the poet was "free to exploit history's romantic side to further his artistic or political ends." Thus, to Vance history has two sides, the romantic and the objective, and Johnson is "romantic" when he neglects to mention negative things about, say, Elizabeth in *London* and "objective" in *Vanity* when he notes, say, failings as well as virtues in Wolsey, Xerxes, and others. The reader who expects analysis to rise from this level later in the book will be disappointed. Johnson is and will remain a good historian to the extent that he refuses to emphasize only the positive aspects of an event or a "personality." (The term "personality" has a quiet eloquence of its own that reveals something about the qualitative reach of Vance's discourse.)

Perhaps nowhere in the periodical papers does Johnson

function more strikingly as an objective, skeptical historian than in *Adventurer* 99, where he "offers to many of his *uneducated* readers a brief lesson in *historical truth*" (p. 38, my emphases). To Vance, Johnson is a good historian here primarily because he points to the defects as well as to the virtues of such military or political "projectors" as Caesar, Catiline, Xerxes, and Alexander the Great. Anyone familiar with this essay will immediately see the baneful consequences of Vance's failure to consider Johnson's statements within their rhetorical, argumentative context, and will be struck by the naiveté of Vance's discussion. Johnson's essay takes up the issue of why the success or failure of enterprises should determine posterity to hold in esteem some projectors and to heap obloquy and opprobrium upon others. He subsequently distinguishes between the benefits to mankind to be derived from military or political *and* learned projectors, regretting that of the heroes and conquerors "he that accomplished mischief should be glorious," while "he that only endeavored it should be criminal" (he wishes that "Caesar, Catiline, Xerxes, Alexander, Charles, and Peter [were] huddled together in obscurity or detestation"). In the end, Johnson avers that if even *successful* martial leaders deserve our disdain, even *unsuccessful* intellectual projectors deserve our admiration, for "from such men, and such only, are we to hope for the cultivation of those parts of nature which lie yet in waste, and the invention of those arts which are yet wanting to the felicity of life." The writer with a sufficiently capacious understanding of Johnson's "historical sense" would find in this essay not only an application of "history" to morality, but a set of assumptions and interests that characterize Johnson's thought and reveal an enduring preoccupation with *intellectual history*, with the progress of the mind, the capacities of man, with, that is, a certain kind of history. But Vance is preoccupied with his romantic and objective categories, exhibiting here, as he does throughout the book, a simple faith in the "objective" truth and in the historian's being able to locate the "real" truth of "things as they are," as though the facts and events of history were not, as some affirm, *constituted by* or, as others more nearly allied to Johnson would say, *filtered through* a particular framework of terms, assumptions, methods, and purposes, as though the "truth," even if supposed to be there (as Johnson supposed), were not shaped, emphasized, ordered, or colored by interest, purpose, and so on.

As always, the best defense against Vance's assumptions is Johnson himself. In *The False Alarm,* Johnson writes: "Every diffuse and complicated question may be examined by different methods, upon different principles, and that truth, which is easily found by one investigator, may be missed by another, equally honest and equally diligent."[6] Thus, for Johnson truth was not inaccessible, only various and variously dependent upon aims and interests. The histories that Johnson disliked were not lacking in truth; they simply contained too few of the truths in which he was most interested, too few truths that could be applied to life. It is not the truth "of things as they are" that Vance should be after, but the "truth" that Johnson regularly and deliberately seeks.

Elsewhere, especially in his account of Johnson's responses to monarchs, Vance's general refusal to consider passages in their rhetorical or social contexts makes possible the identification of a species of "historical remarks" that is essentially phatic or ornamental. Repeatedly, Vance cites passages or remarks which Johnson introduces, not to make a "useful analogy" or to "illustrate a moral position," but to give vent to the "irrepressible pleasure" he took in noting the particulars of history. He took "much *delight* in recalling the famous personalities and events of the past without *consciously* employing them for educative or *moralistic* ends" (p. 31, my emphases). The perceptive reader will rarely find in Johnson's works an instance of such extraneous, unattached delight in personalities or events. A useless digression or two, a miscellaneous remark or two may be found (none springs immediately to mind), but, generally, what appears to be a piece of miscellaneous information (the history of periodicals in the *Life of Addison,* of witchcraft in the *Observations on Macbeth*) is calculated to provide necessary background to an event or action, to illuminate the conditions in which achievement was accomplished, to expose the broader implications of particular opinions or passions, to call something neglected but estimable to our attention, and so on. There is more vegetable exuberance in Johnson's Scotland than there is useless, ornamental matter in Johnson's writings. The more respect we pay to Vance's instances of sheer delight, the less we can pay to Johnson's character as a historian; Johnson becomes an enthusiastic trifler, and we become virtuosos, collectors of shining, useless ornaments.

Quoting from many sources, Vance in the rest of the chapter shows Johnson fluctuating between romanticism and objectivity in his comments on monarchs and the Civil War. The only thing in all this that need detain us even momentarily is Vance's assertion that "of all the historical periods he considered, none was more memorable or influential in the *shaping of his philosophy* than the English Civil War" (p. 53, my emphases). From this announcement one expects Vance, finally, to lay open before the reader the foundational elements of Johnson's conception of history. Instead, one discovers that in his responses to this event Johnson is sometimes objective, sometimes romantic. For example, the war "captured and sustained his imagination," but because he did not pay sufficient attention to the concerns of "the many devout and rational men and women who supported Parliament's and Cromwell's cause," we can see that "his normal historical objectivity was not always operative" (p. 54). How this period, which Johnson never views with the steady eye of the objective historian, "shaped his philosophy" in any particular way we never learn. In the end, we learn only that Johnson achieves objectivity at times, observes both the negative and positive aspects of some matters, perceives the partiality of "party" historians, and indulges more than occasionally in delightful recollections of personalities and events. The opinion is not hasty or ill-natured which suggests that by means of Vance's categories of judgment the distinctive power and subtlety of Johnson's mind will not be captured.

Of Chapter 3, on Johnson's attitudes toward antiquarianism, much could but little need be said. Vance is determined to show, once again, what no one has denied, namely, that even though Johnson occasionally had fun at the expense of antiquaries in his periodical papers (notably in *Ramblers* 82, 83, and 177, and *Idler* 56), he also evinced throughout his life an interest in antiquarian scholarship, established friendships with many antiquarians (Bishop Percy and Thomas Warton most conspicuously), and encouraged the research efforts of many interested in various aspects of antiquity (for example, Thomas Patten, Thomas Astle, Thomas Wilson, Warren Hastings, and Evan Evans). We are also informed that Johnson "enjoyed and *drew inspiration* and philosophical insight from the many historical structures he visited in his lifetime" (p. 73, my emphasis; "drawing inspiration" is what Vance often finds Johnson doing, and when Johnson is *excited* by historical facts, he responds *enthusiastically* and writes with *enthusiasm*). The reader who expects Vance to examine in detail the nature of the *philosophical insights* that Johnson drew from historic structures will only learn something about the folly of vain wishes.

Nevertheless, in support of his notion of development in Johnson's thinking, Vance asserts that in his remarks to Patten, Astle, and Wilson, expressed in 1781 and 1782, Johnson gives an indication of "how far he may have come in his appreciation of antiquarianism from the satire and criticism of the 1750s to the last years of his life" (p. 66). A moment's reflection undoes whatever credit credulity is willing to extend to this opinion. In the very papers in which Johnson attacks the collectors, especially *Rambler* 83 and *Idler* 56, he also expresses a wise appreciation of the potential value of even apparently useless collections of "ancient" (and modern) materials; Johnson is himself working on the Harleian collection in the 1740s, is meeting with and supporting the efforts of Percy and Warton in the 1750s, and so on. Neglecting the evidence which his own book has accumulated against his position, Vance at this point simply isolates two kinds of remarks provoked by and responsive to different occasions and purposes, treats them as representative of Johnson's attitude in the fifties and eighties respectively, and then declares, on the basis of their evident differences, that Johnson achieved in the eighties a new appreciation of antiquarianism. Because there are so many fish in Vance's barrel, even the tyro rifleman with his Christmas air gun can take no pride in his marksmanship.

We can conclude this discussion with a look at what is apparently Vance's final position on Johnson's attitude toward antiquarianism. At the end of the chapter, Vance finds ambivalence in that attitude. "Because Johnson deeply respected serious scholarship and knew there were many pedants and faddists engaged in antiquarian studies, he was *forced* to maintain an ambivalent attitude about antiquarianism *as a whole*; he was never able, regardless of the friends who showed him the *best side* of such work, to embrace enthusiastically all efforts at *recalling* and studying the past" (p. 80, my emphases). That Johnson, like all sensible human beings in all times and places, failed to embrace enthusiastically all projects should not lead us to believe that, like Vance, he was incapable of making sharp distinctions and valuing different enterprises on the basis of discernible differences in their real or potential merit. The culminating proof, however, of Johnson's general ambivalence or tentativeness Vance finds, oddly enough, in *Rambler* 83, a product of the early fifties. Allowing no room now for a "late conversion," Vance discovers in this paper what is "representative of his position *throughout his mature years*" (p. 81, my emphases). From this paper Vance quotes passages that seem alternately to raise and sink antiquarianism, and he concludes: "Rarely do we find Johnson so tentative in his observations; he appears torn between the undaunted critic and the timid friend of *all learning*" (p. 82, my emphases). I think it is fair to say that Vance seriously misreads this essay and completely misses the significance of Johnson's rhetorical strategy and the principled basis of his defense of collections and collectors.

What Vance takes to be tentativeness is characteristic of Johnson's writing everywhere, especially in the periodical papers; it is a feature noted by many scholars and critics, but never fully analyzed. Habitually, Johnson seems to exhaust a topic, and then he turns it a new way and then another way and still another way; or, as he moves from one paragraph to the next (or from one proposition to the next within a series of paragraphs), his argument takes the form, "there's this, *but* then there's this," or "there is this, *yet*, on the other hand, there's this." To my knowledge, no deconstructionist has given his full attention to this persistent feature of Johnson's writing, but every Johnsonian recognizes that Johnson only *seems* to build and then unbuild, to establish and then cancel, to write and then erase. Every Johnsonian knows that Johnson is no fickle, imperious master who arbitrarily giveth and then quixotically taketh away. Perhaps our nearest approach to a satisfactory understanding of this salient aspect of Johnson's writing, exhibited most extensively in *Rasselas*, can be found in that section of Hoyt Trowbridge's recent essay, "The Language of Reasoned Rhetoric in *The Rambler*," in which he comments on Leo Braudy's term "epistemological doublets":

In his interesting comparison of fictional with historical narrative in Fielding, Hume, and Gibbon, Leo Braudy coins the useful term *epistemological doublets*. These are pairs of terms, found everywhere in Gibbon's *Decline and Fall*, which designate alternate possible causes of some event, policy, or belief without choosing between them; the pairs are "epistemological" in the sense that they reflect a theory of knowledge in which historical events are not certainly knowable, though effects are more clearly determinable than causes. Braudy's point could be put more technically and precisely by saying that in probable reasoning we must often resort to hypotheses to explain causes of observed and recorded effects, and that two or several alternative possibilities are sometimes equally plausible.[7]

A proper understanding of Trowbridge's remarks and their ramifications would carry us a long way toward explaining the structural dynamics of many of Johnson's arguments. Causes are often unknown; probabilities consistent with reason and experience are often multiple, and consequences similarly consistent with reason and experience are generally uncertain.

But of course Johnson regularly does more than open up before us a range of possibilities and modifying, qualifying conditions; as always, he is an enabling critic, interested in disentangling perplexity, invigorating our flagging energies, activating our efforts. He not only exhibits but confers powers, instructing in the ways of useful reflection as he displays them, and hence contributing to as he fits the reader for useful endeavor. Johnson's turns usually do not overturn what has been asserted antecedently. Rather, Johnson makes us aware of the various complexities, the various principles (or the various modes and combinations of possibilities) that may determine as they complicate human behavior. It is not that one proposition cancels another, but that the subsequent one shows the situation from a different angle or perspective, or as it is complicated by different motives or circumstances. And as we read, Johnson invites us to anticipate his moves and to validate from our own experience his developing argument. Of course, sometimes (and frequently) the turns display a progressively deepening conception of the general problem, and even if cancellation of some sort takes place along the way, we are not left at the end with a self-consuming essay, but with an enriched sense of the phantoms that may delude judgment or mislead action. What we know from the testimony of our experience of Johnson's essays is that we are not in greater perplexity or less well equipped to be useful to ourselves and others at their completion. We feel that we have new knowledge of or new access to the genuine springs of human thought or behavior. This experience is not a likely consequence of a series of propositions progressively cancelling or immolating one another. There is no cancellation because there is no contradiction.

The practical efficacy of these general remarks cannot be fully or even adequately illustrated here, but something of their utility can be seen in a brief examination of *Rambler* 83, in which Vance discovers only ambivalence, vacillation, and tentativeness. The first thing to notice about number 83 is that it serves as a balance weight to number 82, in which Johnson's fictional correspondent, Quisquilius, recounts, to our amused delight, the history of his life as a collector of such natural and artificial curiosities as the "sting of a hornet," "three species of earthworms not known to naturalists," a "fragment of Trajan's bridge over the Danube," "brine that has rolled in the Pacific Ocean," a "lock of Cromwell's hair," and "a boot of Charles of Sweden." At the outset of number 83, Johnson readily admits that there are indeed "many subjects of study which seem but remotely allied to *useful knowledge,* and of little importance to *happiness* or *virtue,*" and to these subjects Quisquilius has given his nights and days, sacrificing on the altar of his preoccupations both his inherited wealth and his well being. (I have added the emphases to the material quoted above in an effort to accentuate silently the sort of knowledge, whether derived from history or some other branch of inquiry, that Johnson is most interested in having.) Already, with the words *seem* and *remotely,* Johnson is preparing us for his turn. After briefly flashing a patronizing smile at the assiduity of trifling industry, Johnson goes on to look closely at collections and to rank them in a hierarchy of potential usefulness.

He begins with natural curiosities: "A man who thinks only on the particular object before him, goes not away much illuminated by having enjoyed the privilege of handling the tooth of a shark, or the paw of a white bear; yet there is nothing more worthy of admiration to a philosophical eye, than the structure of animals, by which they are qualified to support life in the elements or climates to which they are appropriated." What Johnson does here with natural curiosities he does persistently with objects and artifacts throughout the *Journey to the Western Islands*: he reasons from the objects to the grounds of their existence, attempting to learn something about the art of our necessities in various situations and stations of life, about how life is maintained and what conditions account for the nature and structure of huts, towers, castles, and so on. On his tour to Scotland, Johnson is regularly the *historian* of men and manners. Moving next to collections of the "productions of art" and "of examples of mechanical science or manual ability," Johnson discovers that they are useful, "even when the things themselves are of small importance, because it is always advantageous to know how far the human powers have proceeded and how much experience has found to be within the reach of diligence." More important, such knowledge of our capacities and powers may "promote the invigoration of faint endeavors by shewing what has been already performed," and the "same principles and expedients" that produce trifles may be "applied to more valuable purposes." The "movements which put into action machines of no use but to raise the wonder of ignorance, may be employed to drain fens, or manufacture metals, to assist the architect, or preserve the sailor."

Moving further down the scale of utility and value, Johnson finds that even collections of utensils, clothing, arms, and the like are not all "equally useless," since they may sometimes "contribute to the illustration of history, and to the knowledge of the natural commodities of the country, or to the genius and customs of its inhabitants." And even the most apparently useless collections, those containing items associated with great events or persons (a lock of hair, a stone from a field of battle), may serve as an "incitement to labour, and an encouragement to expect the same renown, if it be sought by the same virtues." There is no "tentativeness" in Johnson's attitude here, and anyone interested in the relatively stable body of assumptions and questions which Johnson brought to virtually every sort of inquiry, including (and perhaps especially) history, could profit from looking closely at how Johnson examines and divides issues with a philosophical eye in this *Rambler*. Taken together, *Ramblers* 82 and 83 do not cancel one another or exhibit a Johnson wavering in his commitment to learning or, more narrowly, antiquarian research. He is not confusing the diligence of Quisquilius and other virtuosi with that of Percy, Warton, O'Connor and others; rather, he is showing us how to understand the potential value of apparently useless materials and how to recognize the opportunities in our midst to extend our knowledge, increase our happiness, alleviate our pain, and exercise our virtue.

Our task is to see more than the object directly in view, to see with a philosophical eye alert to causes and consequences. Of two men looking at an overturned wagon, Johnson says: "He who has no genius, will think of the wagon only as he sees it, overturned, and walk on; he who has genius, will paint it to himself before it was overturned—standing still, and moving on, and heavy loaded, and empty."[8] Johnson had no difficulty understanding the value of the antiquarian projects he encouraged, but he also knew how it might be possible to profit from even the apparently trifling industry of certain virtuosi.

At the farthest reach of justification, Johnson could say of the collectors of thoroughly useless materials that "he who does his best, however little, is always to be distinguished from him who does nothing. Whatever busies the mind without corrupting it, has at least this use, that it rescues the day from idleness, and he that is never idle will not often be vitious."[9] Not every reader, of course, is obliged to show how Johnson's views on antiquarian study can be fruitfully related to his most persistent concerns, but no one should come away from this topic (or from *Rambler* 83) believing that Johnson vacillates in his approval of it or is "torn between the undaunted critic and the timid friend of all learning."

Chapters 4 and 5 can be considered together, since they are companion pieces, both concerned with "Johnson as Historian," with examining—or, more exactly, pointing to—Johnson's actual writing in the "historical vein." In Chapter 4, Vance looks at a selection of Johnson's "historical" remarks in reviews, in the "Preface to Shakespeare," and in a few early lives ("Cheynel," "Blake," and "Drake" primarily) and then talks about Johnson's contributions to Chambers' Vinerian law lectures. (It is significant, I think, that Vance makes no attempt to ascertain what Johnson may actually have contributed to the lectures—he relies entirely on McAdam's determinations—and that in his remarks on, for example, the "Life of Drake" or *The World Displayed* he makes no effort to separate Johnson's views from those found in his sources. There is in the book, then, nothing that approaches original research and nothing that has the appearance of aspiring to scholarship.) In Chapter 5, Vance concentrates on Johnson's political/historical writings of the 1750s and 1770s, but here as elsewhere he fails to examine the rhetorical structure or the argumentative and political contexts of these pieces, giving priority instead to isolated passages and statements, to "romantic" and "objective" commentary, and to those effusive moments when Johnson simply sits back and gives way to his "irrepressible desire to write in the historic vein" (p. 106).

On the matter of context, a brief illustration might prove helpful. Vance is convinced that Johnson is a thoroughgoing, objective historian in *Taxation No Tyranny*. The argument that proves at once Johnson's objectivity and independence from "party" influence is simply and efficiently stated: "Johnson's employment of history in *Taxation No Tyranny* does not support the assumption that he was *indulging* in a bit of party propaganda, *for* his knowledge of the history of colonization compelled him to draw several derogatory conclusions about the English as well as the French settlers, conclusions that would not have amused many who supported Johnson's general attack on the American position. Few in government would have applauded his refusal to endorse the patriotic cant extolling the colonization of foreign lands by a superior English people, as if such settlements were the nation's *manifest destiny* or global noblesse oblige" (p. 132, my emphases). This is not all folly, of course, but it is grossly misleading. One could wear out a night in Russia when nights are longest there before one accomplished with annotation whatever annotation could accomplish to correct or to add appropriate qualifications to these remarks. Yes, in this piece, as always, Johnson attacks the rapacious behavior of those who ruthlessly exploited and corrupted native populations, but one must go elsewhere to learn that Johnson's essay was written at the instigation of the government and published with its imprimatur after having been revised by government hands. Moreover, in it, as Greene notes, Johnson is "making the British case" and responding more and less directly to a series of "resolves" articulated in a set of documents published by the First Continental Congress in 1774. He is providing a "quasi-official reply to this highly important and influential manifesto."[10] Similarly, when Vance turns to *The False Alarm*, he provides no nice analysis of how Johnson orders his essay to meet the specific arguments of his opponents, especially those of Sir William Meredith.[11] Vance knows, however, that this piece is polemical and thus not without a rhetorical slant. Nevertheless, since his chief concern is with objectivity, he preserves as much of the objective historian as he can: "Certainly, Johnson exploits history for a polemical purpose here [though apparently not elsewhere in the pamphlets of the 1770s], but his point has *far more than a semblance of truth* behind it. Although his views in *The False Alarm* have not been universally seconded [were his views in any of these pamphlets so seconded?], we should not fail to recognize that his fine sense of *historical perspective* as well as his *desire* to engage in political argument affected the composition of this pamphlet" (p. 128, my emphases). Vance's argument attains no higher degree of subtlety than this, and he nowhere attempts to explain why Johnson thought the piece was the best of his political writings, containing more "subtlety of disquisition" than his other essays. (Greene thinks "subtlety of disquisition" refers in part to the "array of precedents" he cites from "parliamentary history," about which we hear nothing from Vance.)[12]

There is space here to glance at only a couple of points made by Vance in these chapters. In his review of William Tytler's *An Historical and Critical Enquiry into the Evidence Produced . . . Against Mary, Queen of Scots . . .* , Johnson writes: "When an opinion has once become popular, very few are willing to oppose it. Idleness is more willing to credit than enquire; cowardice is afraid of controversy, and vanity of answer." These remarks many Johnsonians would immediately relate to companionable expressions in several *Rambler* essays and to persistent emphases in Johnson's moral thought. To Vance, however, they are rich in "historical" significance: "Few bits of Johnsonian wisdom express as well the philosophy behind his historical outlook: in order to be a good historian, one must reject popular interpretations of events, no matter how widely accepted, and make the effort to question the validity of a view and then search for contrary evidence. His words could serve handsomely as the historian's credo" (p. 86). Although at once philosophy and credo to Vance, these remarks to most readers would not seem to express either one or the other. (It is possible that by philosophy Vance means what the bartender means by philosophy when he says, "My philosophy is 'take while the takin's good.' ") To Johnson, of course, these remarks constitute neither philosophy nor credo. Although he did not always concur with common judgment, he never—whether speaking as historian, critic, or moralist—began the process of reasoning by rejecting common opinion. If Vance were content to affirm only that on many historical issues popular judgment could not always be trusted, few would disagree, but Vance does here what he does throughout the book—he adjusts Johnson's capacious views to his own narrow bed of ideas, managing, thus, to both trivialize and misrepresent the mind he comes to celebrate.

Vance subsequently calls Johnson's review of Thomas Blackwell's *Memoirs of the Court of Augustus* "the most interesting of these major reviews . . . because more than a criticism of the author's book, the review is important to our understanding of Johnson's impressions of ancient Rome" (p. 87). Anyone who consults this short review, however, will immediately discover that Johnson says almost nothing about ancient Rome and concentrates instead on Blackwell's vanity and affectation (his *personal* engagement with the decisions of the Roman Senate) and on his stylistic excesses, a focus determined by the fact that Blackwell adds almost nothing to our stock of knowledge. In short, this is not a major review, and if it discloses something characteristic of Johnson—his willingness, say, to value works that, while contributing nothing to our knowledge, present received ideas "more intelligibly or more delightfully"—it is not a document central to our understanding of Johnson the historian.

As a final example of Vance's failure to understand the radical significance of Johnson's "historical" commentary, we can take his remarks on the "historical" section of the "Preface to Shakespeare": "At one point Johnson seems to pause—*apparently for effect*—and states uncategorically: 'Every man's performances, to be rightly estimated, must be compared with the state of the age in which he lived, and with his own particular opportunities.' Given the qualifications to his position mentioned above—that a writer may be judged by universal standards transcending time and place—Johnson endorses the historical method of criticism" (p. 92, my emphases). Indeed Johnson does endorse the method, but Vance neglects to examine what the method is or entails or how it functions in or is crucial to both his critical and moral writings. To Vance, Johnson suddenly shifts to the historical mode, "apparently for effect." At this point, of course, having established that Shakespeare is the poet of nature and having traced our enduring pleasure in Shakespeare's plays to its sources, Johnson attempts to determine how much of his success may be attributed to his native genius and how much to his circumstances, to determine how much Shakespeare owed to his age and how much his age owed to him. And since the works themselves are ambiguous signs of greatness, Johnson must consider both the state of learning at the time Shakespeare wrote and the extent to which he may have been influenced by it. Only by considering Shakespeare's achievement within its circumstantial setting can Johnson determine the peculiar nature of Shakespeare's genius and his contribution to our understanding of the capacities of man. Johnson's focus in this section of the "Preface" is determined by the antecedent argument and, primarily, by the special emphases of his kind of criticism. The method exemplified here, which is grounded in a stable body of assumptions, principles, and aims, is central to Johnson's approach to the *facts* and *events* of history, biography, literature, and life. But here, as throughout these two chapters, Vance puts the emphasis on isolated comments and refuses, in general, to consider them in their internal and external contexts or in relation to Johnson's larger concerns. Looking for Johnson the historian, Vance lets the man pass by to get a better look at his shadow.

Chapter 6, the last to be discussed here, is Vance's most ambitious and least satisfying; it is here that he attempts to define the theoretical bases of Johnson's approach to history and succeeds only in showing that he is a retailer of trite commonplaces, a dealer in flocculence, peddling old bags of wool. Recognizing that the figure standing in the way of a proper appreciation of the importance of history to Johnson is Johnson himself, Vance begins by recalling all those passages scattered in Mrs. Thrale's ancedotes, Boswell's *Life*, and Johnson's works in which Johnson declares his distaste for "history." To Mrs. Thrale, for example, he declares that "he never desired to hear of the Punic War while he lived"; such conversation was "lost time"; it "carried one away from common life, leaving no ideas behind which could serve *living wight* as warning or direction."[13] The image of Johnson the hater of history created by passages such as this one could be removed by bringing to attention the occasions or persons provoking Johnson's rejoinders; by reminding the reader of Johnson's steady disapproval of the fashionable practice of historical analogizing, especially when exercised by those of "Whiggish" inclinations; by noting that in Johnson's view, most histories, like most biographies, were written by people who did not know what to observe or who had no opportunities to observe what could be most useful (we need search no further to explain why he *could praise* Clarendon's *History* and the Duchess of Marlborough's *Memoirs*; the writers of these works, like autobiographers, had the "first qualification of an historian, the knowledge of the truth"; as parties or witnesses to the decisions on which national policy or royal behavior was based, they could show events from the perspective of motives, desires, fears, and passions); by observing that Johnson's attacks, far from evincing disdain for history, reveal how much potential he saw in the study of history, properly conducted; by reminding the reader that Johnson himself not only encouraged and practiced history writing but also showed—in "An Introduction to the Political State of Great Britain," "Observations on the Present State of Affairs," and other works—how the kind of history he was most interested in could be written (in these works we see nations acting, as individuals do, according to common principles of reasoning, in conformity with one or another natural or adscititious passion); by noting that against the opinion of Bolingbroke that England had produced no good historians he gave as evidence to the contrary the accomplishments of Raleigh, Clarendon, and Knolles; by recalling the range of Johnson's historical interests (e.g., his interest in the development of languages, in the genesis and progress of literary compositions—Milton's *Paradise Lost*, for instance—in the rise and fall of learning, in biography, in the history of a garret, the history of Rasselas, the histories of all those characters in the periodical papers who listen to the call of one or another

Samuel Johnson and History

wish or desire, and so on and so on); and by showing, finally, how in all his efforts to understand what we have done and can do as creative and moral beings he relies on comparative judgment, which has its basis in a "historical method" of reasoning.

Although Vance is interested in some of these matters, by and large it is not by any systematic exploration of these facts, conditions, or extenuating circumstances that he seeks to dispose of the false image of Johnson. Instead, he gives us a figure caught in a transitional moment when the *humanist* was yielding to the *Rationalist/scientific* approach to the study of history and when the reconciliation of conflicting demands was the hard task of the historian. The progress of Vance's argument is not always easy to follow, but the end of it is to show that Johnson's place in the contemporary "debate" was at the cutting edge and that his views were perfectly consonant with those of the best historical minds of the period, especially with those of Bolingbroke, Gibbon, Robertson, and Hume. What Vance succeeds in showing, however, is that, when considered apart from their particular contexts and from the principles and assumptions informing them with specific meaning and value, a variety of large, general opinions can appear to be perfectly compatible with one another. And Vance's "debate" is without debaters; we see no real spokesmen joining real issues, no contradictory positions locked in combat, and no particular set of ideas working to undermine another particular set. From Vance's satellite we see only clouds joining together or drifting apart.

To Vance, Johnson's enthusiasm for those inert facts which he "freely added . . . to his narratives" and for the "details of chronology" betokens a scientific spirit (p. 140). On the other hand, when Johnson uses history to make a moral point, he indulges in "exemplary history," which is part of the humanist tradition. As a historian, then, Johnson is alternately romantic and objective, a humanist and a scientist. As a humanist, Johnson does not of course stand alone; many wrote in the "exemplary" vein, enforcing moral points with examples from the past (or present). To show that this form of writing has both a venerable past and an active present, Vance quotes statements from writers as diverse as Polybius, Tacitus, Bolingbroke, Gibbon, Robertson, and Hume, each of which affirms in one way or another that we can learn "proper behavior from the examples and experiences of others." (At this level of pronouncement, these writers express opinions with which most scholars, professional wrestlers, and high-school football coaches would be hard pressed to disagree.) Having moved from the garret to the cockloft, Vance may not be able to hear the homely truth circulating among the crowd on the street. That is, even though Hume, for example, appears to betray a deep affinity with Johnson when he says that the chief use of history "is only to discover the constant and universal principles of human nature,"[14] we cannot know with certainty whether indeed he and Johnson share similar views without looking at their ostensibly consanguineous ideas in the particular contexts of their articulation. From a common stock of ideas a multiplicity of particular historical or critical positions can be constructed, and many disparate, different, and even contradictory essays, treatises, and histories can spring from shared assumptions. At any rate, what we need to know, according to our writer, is that exemplary history forms a major part of "the 'humanist' school of historical theory, one to which Johnson subscribed enthusiastically" (p. 143).

Expanding his argument, Vance goes on to say that "like other eighteenth-century thinkers, [Johnson] was *unable* or at least *unwilling* to *break the grip* of the humanist tradition, even though he *saw* that it *held back* the rapid development of a scientific approach to history" (p. 143, my emphases). Yet if, with Hume, Gibbon, Bolingbroke, and Robertson, Johnson thought that history "should discover the constant and universal in human nature and that it should be used as an educative tool," he, like Hume, Robertson, Bolingbroke, and Gibbon, was not a reactionary obstructionist, obstinately and truculently determined to stand "squarely in the way of the emerging scientific approach to history, which held that historians should tell things as they were rather than concern themselves with philosophical and moral emphases" (pp. 144,

145). No, one and all, these writers parked themselves at the crossroads and saluted both tradition and science. As Vance says, "historiography was in a period of transition, in which the historians were pulled in two directions: by tradition and by an increasing acceptance of a more scientific emphasis" (p. 145). (N.B. The "problem" here is not with the notion of a "period of transition"—about that there is general agreement—but with the nature and quality of Vance's analysis.)

This new scientific emphasis merges with or at least is not sharply distinguished from what Vance, appealing to R. N. Stromberg's categories, calls the "Rationalist" or "Enlightenment" school of historiography, which broadened the scope of historical inquiry to include "social history, the history of trade, law, institutions, literature, families, music, taste, travel, customs, exploration, colonization, ideas, and the histories of lands far removed from Britain" (p. 145). Of course, Johnson is interested in all these—though Vance has referred to a scant few of them in his book—but it is important to remember that two writers agreeing on the importance of these topics might agree on nothing else; these are topics that can be discussed in an almost infinite number of "scientific" and unscientific ways from a variety of perspectives informed by a diverse number of first-order principles. And we come no closer to an understanding of the theoretical bases of Johnson's historical thought by aligning Johnson with these topics than we would to an understanding of the peculiar principles of his criticism by listing a series of commonplaces with which Johnson and many other eighteenth-century critics agreed. By means of Vance's procedure, Johnson could be shown to be in perfect agreement with any number of ancient and modern writers.

Nevertheless, Vance is content to work at this level of discussion, where all distinctions are lost in empty categories and shared commonplaces. "Not restricted by his humanistic historical assumptions, Johnson would take the magnifying glass of the scientist [and Rationalist presumably] and search diligently for the particles of history—the unglamorous and often ignored data of 'common life'—that, when pieced together, gave him a far more accurate depiction of the past than the more impressive accounts of famous battles and reigns. His own work pointed in the direction toward which the best historical minds wanted the study of history to go" (p. 147). The confusion here is not easily straightened out, but we should note, among other things, that when Johnson is most what Vance calls the scientist, when he is concerned with men and manners and the details of common life, he is most what Vance elsewhere styles the *humanist* (there is no conflict or struggle between the humanist and scientist in Johnson, though there is something approaching what none would call wisdom in consenting to restrict discussion to Vance's categories); that there is nothing peculiarly scientific or "Rationalistic" about a focus on manners, institutions, and law; that Johnson is interested in the "particles" (the details that disclose motives and desires) of military and political as well as social history, and that wherever he turns his gaze Johnson is concerned with the capacities of man, the springs of actions, the art of our necessities, and the employments that the hunger of the imagination instigates.

As it is with social history to Vance, so it is with small tracts, pamphlets, and public records: "His appreciation and advocacy of the smaller though more crucial tools at the historian's disposal suggest that in this matter his eyes were turned away from the humanist tradition of historiography and toward the emerging scientific response to history" (p. 154). Once again, it is important to note that Johnson values such things, as he does other "historical" materials, for what they can disclose about the nature and capacities of man, or what they can reveal, as he says in *Rasselas*, about "the progress of the human mind, the gradual improvement of reason, the successive advances of science, the vicissitudes of learning and ignorance . . . the extinction and resuscitation of arts, and the revolutions of the intellectual world"; or, finally, from these materials we may "enlarge our comprehension by new ideas, and perhaps recover some art lost to mankind, or learn what is less perfectly known in our own country."[15] Nothing, it seems to me, is less well qualified to illuminate the richness of Johnson's conception of history and history writing than Vance's method of reasoning, supported as it is by infirm distinctions.

In the remainder of his "theoretical" chapter, Vance argues that like Bolingbroke, Gibbon, Hume, Robertson, et al. (indeed, it would be difficult to find historians in this or any period who did not hold the opinions that to Vance signalize Johnson's intellectual achievement as a historian), Johnson is 1) "skeptical" (though his, like Hume's, is a "healthy skepticism," not a "debilitating" one, such as afflicted Pierre Bayle, who was too much of a Pyrrhonist for his own good), 2) much interested in "accuracy" and 3) convinced of the value of an "effective style."

Enough has been said, I think, to indicate that by means of Vance's method of analysis we can never arrive at a knowledge of the distinctive nature of Johnson's approach to history or history writing. Vance has a large and important subject before him, and he has read and assembled at least the primary materials that must form the bedrock of any analysis of Johnson's understanding of and contribution to historiography. But what he has written can only make his readers feel more intensely than ever before the need for a book that is answerable in style and argument to the subtlety and complexity of Johnson's sense of history.

Notes

1. The language here is adapted from the conclusion to *Rambler* 60.

2. W. K. Wimsatt, *The Prose Style of Samuel Johnson* (New Haven: Yale Univ. Press, 1941), p. 96; Joseph Wood Krutch, *Samuel Johnson* (New York: Holt, 1944), p. 75; John Butt, *The Mid-Eighteenth Century*, ed. and completed by Geoffrey Carnall (Oxford: Clarendon Press, 1979), p. 191.

3. Godfrey Davies, "Dr. Johnson on History," *The Huntington Library Quarterly* 12 (1948), 1-21.

4. William R. Keast, "Johnson and Intellectual History," in *New Light on Dr. Johnson*, ed. Frederick W. Hilles (New Haven: Yale Univ. Press, 1959), p. 256.

5. Samuel Johnson, *A Journey to the Western Islands of Scotland*, The Yale Edition of the Works of Samuel Johnson, IX, ed. Mary Lascelles (New Haven: Yale Univ. Press, 1971), p. 40.

6. Samuel Johnson, *Political Writings*, The Yale Edition of the Works of Samuel Johnson, X, ed. Donald J. Greene (New Haven: Yale Univ. Press, 1977), p. 324.

7. Hoyt Trowbridge, "The Language of Reasoned Rhetoric in *The Rambler*," in *Greene Centennial Studies: Essays Presented to Donald Greene in the Centennial Year of the University of Southern California*, ed. Paul J. Korshin and Robert R. Allen (Charlottesville: Univ. Press of Virginia, 1984), p. 211.

8. Madame d'Arblay, *Diary and Letters*, ed. Charlotte Barnett (London: Macmillan, 1904-05), II, 271-72.

9. *Rambler* 177.

10. Donald Greene, *Political Writings*, pp. 401-02.

11. See *Political Writings*, p. 315.

12. See *Political Writings*, p. 316.

13. Hester Lynch Piozzi, *Anecdotes*, in *Johnsonian Miscellanies*, ed. George Birkbeck Hill (Oxford: Clarendon Press, 1897), I, 202.

14. This remark is quoted by Vance on p. 143.

15. *Rasselas*, Chapter 30.

Framing Caws

Gerhard Joseph

Mary Ann Caws. *Reading Frames in Modern Fiction.* Princeton: Princeton University Press, 1985. xii, 312 pp.

Whatever its rewards, academic reviewing may also generate a sense of wasted energy in the reviewer. Why, when as an allusive Carlyle warns us, "the Night cometh, wherein no man can work," does one expend precious time framing other people's secondary work—not even elaborating one's own commentary but rather summarizing someone else's? For surely the reviews in this volume—and certainly this one—exist at an even further remove than the critical work under inspection from the central thing itself—if not from a primary, originating "life" then at least from the great creative poem or novel which generates the illusion of representing that life with consummate verisimilitude. Presumably the critic, especially if he or she has chosen wisely (and how much better can one choose than to move, as Mary Ann Caws does in *Reading Frames in Modern Fiction*, from Austen, Melville, and Hardy to James, Proust, and Woolf?), has come closer to it than the reviewer, who is at a third remove. For whatever our theoretical positions, we are all at least in our unguarded moments mostly naive Arnoldians who believe that the function of criticism (and of reviewing, for that matter) is "to see the object as in itself it really is," whatever the degree of removal of that object from nature. But already in the Victorian heyday of such a belief in "disinterestedness" or "objectivity," in the possibility of unmediated vision, Arnold's famous dictum undermines itself by self-framing—by a redundancy ("in it*self*," "as it *really* is") that betrays cognitive anxiety. In one of Caws's opening epigraphs—Henry James's assertion in the Preface to *The Tragic Muse* that "I'm fond of representation—the representation of life: I like it better, I think, than the real thing"—we have taken a step further toward modernist skepticism, though there remains a hint of the Arnoldian view of representation in James's (conceivably ironic, in the light of *The Tragic Muse* itself) implication that it is a matter of preference, that one could break through to the "real" if one wanted to.

Of course it is precisely the existence of the Real Thing, or at least the possibility of "seeing" it, that modernist reflexiveness both in theory and fictional practice calls into question, and *Reading Frames* charts the historical process by which this happens through a far-ranging, subtle treatment of the literary and conceptual frame. For while Caws demonstrates that the passion for framing is part of a current collective literary fascination (witness her allusion to that interest in Derrida, Felman, Hamon, Johnson, Kermode, Lotman, Miller, Said, Smith, Todorov, et al.), she buttresses her discussions of literary framing with homologous ones from art history (Gombrich and Schapiro), psychology (Dennett and Hofstadter), sociology (Bateson and Goffman), and computer science (Minski).

Her theses are three interlocking ones: first, in major literary works, the foregrounding of certain passages via architectural, verbal, or diegetic cues leads to the cropping off of what is not stressed, and this intensification of focus is the simplest form of literary or visual framing. Secondly, such stressing often enables the intrusion of another genre into the primary narrative, generic mixture being a characteristic of texts we call "modernist." Finally and most importantly, "pre-modernist" texts have gradually given way historically to "modernist" ones. In the former (pre-eminently, the novels of Austen and Hardy) the narrative frame defines a field of observation, and the progression of a text focuses down upon a series of enclosed and cropped scenes; whereas in modernist works it is the framing process itself which becomes the writer's center of interest as the observed field, object or origin—a Jamesian "sacred fount"—recedes ever in *en abyme* fashion before the framer's obsessive, inwardly moving eye.

The first of her theses derives rather directly from Caws's earlier work on surrealism. In *A Metapoetics of the Passage:*

Architexture in Surrealism and After (1981) she had first concerned herself with the self-referential metaphors of rupture—of "fissure, fault, break, breach, gap, split, crevice, vacancy" (p. 6)—in the vocabulary of contemporary theory, and of the ways in which such ruptures are both accentuated and traversed in surrealist and post-surrealist works. Such explorations of an aesthetics of liminality, of a concern with "passage," were intensified in *The Eye in the Text: Essays on Perception, Mannerist to Modern*, where, ranging from the English metaphysical poets to contemporary French writers and painters, she examined the transactions between "the outer object and the inner seen," described "how to look from the inside at what we perceive outwardly, how to include ourselves in writing which we, after all, only read."[1] It is this passion for readerly self-inclusion that informs her sense of the modernist text in *Reading Frames*. For in pre-modernist works an opposition of framing and framed, of outer and inner, is relatively easy to maintain, and Caws's discussion of Austen and Hardy posits that comfortable phenomenological orientation, whatever the thematic dislocations that mar the surface of nineteenth-century texts. But in modernist texts the constancy of frame shifting makes for an epistemological vertigo that draws the reader in, that makes him "look from the inside," whether he wishes to or not.

When we get to James and Proust, we are in the presence of the two masters of "high modernist framing" and at the climax of Caws's argument. For if James is the writer with the most sophisticated spatial sense of setting and oversetting, of positioning and superpositioning, of "frame" and "fill" (in Gombrich's useful distinction), Proust is the modernist with the most refined temporal framing sense. Of the two, James gets the greater space and is the more important, perhaps because those who came after him (especially the Virginia Woolf of the book's closing section) learned their high framing in large measure from him. For the term "high" is one of James's two spatial metaphors for framing. This vertical figure that he continually uses in the sense of great visibility derives from his inclination toward scenes set in lofty and privileged places (balconies, stairs, high rooms), toward actions inset or outlined against high windows or doors, toward the raising of characters upon symbolic pedestals. Alternatively, James's framing metaphor is one of depth as he strains for effects of authenticating density: "We want it clear, goodness knows," as he says in the New York Edition of *Novels and Tales*, "but we also want it thick, and we get the thickness in the human consciousness that entertains and records, that amplifies and interprets it."[2]

While never embracing reception aesthetics in any formal way, Caws's own deepest frame is always the eye/I in the text, the reader's interpretive fusion with the object, and her particular "I" is alternatively shrewd, playful, and intensely lyrical. In exemplification of that last quality, I cannot resist quoting from her summation of Maggie Verver's generosity toward her husband at the close of *The Golden Bowl*, Maggie's exquisite rise in moral stature by which the novel's "vocabulary of value received and appreciated, of debts and accounts to be settled, can be thrust aside with all the trappings of gold, paying, amount, number, moneybags, and even all reward." The moment turns upon her husband's recognition, his final framing of what Maggie truly is:

"It kept him before her therefore, taking in—or trying to—what she so wonderfully gave". . . . That his statement, on which this novel of seeing and picturing and consciousness concludes, can be so diversely interpreted indicates that the last essential work of framing is to be left to each reader: "close to her, her face kept before him, his hands holding her shoulders, his whole act enclosing her, he presently echoed: 'See? I see nothing but *you*.' And the truth of it had, with this force, after a moment so strangely lighted his eyes that, as if for pity and dread of them, she buried her own in his breast" (*GB*, p. 547). For "pity and dread": Maggie's own long ordeal has here its Aristotelian catharsis, in the drama finally enclosed in her husband's eyes for its only frame, now that the others have departed—characters and props alike. There are no more objects in this final scene, neither paintings nor bowls, nothing to collect or to recollect, in the bare light. [p. 205]

I isolate this particular passage because it illuminates both Caws's celebratory spirit and her penchant for focusing down upon those textual moments in which the frames of those three necessary fictions—author, character, and reader—seem most intensely to coalesce: the Prince's *"you"* is the epiphany toward which all three have been converging. But Caws's point about such moments is that they are marked by absence as much as presence. The Maggie that the Prince and the reader finally "see," in the full Jamesian sense, is the ever elusive figure in the modernist carpet, a mystery that teases us out of thought. For in the late James the inexorable process of frame shifting undermines the existence of the fill: the focus turns to the focusing border, the view to the act of viewing, and it is the frame which turns out to be the only Real Thing. The study of the frame is finally self-reflexive, is always "a self-study of our reading habits as well as the picture itself; by the sharp cropping of its sides, it shows its self-reflection to be at once finished and contained" (p. 265).

High modernist framing thus combines a passion for the greatest order and the greatest plenitude; as such it is the latest reflex of a Romantic passion for totalization, for getting it all in. The thicker the layering before one has worked through to the outer border or the inner center (for the striving stages itself alternatively in centrifugal and centripetal directions), the more aesthetically powerful the fiction that one has, like God, included everything. But of course Caws, like her Master (James, rather than God), fully understands that such totalization of perspective is an illusion; she is fully in touch with the Derridean 'parergonal" view of the frame with its quotable quotation— "Frames are always framed: thus, by part of their content," followed by Barbara Johnson's frame of Derrida: "The total inclusion of the frame is both mandatory and impossible. The 'frame' thus becomes not the borderline between inside and outside, but precisely what subverts the applicability of the inside/outside polarity to the act of interpretation" (Caws, p. 278, quoting Barbara Johnson, quoting Derrida . . .).[3]

As subtle and all-inclusive as a critic's act of framing thus tries to be, her reviewer, even were he to strive for the absolute subordination of "mere" paraphrase, would be forced into framing, into the sense of the outside (though the word "review," "seeing again," suggests the temporal rather than the spatial aspect of framing). He would be tempted into "criticism" in the competitive—or even hostile—sense of that word. (In this respect a frame, however humble in intention, always approaches the agonistic condition of a frame-up, with its implication of greater cognitive leverage.) Which is why one of the conventions of the laudatory review is the closing cavil or two, thus:

Caws's struggle for inclusiveness is qualified by a relatively European outlook. The choice of James and Proust as paradigms of modernism suggests that her range is French and Anglo-American culture, a limit that characterizes all three of her books on liminality. (To be sure, in her most recent turn of the screw, "Willing Frame-Ups, After Henry James,"[4] she has widened the net to include South American fiction, or at any rate the work of Borges and Cortázar.) Furthermore, her consideration in *Reading Frames* of what happens to the Poe short story, "The Oval Portrait," when translated by Baudelaire into the poem "Un Fantôme" is unique in its geometry: that "egg-shaped rebirth" (p. 100) is the exception to the rule of rectilingularity for all of the other frames Caws discusses. Her signifying doors, mirrors, windows, etc., that is, derive in one sense or another from a Western conception of the house—and more specifically from post-Renaissance laws of artificial perspective defined by a vanishing point and a single viewing point. Crucially dependent upon the invention of the glass window,[5] such a perspective tends to privilege a static binary opposition between room and surrounding landscape, interior and exterior, the intrinsic and extrinsic—i.e., tends to reenforce the separation of self and other. The phenomenological school to which Caws is indebted accepts as one of its assumptions the possibility that consciousness and the objects of consciousness can be distinguished for the sake of discussion, even when such divisions traceable back to a Cartesian dualism may then be undermined. Characteristically, Caws has herself promised such a self-deconstruction in the future, such a delving one yard below her previous mines, in "Willing Frame-Ups." "All the tales alluded to here," she says in summarizing her treatment of Hawthorne, Poe, Flaubert, Borges, Cortázar, and Robbe-Grillet, "could be retold within a currency of exchange poetics, where dialogue might lend to the flexibilization of inside and outside, to the complexification of the framing categories. That will have to be for a future frame."[6]

That last sentence implies the paradoxical cage in which she will continue to struggle toward a fading marge, toward the critical stance from which she can "frame it all," to quote another of her epigraphs from James, this one from "In the Cage." After 265 pages of words, Caws provides a visual conclusion for *Reading Frames:*

> It strikes me that it might all end with a picture.

In emulation of that playful spirit,

> It strikes me that this review might end with yet another picture: "She had framed it all."

Notes

1. Mary Ann Caws, *The Eye in the Text: Essays on Perception, Mannerist to Modern* (Princeton: Princeton Univ. Press, 1981), p. 20.

2. Henry James, *The Novels and Tales of Henry James*, The New York Edition (New York: Scribners, 1907-17), 18, xix.

3. Barbara Johnson, *The Critical Difference: Essays in the Contemporary Rhetoric of Reading* (Baltimore: Johns Hopkins Univ. Press, 1981), p. 128; Jacques Derrida, "The Purveyor of Truth," *Yale French Studies*, 52(1975), 99.

4. Mary Ann Caws, "Willing Frame-Ups, After Henry James" in *Notebooks of Cultural Analysis, II* (Durham: Duke Univ. Press, 1985), pp. 169-89.

5. For a survey of alternative possibilities, see Edward Wachtel, "The Influence of the Window on Western Art and Vision" in *The Structuralist*, 17/18 (1977-78), Saskatoon, Canada: Univ. of Saskatchewan Press, pp. 4-10.

6. Caws, "Willing Frame-Ups, After Henry James," p. 171.

Literary Stepchildren: Nineteenth-Century Dramatists

Brenda Murphy

Plays by Dion Boucicault. Edited with an Introduction and Notes by Peter Thomson. Cambridge: Cambridge University Press, 1984. xii, 238 pp.

Plays by Augustin Daly. Edited with an Introduction and Notes by Don B. Wilmeth and Rosemary Cullen. Cambridge: Cambridge University Press, 1984. xii, 208 pp.

The editors of these two volumes took on a tremendous task. The material that fills the approximately two hundred pages of each had to be selected from among a prodigious number of plays — original works, collaborations, and adaptations — by these two prolific nineteenth-century playwrights. Sorting through the dubious attributions and the casual collaborations undertaken by two very busy theatrical managers in the process of getting a theatrical season together or keeping a tour on the road is a challenge in itself. Peter Thomson lists 141 plays that Boucicault had a hand in writing. According to Don Wilmeth and Rosemary Cullen, Daly was involved in creating more than ninety, of which he had more than fifty printed as his own work or the result of a collaboration.

There is an additonal complication in the fact that Augustin Daly and Dion Boucicault are important and well-known figures in Anglo-American theater history, but their reputations do not rest solely, or even mainly, on their plays. As the introductions to these volumes carefully demonstrate, both men were, in their very different ways, important managers and producers who had a significant effect on the way our theater developed. Boucicault, for example, is given the dubious credit of introducing the "road company" that was the death knell of the provincial stock company. Daly was an early champion of ensemble acting in America and a potent force in the destruction of the early nineteenth-century "star system," as well as a precursor of the modern director who oversees every aspect of a production at the same time he gives the lion's share of his attention to training and rehearsing the actors. Boucicault was also a well-known, if not very skilled, actor, and Daly was an accomplished theater critic as well as a playwright and manager.

In approaching what is of necessity a very small percentage of each author's work, it is important to keep the purpose of the collection well in mind. These two volumes are part of a Cambridge University Press series called British and American Playwrights 1750-1920, which has as its primary aim, according to the General Editors' Preface, "to make available to the British and American theatre plays which were effective in their own time, and which are good enough to be effective still. . . . These are not plays best forgotten. They are plays best remembered. If the series is a contribution to theatre history, that is well and good. If it is a contribution to the continuing life of the theatre, that is well and better" (p. v). The editors of the series, at least, are not content to accept the common critical position that these nineteenth-century plays are of interest only as historical documents, necessary exhibits to show how far the drama has come since they were written. They make a claim for the enduring aesthetic quality of the plays themselves, a claim that bears serious consideration.

The editors of these two volumes have different ideas about the relative importance of aesthetic quality and historical significance for selecting their texts. Thomson clearly wants to rescue Boucicault from "an unmerited posthumous obscurity" (p. 1). He claims that "it is by his best plays that Boucicault deserves to be remembered. He can be fairly credited with having written two of the best comedies and three of the best melodramas of the nineteenth century" (p. 13). Wilmeth and Cullen, on the other hand, make a case for Daly's significance as a playwright on the basis of his broader historical significance: "Even if today Augustin Daly is remembered primarily by historians as the first modern American director and, to some degree, as a great teacher of actors, Daly's contributions cover the entire range of the theatre arts, and despite justifiable criticism of much of his work as a playwright and manager . . . he deserves a prominent place in the history of the nineteenth-century theatre as a theatre manager, director, original playwright, adapter of foreign plays, producer and adapter of Shakespeare (and other writers of established fare), and a manager of an ensemble of actors that successfully carried Shakespeare and other drama to Europe and all parts of the United States" (p. 1). Both of these judgments are well-considered and just. But what do they signify about the contents of the volumes?

Readers who have been primed by Thomson's concise but effective introduction might justifiably expect to find "three of the best comedies and two of the best melodramas of the nineteenth century" in this volume, and be ready to reassess their views of Boucicault on the strength of these plays. The most familiar of Boucicault's plays, that is, the most often anthologized, revived, and mentioned in theater histories, are *London Assurance*, an early comedy; *The Poor of New York*, an adaption of a French melodrama; *The Octoroon*, one of the best-known melodramas of the nineteenth century; and his three "Irish" plays, *The Colleen Bawn, Arrah-na-Pogue*, and *The Shaughraun*. In editing the Boucicault volume for the America's Lost Plays Series in 1940, Allardyce Nicoll and F. Theodore Cloak chose *Forbidden Fruit, Louis XI, Dot, Flying Scud, Mercy Dodd,* and *Robert Emmett*.[1] Thomson doesn't make it entirely clear which of these plays he would include among the three comedies and the two melodramas he considers Boucicault's most important work, and he further confuses the issue by calling the three Irish plays "comedy-melodramas."

In any case, Thomson clearly has a rationale for selecting the five plays that appear in this volume other than simply preserving the best of Boucicault. Included here are *Used Up*, an adaptation from the French of a short comic afterpiece that a twenty-two-year-old Boucicault collaborated on with Charles James Matthews (Thomson tells us that "We can never know the extent of the Boucicault-Matthews collaboration on the text of *Used Up*, though Matthews later went so far as to dispute Boucicault's claim to authorship in the Court of Chancery" [p. 4]); *Old Heads and Young Hearts*, another collaboration with Matthews modeled on Restoration and eighteenth-century British comedy; *Jessie Brown; or the Relief of Lucknow*, a "contemporaneous melodrama" which "is included in this collection as an outstanding example of formula writing" (p. 7); *The Octoroon*; and *The Shaughraun*. It is clear from his introduction that Thomson does not consider these five plays Boucicault's best, and thus his selection does not represent a reassessment of the relative value that theater history has accorded Boucicault's work. Instead he has given us a representative selection of the kinds of plays Boucicault wrote at various times in his career: a piece of juvenilia, an imitative melodrama, and an "Irish" comedy-melodrama.

This selection would be entirely appropriate if Boucicault were a playwright whose reputation was beyond question — a Shaw or an O'Neill, for example. But for a playwright whose work has been either lost or relegated to anthologies, which, as Thomson and his fellow series editor Martin Banham say in their General Preface, is "scarcely distinguishable from anonymity" (p. v), it does not serve to bring Boucicault out of his "unmerited posthumous obscurity" as well as would a volume that offered only his best work.

Wilmeth and Cullen make less of a claim for the quality of Daly's work, and their principle of selection is more overtly stated as representativeness. While they avoid duplicating the contents of the Daly volume in the America's Lost Plays Series (*Man and Wife; Divorce; The Big Bonanza; Pique; Needles and Pins*),[2] they base their selection on the categories established by Marvin Felheim[3] for Daly's original plays and on their own belief that his adaptations from the German "deserve recognition for their originality and imaginative recasting" (p. 28). Thus, they include *Love on Crutches*, adapted from the German original as a vehicle for Daly's famous "Big Four" actors, Ada Rehan, John Drew, James Lewis, and Mrs. Gilbert, as well as the representative melodrama *A Flash of Lightning* and Daly's innovative frontier play, *Horizon*. The justly better known

Under the Gaslight might have been a better selection than *A Flash of Lightning* to display Daly's skill at writing sensational melodramas of contemporary urban life, but the three plays as a whole are excellent choices to show Daly's range as a playwright.

Despite different emphases in the Introductions, then, both volumes are intended to give the reader a representative selection of the plays written or adapted by these two neglected nineteenth-century playwrights. The question now is, how should we read them? What is their context? Some of the plays suggest earlier models. Boucicault's *Old Heads and Young Hearts*, for example, invites comparison with Congreve and Goldsmith. *The Shaughraun* anticipated Synge's treatment of the Irish peasant and helped establish many of the stereotypes that were to appear in the plays of the Irish Renaissance. Daly's *Horizon* has long been recognized as a repository of local-color characters and situations that were to become the stock-in-trade of the Western, whether play, motion picture, or television series. Parallels and anticipations such as these suggest a historical reading, and one way to read these plays is certainly as important documents in the development of Anglo-American drama.

The context needs to be broadened, however. Both Boucicault and Daly were primarily melodramatists, and their plays should be assessed as melodrama. The problem is that this word has become little more than a derisive comment on popular entertainment to a critical establishment that sees nineteenth-century Anglo-American drama primarily as a rather dismal hiatus between the comedy of Sheridan and Goldsmith and the dramatic renaissance at the turn of the century that produced Shaw, Wilde, and Galsworthy, Synge, Yeats, and O'Casey, and finally O'Neill and his successors. As Thomson suggests in his Introduction, "Our understanding of melodrama has been blurred by literary snobbery. It is not an inferior nineteenth-century form merely because it was a popular one"' (p. 6). The recent work of such critics as David Grimsted, John Cawelti, and Daniel Gerould has begun to open up the melodrama to more sophisticated critical analysis, but the study of melodrama as a form lags far behind the study of tragedy, comedy, or even the discussion play, and the typical education in English and American literature still leaves most of us woefully ignorant of melodramatic texts, particularly those of the nineteenth century.[4] If we are going to understand and evaluate these texts, or the melodrama in our contemporary culture, we need to build a much better context for reading melodrama and comedy-melodrama.

The present series is already doing a great deal toward filling this need. Once these volumes of plays by the likes of Tom Robertson, Henry Arthur Jones, William Gillette, Arthur Wing Pinero, and Tom Taylor take their place among the nineteenth-century literary texts, the context for reading melodrama will be significantly broadened, and perhaps deepened as well. Meanwhile, *The Octoroon* and *Horizon* are recognizably effective melodramas by the critical standards we have begun to develop. There seem to be two elements that are essential to effective melodrama. The first is the creation of an illusion of verisimilitude, through the surface details of stagecraft and costume, which convinces the audience of the immediate realism of the play's world and allows for the suspension of disbelief. The second is the evocation of the universal deep structure in the melodrama's inevitable narrative sentence. The audience must identify both with the figure of endangered innocence usually represented by the heroine and with the figure of active virtue that is the hero, and it must hate the personification of evil that is the villain. And the audience must feel deep satisfaction at the preservation of innocence through the triumph of virtue over evil. Both *The Octoroon* and *Horizon* not only succeed at combining these two essentials of effective melodrama, they also touch the deepest psychological currents of our national experience through the particular American cultural phenomena of race consciousness and that shadow zone between civilization and lawlessness, the frontier. They also preserve enough verisimilitude through local-color detail to produce an effective illusion of reality for the audience.

There is a great deal to be learned simply from the study of this combination of melodramatic elements. Clearly, they reach the audience at very different levels of consciousness. How

Nineteenth-Century Dramatists

do they interact to produce audience response? What are the deep cultural currents that allow the melodramatist to evoke such a strong response from such a simple vehicle? What are the aesthetic aims of melodramatic dialogue? How does the conception of character in melodrama differ from that in comedy or tragedy? Reading, producing, and watching representative melodramas like these can bring us closer to understanding melodrama's aesthetic form and its cultural function.

Of course there is a much fuller context already available for the study of comedy, and in this context both Boucicault's *Old Heads and Young Hearts* and Daly's *Love on Crutches* hold their own. Though not as witty as the plays of Congreve and Sheridan that preceded them or those of Wilde and Shaw that followed, they represent a uniquely nineteenth-century wedding of farce to wit and wholesomeness to the sex triangle. The extreme Victorian tensions surrounding cultural, sexual, and social mores that are being worked out behind the bland facades of these domestic comedies make them worthy of further study as cultural documents and as effective comedies. Of the formula comedy *Used Up* and the formula melodrama *Jessie Brown* there isn't much to say except that they do teach us something about formulas that worked. The interesting thing for critics to do is find out why and how they worked.

One other element which must be considered in assessing how well these volumes fulfill their stated purpose is the editing itself. The textual apparatus has been kept to a minimum in both books, and errors have been corrected silently. In the Boucicault volume, the texts have been established from copy-texts that are reasonably close to the scripts for the first performances, and usually they have been collated with at least one edition. In the Daly volume, all of the texts are based on the published versions that Daly had privately printed. Some readers might be disappointed to find that Daly's editors have shortened and standardized the stage directions, and omitted those that "seemed overly restrictive for a modern performance" (p. 47). Though the shorter stage directions probably make for easier reading, one can't help wondering what is lost in not learning what we can about Daly's production methods and the semiotic elements of the performance text such as space, color, gesture, and facial expression.

Clearly these volumes are not meant to present definitive texts of the plays. Rather they offer reading versions intended to make the plays available to a wider public. Each book includes valuable features such as a chronology of the playwright's life, a list of known plays, and a bibliography. Both introductions provide useful assessments of the place each playwright has in the history of the Anglo-American theater, and Wilmeth and Cullen's is particularly full and well-informed.

Referring to the criteria the general editors of the British and American Playwrights 1750-1920 Series have given us for evaluating the contents of these volumes — enduring aesthetic quality and historical importance — I must say that the editors have convinced me more on the second count than on the first. These are clearly representative selections by playwrights who were important forces both in developing Anglo-American drama and in shaping the American theater of the twentieth century. They are also representative examples of the important dramatic genres of the nineteenth century — melodrama, domestic comedy, comedy-melodrama, the Western play, and the Irish play. But are they good plays? To answer that, we have to ask, are they good melodramas? Are they good Westerns? These are questions that require a good deal more thought about melodramas and Westerns than the academy has thus far been willing to give them. Editions such as Thomson's and Wilmeth and Cullen's help to keep the issues before us.

Notes

1. *Forbidden Fruit and Other Plays*, ed. Allardyce Nicoll and F. Theodore Cloak (Princeton: Princeton Univ. Press, 1940).

2. *The Plays of Augustin Daly*, ed. Catherine Sturtevant, America's Lost Plays, vol. 20 (Princeton: Princeton Univ. Press, 1942).

3. Marvin Felheim, *The Theatre of Augustin Daly* (Cambridge: Harvard Univ. Press, 1956).

4. For discussion of melodrama, see David Grimsted, *Melodrama Unveiled: American Theater and Culture 1800-1850* (Chicago: Univ. of Chicago Press, 1968), John Cawelti, *Adventure, Mystery, and Romance* (Chicago: Univ. of Chicago Press, 1976), and David Gerould, Introduction, *American Melodrama* (New York: Performing Arts Journal, 1983).

Wordsworth and the Genius of Burke

Jeffrey C. Robinson

James K. Chandler. *Wordsworth's Second Nature: A Study of the Poetry and Politics*. Chicago: University of Chicago Press, 1984. xxiv, 313 pp.

In a limited but important way *Wordsworth's Second Nature* reads like a detective novel. The book is not so much a "who done it?" as a "how early in his career did he do it?" What Wordsworth did was to renounce radicalism for a Burkean conservatism; this much everyone knows although no critic has ever identified his conservatism so convincingly and comprehensively as Chandler has. But when Wordsworth "converted" to a conservative poetry and politics has always been in question, or, rather, the traditional conviction that it happened some time shortly after the Great Decade (1797-1807) of his poetry has recently come up for serious criticism. To question the date of the renunciation of radical politics is to reinterpret much of Wordsworth's poetry. Part of the resistance to such a reinterpretation and to the solving of the mystery of dates comes from Wordsworth himself who continually reinvented his life story so as to deny the possibility of conversion or renunciation altogether. For example, when in "Tintern Abbey" Wordsworth recalls his first visit in 1793, he describes himself as an adolescent in love with nature, not acknowledging that "1793 marks the center of his revolutionary phase." Or, more generally, in a letter to Anne Taylor in 1801 Wordsworth sketches briefly his autobiography but, as Chandler notes, fills a paragraph with mention of many of the important places of his life without saying what he *did* in each place. Wordsworth clearly is the accomplice to his own mystery.

This suggests another analogy for Chandler's book, that of the psychoanalytic reconstruction of a critical moment in the poet's early life that has gone underground through the natural repression of maturation. For the book works backwards chronologically. Whereas we are accustomed to studies of Wordsworth's poetry that trace (as the poet would have wished) the growth of the poet's mind, we encounter here an unfolding of the poetic career in reverse, from relatively late to relatively early. True to the psychoanalytic model, this study reveals a rigidity or determinism in the poet such that the late veneration of Burke (e.g., the "genius of Burke" passage in *The Prelude* written between 1820 and 1828), the traditionalism, the psychologizing and internalizing of history and experience, the anti-rationalism, all are reverberations of early expressions of the same convictions.

And as with any good exercise in psychoanalysis, the apparent background figures become as prominent and guiding as those in the foreground. Just as one learns that the obscure figure in the background of the dream may, upon association and interpretation, be eventually perceived as the most significant, so the figure of Burke—usually relegated to the background when discussing the poetry of the Great Decade—turns out to be a controlling presence. Similarly traditional foreground figures, such as Rousseau and Coleridge, turn out to bear a different weight than we have come to expect. This further suggests that part of what stimulates the analogy to psychoanalysis comes from the effect the book has on its scholar-critic reader: the slow removing of a resistance to the historical interpretation of Wordsworth and Romanticism, the gradual undermining of the idealist tradition in criticism. Romanticism, says Marilyn Butler, "in the full rich sense in which we know it, is a posthumous movement; something different was experienced at the time."[1] Or, as Jerome McGann (Chandler's mentor) says, literary criticism of Romanticism needs to achieve "a critical distance, however provisional, from its own ideological investments."[2]

But psychoanalysis must remain here only an analogy. Chandler has no particular interest in unconscious repression and personal trauma but rather wants to delineate the various ideological choices made by the poet in his work and to mark the occasions of those choices. Indeed, the phrase, "the growth of the poet's mind," accurately representing the category under which Wordsworth would like his poetry to be considered, itself receives interpretation within the larger category of politics filtered through Burkean conservatism.

Chandler encounters the usual reading of Wordsworth as a poet of nature by showing that he is (or that he became) a poet of Burkean "second nature." Immediately the terms assume a political value. "Nature" is Rousseauist, referring to the person in a nakedness with respect to civilization, the past, class prejudice. A person in such a state stands before the world with all mental faculties alert and potentially active and effectual. It follows from being a "natural" man or woman that the mind, an instrument of reflection and reason, defines the person and allows him to act for survival and for the betterment of his and others' conditions. The cover illustration for Chandler's book, "The Apotheosis of J. J. Rousseau and His Conveyance to the Pantheon (October 11, 1794)," is employed here to reinforce Rousseau's revolutionary impact in France based largely upon the value of reason as the weapon of reform and revolution. By contrast, Burke, and Wordsworth after him, consistently denigrate the revolutionary power of reason which is replaced by the power of tradition to guide and chasten one's actions and acceptance of the established English political order. This "second nature" is human nature refined and channeled by habits and customs. If the empowering source in the Rousseauist idea of nature is mind as reason and imagination and will, in second nature that source stands outside the self: one submits to it rather than becomes it.

Wordsworth's Second Nature might be said to reveal an essential set of oppositions current in late eighteenth-century culture and politics and manifest in the ongoing poetry of Wordsworth: mind versus autobiography, history versus psychology, revolution versus continuity, inflammatory writing versus the oral tradition. Burke articulates the second part of these oppositions in every case. To the extent that Wordsworth's poetry is centrally autobiographical, autobiography appears in Chandler's book as the primary manifestation of Burkean thought and politics. Indeed, *Wordsworth's Second Nature* is surely the best study of the politics of the Wordsworthian autobiographical impulse (and is thus largely about *The Prelude*).

Chandler helps us to accept the unexpected relationship between mind as a socially critical and potentially subversive instrument on the one hand and, on the other, mind as subsumed, tamed, and organized by the "organic" category of autobiography. Autobiography seen thus is neither a pure genre nor a pure fact of human life but rather a literary construction with potent political content. If mind employed in the service of social criticism, and possibly social revolution, implies radical changes and discontinuities for the subject—that past may not and should not resemble future—then autobiography implies a mind which encourages not change but the confirmation of what has gone before. Human strength lies not in the ability to throw off a burdensome past but in the capacity to build upon, architecturally (cf. Wordsworth's analogy of *The Prelude* to part of a Gothic church), the past into the future. For Burke as well as for Wordsworth (following him closely), personal strength through autobiography radiates into national, i.e. English, strength, so that in Wordsworth's autobiographical poetry the representation of successful personal negotiation of past into present and future is a civic glory as well. Not surprisingly mind itself—since it naturally and morally tends towards the criticism of the humanly unjust—becomes for Wordsworth less significant than the feeling which registers and affirms more readily the links to the past:

> So feeling comes in aid
> Of feeling, and diversity of strength
> Attends us, if but once we have been strong.

Burke and Wordsworth denigrate as "upstart theory" those formulations of human and social life as they should be according to the principle of liberty for all.

It is powerful to discover that the onset of Wordsworth's main drive towards the autobiographical representation of experience coincides with what Chandler dates as the poet's conversion to Burke, around 1797. Then and shortly thereafter Wordsworth begins the early versions of *The Prelude* and elaborates the autobiographical history of the Pedlar, the narrator of *The Ruined Cottage*. Let me disgress (only apparently) from autobiography to the story of Margaret to remark Chandler's fine distinction between *The Ruined Cottage* and its predecessor *Salisbury Plain*. Chandler observes the similarities between the two poems in order to show that the later poem is more Burkean: that is, rather than explaining human tragedy and alienation in terms of social inequities and class manipulations as he does in *Salisbury Plain*, Wordsworth in *The Ruined Cottage* reverts for explanation to a kind of natural entropy; the pedlar-narrator becomes moreover a teacher, even a master, in the ways of human nature, one who can convince the neophyte poet that the deep beauty of nature herself should demand that one accept the authority of nature's ways, even if they presume upon the life of a young woman. The autobiography of the Pedlar, an autodidact who has let nature be his teacher, lends force to the authority of nature herself. Or rather, it lends force to the "lore," or second nature, the oral tradition that Burke favored over writing itself which made room for inflammatory tracts, an oral tradition of which the story of Margaret becomes a part.

Autobiography casts another Burkean influence on the representation of experience, the psychologization of experience. Here the "spots of time" are the characteristic structure of experience in *The Prelude*, moments in which the poet's response to the event counts more than the event itself. In this regard I think of a moment in *The Prelude* where such internalization is refused, a moment that isolates the Burkean-Wordsworthian limits to represent experience. In Book x, Wordsworth recalls sitting in his Paris garret contemplating the Square below which had witnessed recently the "September Massacres." The thought of the genial hopes of the Revolution turned into the brutality of mass murder is impossible for him to assimilate. His simile for this impasse is revealing. He was:

> . . . upon these
> And other sights looking as doth a man
> Upon a volume whose contents he knows
> Are memorable but from him locked up,
> Being written in a tongue he cannot read,
> So that he questions the mute leaves with pain,
> And half upbraids their silence.
> [1805, X, 47-54]

That is, he cannot possess—internalize, psychologize—the bitter historical truth. Later in the same passage he is "Defenceless as woods where tigers roam," where "defenceless" means "unable to defend against harsh experience by internalizing it and converting its pain into pleasure or the bliss of solitude."

The "scene," in this regard, serves an ideological purpose opposite to that which Diderot (revived by Brecht and Barthes) proposed: that it convey the defining contradictions inherent in a modern, industrial society. The process of internalization and psychologization converts social contradiction into nurturing for the individual.

Historical (irreversible) time is converted into timelessness: autobiography is the picture of a being for whom time and event serve to confirm his existence outside of time, an instance of typical Romantic "essentialism." Chandler observes this view of time repeatedly in Wordsworth's poems when he notes the time or tense confusions between past and present. Similarly Chandler interprets Wordsworth's preoccupation with "restoration" and renovation, or the wish—as the poet says in "To the Cuckoo"—to "beget that golden time again."

The way for the individual to assert his relationship to history opposite to that of autobiographical assimilation of time is the way of systematic thought. Here history and society are confronted, not assimilated, by mind. Chandler is excellent on repeatedly showing how Burke and, following him, Wordsworth consistently deplore the use of systematic thought and "upstart theory" to confront history and prefer instead the consoling links to the past provided by the oral tradition. Similarly he demonstrates how, in poems like "Expostulation and Reply" and "The Tables Turned," Wordsworth dramatizes the preference for the abandonment of questions and answers altogether. This is one of Wordsworth's most characteristic epistemological scenes in his poetry; it follows the pattern of what Geoffrey Hartman two decades ago labelled "surmise": one asks a question in an "either-or" grammar (Is it "x" or is it "y"?) but then refuses to choose an answer. The *locus classicus* in Wordsworth is "The Solitary Reaper" where the halted traveller asks the theme of the Reaper's song, proposes two alternatives, but then dissolves the need to choose:

> Whate'er the theme, the Maiden sang
> As if her song could have no ending; . . .
> The music in my heart I bore,
> Long after it was heard no more.

To have stayed with the original plan of questions would have demanded that the poet seek out the answers by approaching the Maiden or someone else instead of remaining pleasurably in the lake of his own imagination. The poet would have had to enter history. The message at the end of this poem is clearly that it is better to convert thought and subsequent interaction with another into feeling and to convert words into music.

This study, I have tried to suggest, goes far towards enhancing our understanding of the political and ideological valences of "mind" at the end of the eighteenth century. My only criticism of (or queries about) the book concerns the question of mind in the work of two major though still peripheral figures in Chandler's cast of characters, Rousseau and Coleridge. He sets Wordsworth against Coleridge by asserting that the latter criticized the former's abandonment of mind as a determining and critical principle. A valuable point, but throughout the book Chandler has primarily associated the preference for systematic thought with radical politics; thus it is hard to see the value of concluding the book with a chapter on the Coleridge of the *Biographia* whose allegiance to mind belongs to a now conservative thinker. Are we to believe that the politics of mind has been changing from the time of Burke to that of Coleridge in 1817? And if it has not been changing, then what is the point of Chandler's contrast of Wordsworth and Coleridge on this subject?

The problem with Rousseau is similar. He appears in this book as the radical precursor to Romanticism, the clear antagonist to Burke. His is the line that Wordsworth chose to abandon. His opposition to Wordsworth is easy to assume as long as "mind," pure and simple, remains the point of contrast. But the radical status of, for example, Rousseau's *Emile* as an educational tract, becomes less clear when the categories are slightly shifted. Rousseau may advocate the development of mind as an analytical tool, but the education of Emile hardly produces a young adult bursting with radical sentiments and views. Rather, mind in *Emile* aids in the avoidance and then sublimation of the revolutionary implications of late adolescence: how far is Emile from an Orc or a Los or a Caleb Williams! For Blake, Schiller, and Godwin adolescence brings systematic thought and sexual and rebellious feeling into a powerful if uncontrolled synergism. Not so for Rousseau; the dominating though serene figure of Emile would fit more with the young adulthood Wordsworth wished for himself. Then there is the problem that the radical Mary Wollstonecraft confronted in her *Vindication*: the education of Emile, with its emphasis on reason, may work for the boy, but the young Sophie deserves and does not get the same. Something in Rousseau's view of mind and education, and what they act upon, seems to reinforce the traditional subordinate role of women. Wollstonecraft speaks brilliantly on Rousseau's neurotic experience of sexual desire and his subsequent distortion of the meaning and effect of the passions. The question of the politics of "mind," in other words, seems to me more complex than Chandler presents it. It is perhaps indicative of this oversimplification that Chandler does not bring Hazlitt more centrally into his argument; for Hazlitt, more than any other English thinker of the time, embodies and can speak to the political significance of mental activity in Romantic poetry as a socially critical instrument.

Notes

1. Marilyn Butler, *Romantics, Rebels, and Reactionaries* (New York: Oxford Univ. Press, 1981), p. 2.

2. Jerome J. McGann, *The Romantic Ideology* (Chicago: Univ. of Chicago Press, 1983), p. x.

Living at a Gallop

R. C. Terry

N. John Hall, ed. *The Letters of Anthony Trollope*, 2 Vols., Stanford: Stanford University Press, 1983.

Anthony Trollope's reputation has always been safe with the general public. Apart from a short period soon after his death it has gone on growing, boosted in recent years by televised versions of his best known Barsetshire and Palliser novels. But only comparatively recently has Trollope begun to receive the critical attention his work deserves. When Bradford Allen Booth published the first edition of his letters in 1951, he referred to "Trollope's long banishment from the ranks of distinguished novelists,"[1] and in my own experience Eng. Lit. at the university gave him short shrift up to the 1960s.

Since then there has been a dramatic increase in Trollope studies, and his centenary was celebrated in 1982 with an international conference in London and an issue of *Nineteenth-Century Fiction* (appropriately enough since Booth had founded the periodical as *The Trollopian* in 1945) solely devoted to the novelist. Regrettably, no complete edition of his work exists, and there is little sign of an enterprising publisher to undertake it. Some of his lesser novels are still hard to come by, although a valiant attempt was made a few years ago with a reprint series under the general editorship of N. John Hall.[2] Hall now adds luster to his status in the world of Trollopian scholarship with this meticulous edition of the letters.

Reviewing Trollope studies in 1978, Ruth apRoberts reminded us that the challenge was still "to define the very qualities of the man, both as a writer and as a personality."[3] A new edition of the letters brings us a good deal closer than we have so far managed to get, notwithstanding the pioneering biography of Michael Sadleir and further efforts by C. P. Snow and James

Pope Hennessy.[4] The two volumes provide a treasurehouse of anecdote and reminiscence, updating Booth's work with what amounts to a fascinating picture of this many-sided man.

Booth's collection, an important contribution in its day, drew upon the Morris L. Parrish Collection at Princeton University, 83 letters owned by Miss Muriel Rose Trollope (Anthony's granddaughter) and 53 in the possession of Mrs. Reginald Smith, daughter of his friend and publisher, George Smith. Others came from individuals, booksellers and libraries. A generation later, Hall can draw on far wider sources, including the National Library of Scotland, Post Office Records, the Royal Literary Fund, the archives of many publishers and the University of Melbourne, this last a veritable goldmine of letters from G. W. Rusden, as I shall show. These *Letters*, therefore, contain 1,826 entries, compared with Booth's 932, plus full versions of over 300 Booth had summarized (helpfully indicated in the text by the initials "SB"). In addition there are 85 letters to Trollope and 16 about him. It is good to have, for example, George Eliot's splendid words on his novels: "They are like pleasant public gardens, where people go for amusement, and whether they think of it or not, get health as well" (p. 238).

Impeccable editorial methods characterize this edition, and credit is given to the assistance of Nina Burgis. The two volumes are attractively presented, with enough margin and space between entries to rest the eye (with so much information no small asset) and thirty-six well placed plates. Rather than being numbered, as in Booth, which had led to confusion with page numbers, each letter is identified by manuscript location with date and address, and sequential pagination over the two volumes; further aid to identification comes from a comprehensive General Index and an Index of Correspondents. Some normalizations have been made to conform to conventional practice in such cases as supplying periods at the ends of sentences and offering consistent punctuation where quotations need them. Otherwise the editor has scrupulously maintained Trollope's idiosyncrasies of style, such as abbreviations of "Mss" for "MS" and his fondness for the comma-dash. Where Trollope's notoriously difficult hand makes for uncertainty conjectural readings are preceded by question marks in square brackets.

As N. John Hall observed on the occasion of Trollope's centenary in 1982, we *can* find out what kind of man he was from the letters—but we have to work at it.[5] The effort is certainly worthwhile. These letters, written off the cuff (often on the run) and strictly functional—virtually a log-book, as Booth asserted, of the busiest man of Victorian letters—have hundreds of self-revealing moments which inspire gratitude in all of us still eagerly searching out scraps to define this elusive man.[6]

We know Trollope already in outline: the blustering Post Office surveyor, the meticulous human word-processor who produced forty-seven novels, five volumes of short stories, plus four travel books and other non-fiction, the indefatigable traveller who went twice round the world, the disappointed parliamentary candidate, the robust sportsman, clubman, editor—and always, the outsize, roaring, wild-maned character. Thus his contemporaries: "An incarnate gale of wind . . . he turned my umbrella inside out" (Wilkie Collins); "a conversational stove" (Julian Hawthorne); "manners were rough and, so to speak, tumultuous" (James Payn); "outwardly a curmudgeon, inwardly the soul of good-fellowship" (Walter Sichel).[7] Comparisons with the more ferocious jungle beasts are often made, and Hall quotes one from Charles Kent about the leonine face and bold look "but a mask before a nature intensely sympathetic" (p. 547). Of course, we know he had a softer side and that he wore the social mask to keep the world at bay; but he was an intensely private man and, as Hawthorne concluded, something of a paradox.

If biography needs the tiniest facts, the careful reader of these letters is well served. We learn that Trollope ordered his cigars in vast quantities and liked distributing them among his friends; that he fumed about strikes and the cost of living; that he worried about his weight and went on a popular diet; that he thought Disraeli "the meanest cuss we have ever had in this country" (p. 700); and that he wrote awkwardly to Gladstone asking if he had offended the great politician (p. 864)—an awkward letter from an awkward and undeniably cranky, disputatious man.

Hall notes an evening with the Boston Brahmins in 1861, when Trollope and Holmes fired salvoes across the dinner table while Emerson, Hawthorne and Lowell crouched out of range dodging the grapeshot. When he was in company and on show, Trollope's tongue always ran away with him and, at that time, with *Framley Parsonage* behind him, he was heady with success.

The other Trollope, quieter, sensitive, generous, of whom it was once said that no one in society was more popular, is also abundantly shown in these letters, and nowhere better than in the sphere I now wish to consider. Trollope, the home body, is still something of a mystery, but the letters do get us past the front porch and into the parlor. He loved his various homes, first Waltham House, Hertfordshire, where he lived from 1859 to 1871, next his London house in Montagu Square, occupied between 1873 and 1880, then his final country home at Harting in Sussex. Waltham was his favorite, and it was distressing for him to leave it for a lengthy tour of Australia in 1871. Likewise, when it came time to get out of town in 1880, he loathed the move: "Oh, the books—and oh, the wine!" he wailed (p. 865). He was a great connoisseur and fussed over his cellar, typically working with furious zeal after the move:

Yes, we have changed our mode of life altogether. We have got a little cottage here, just big enough (or nearly so) to hold my books, with five acres and a cow and a dog and a cock and a hen. I have got seventeen years lease, [this was in 1880] and therefore hope to lay my bones here. Nevertheless I am busy as would be one thirty years younger, in cutting out dead boughs, and putting up a paling here and a little gate there. [pp. 887-88]

He was a much better host than guest. W. Lucas Collins, recalling the Waltham days, observed that on warm summer evenings the party would adjourn to the lawn for wines and fruit laid out under a fine old cedar tree, and "many a good story was told while the tobacco smoke went curling up in to the soft twilight."[8] The letters indicate an extraordinary calendar of visitors and parties. One that misfired apparently had clashed with the Derby. Trollope wrote to Millais: "My wife was awfully disgusted as women always are when nobody comes to eat their pastries and sweetmeats. As for me, I only hope you lost your money at the Derby" (p. 125). Rose, his wife, as we have always known, was his anchor and refuge; it is a pity little new information emerges here about her.

An astonishing amount of the novelist's time was spent on writing to ladies with elephantine skittishness. To one Kate (not his beloved Kate Field remembered in the *Autobiography*), who had invited him to a ball, he responded flirtatiously: "You only offer to put me in a corner to play cards. If you had promised to dance three round dances with me, I should have come at once" (p. 605). The list of female correspondents is long—Cecilia Meetkerke, Mary Holmes, Anna Drury, Anna Steele, and many more. Mrs. Catherine Gould is an early recipient (April 1860) of the favorite metaphor on book-writing as equivalent to shoemaking: "The man who will work the hardest at it, and will work with the most honest purpose, will work the best" (p. 100). He confides to another young woman that Lily Dale will not marry John Eames (he was about to begin *The Last Chronicle of Barset*): "No other marriage would be possible to her in accordance with the poetical justice of romance. But I think there will be no marriage for her in print. As far as she has gone she has been successful to me her literary father, and it is ill meddling with such successes when they have been achieved" (p. 323). Susceptibility to feminine charms, however, did not make the author tender to his female friends' literary efforts, which pursued him almost to the grave. After criticizing Cecilia Meetkerke's poems, he wrote, "You will now be imploring protection from your friends,—who are always the most remorseless of critics" (p. 124). Less than two years before his death he wrote to Annie Rowan, the writer of two unsuccessful novels, as follows:

No word from me could do your novel any good. To whom should the word be spoken? And as to blaming the reviewers you blame them,—do you not?—for not praising it? That begs the whole question of its merit. I do not say but that you have written an excellent novel. But you write as though all that were to be taken as a matter of course. Your publisher published it, no doubt, hoping for some profit.

You wrote it hoping for profit and reputation. You fail, as do so many hundred others,—because you have engaged in a precarious undertaking. You can only abide by the risk which you have run, and, if your spirit be high enough and your heart good enough, try again. . . . There is no path to success but by your own merit. [pp. 884-85]

Dorothea Sankey was possibly the recipient of this strange invitation: "My affectionate and most excellent wife is as you are aware still living—& I am proud to say her health is good. Nevertheless it is always well to take time by the forelock and be prepared for all events. Should anything happen to her, will you supply her place,—as soon as the proper period for decent mourning is over" (p. 144). The convolutions of Victorian humor are sometimes hard to recognize, but it is difficult to imagine Rose falling about with laughter at this example of her husband's wit. His most generous proponent would not claim Trollope's letters approached Dickens's for spontaneous humor or Thackeray's for pointed sarcasms.

The great gains beyond the personal portraiture in this collection arise from material dealing with Trollope's official life in the GPO and with his publishing affairs. Here again, as with his private life, it is not so much a matter of startling new discoveries as of filling in. Items relating to his career as a civil servant add to a growing store of information.[9] Here, as in all aspects of Trollope's life, the keynote is passion for work. With relentless detail he reports on working conditions, mail routes, and international negotiations. Nothing escapes him. "I made no mistake about the pace of camels," he writes from Suez in 1858. "When laden they travelled 3 miles an hour" (p. 74). He is punctilious in dealing with local deliveries, a frequent cause of complaint, asking Charles Merivale if his letters reach him before breakfast: "I have just got back from Rome, where I learned that the Pope has but one delivery daily— his letters reaching the Vatican at 11—all too early and all too often as he thinks. So at least it is whispered among the Cardinals. The Archbishop at Rheims does not get his letters till near ten. The bishop of St. Davids has but one delivery a day. (!!!)

Living at a Gallop

The bishop of Jerusalem has none at all" (p. 133). He also had to deal with tiresome requests from individuals wanting pillar boxes to suit their own convenience. In the pillar box, adopted at his suggestion the length and breadth of the country, he clearly had proprietorial interest. When metal indicators were suggested to show which collection one had just missed, he objected: it "would be too complicated for the class of person by whom they would be worked" (p. 155). In this case he was overruled.

A vociferous committee man, as one would expect, Trollope antagonized the Chief Secretary, Rowland Hill, from the word go. On 2 April 1860 he was named to a committee looking into complaints about poor pay and working conditions of postal employees at the lower levels. Hill suspended the committee, feeling it represented a plot against him. A second committee was set up, again including Trollope, and doubtless to further resentment. (This, like much information in the letters, comes from Hall's full supplementary notes.) In the *Autobiography* Trollope gleefully records his "delicious feuds" with Hill, and the letters bear ample witness to them, particularly the feud which evolved from Trollope's efforts to secure a pay increase for the surveyors in 1864. This involved Hill, Trollope, and Trollope's brother-in-law, John Tilley, then Secretary, who must at times have felt like the meat in the sandwich, having to forward Trollope's blistering memos to the Post Master General, Lord Stanley. When things looked bad for the surveyors, Trollope wrote to Stanley begging him to believe he was not insubordinate— "which is not my nature" (p. 280)—to which Tilley penciled a query. Trollope concluded the surveyors had been shabbily treated and his comment (knowing that Tilley would read it first) is deliberate and coy: "It was exactly the way in which Oliver was treated when he came forward on behalf of the Charity boys to ask for more:—and I own that I thought Mr. Tilley was very like Bumble in the style of answer he gave us" (p. 281). Obviously this is a man leaning on his pen with delight. But it is typical that the dispute moulted no feathers between Trollope and his brother-in-law. In 1868 Tilley urged the PMG to give Trollope the task of negotiating a new postal convention with the United States: "It will be necessary to send a strong man" (p. 416). Right to the end they were close. When the fatal stroke occurred, Trollope was at Tilley's house listening to the new popular hit, F. Anstey's *Vice Versa*, being read to the family circle: "Uncle Tony roared as usual; suddenly my father and sister noticed that while they were laughing he was silent: he had had a stroke from which he never recovered" (p. 953).[10]

Was ever man so cantankerous, tactless and abrupt? Trollope was disagreeable to his subordinates, and yet the letters suggest that even when the man bullied and badgered he was somehow likeable. R. S. Smyth, who served under him in Ireland, recorded that he was held out to juniors as a terror, "and my early experience of him was not calculated to remove such an impression"; but Trollope took the trouble to advise him on his future career "in a very friendly, almost a fatherly way" (p. 308). Another striking account from a post office colleague recalls Trollope at work: "I have seen him slogging away at papers at a stand-up desk, with his handkerchief stuffed into his mouth and his hair on end, as though he could barely contain himself" (p. 345). The description suggests a man delirious with the work at hand. As he was in his official post, so he was in his study, wrestling with Mr. Crawley's proud humility or Plantagenet Palliser's overactive conscience. By 1852 he writes to his brother, Thomas Adolphus, that he is "living away at a perpetual gallop. I wish I could make the pace a little slower" (p. 30). He wished nothing of the kind, continuing to live by the same "hard grinding industry" he cited in a letter of 1860 until the day he collapsed—as much from overwork as anything else. The letters document an amazing round by a man of strong physique and mental concentration who (apart from the pre-breakfast, three-hour stint at his writing) busied himself entertaining, lecturing, visiting, clubbing, dining and—the bane of celebrity—attending meetings. "If my success were equal to my energy," he once told John Morley, "I should be a great man" (p. 530). This remark comes almost at the end of the first volume when Trollope was indeed a great public figure although his literary fame had begun its slow decline, his career in the public service was over, and he had blundered into the political arena with a disastrous move to contest Beverley, Yorkshire, in the general election of November 1868.

Even so Trollope's extraordinary energy dominates the second volume of the letters too. Consider his exuberant pursuit of the grand passion of his leisure hours—hunting, the sport that possessed him from his early days working for the Post Office in Ireland and grew when he was able to stable horses at Waltham and join hunts in Essex and other counties. "I have become a slave to hunting" he wrote his publisher George Smith in 1862. "What weather!" he grumbles in 1870. "It is now just a fortnight since I have been on a horse" (p. 500). "In some perfect world," he wrote to Alfred Austin in 1873, "there will be hunting 12 months in the year" (p. 585). And in 1875 he relays to Austin with some relish how he plunged into a muddy ditch, his horse on top of him: "When I saw the iron of his foot coming down on my head, I heard a man on the bank say 'He's dead' " (p. 644). Having eventually to give up the sport was one of life's abnegations he felt most keenly, and he wrote to William Blackwood in March 1878: "Alas—alas— my hunting is over. I have given away my breeches, boots,— and horses" (p. 759).

On publishing affairs the letters amplify much and invite scholars to further investigation. There is a full airing of negotiations with Chapman prior to the establishing of the *Fortnightly Review* (canvassed in the introduction) and of affairs with James Virtue surrounding *St. Paul's Magazine*, which Trollope edited from 1867 to 1870. Exchanges over textual and publishing matters between the novelist and the Blackwoods are well covered, and some expansion of our knowledge is noticeable in correspondence with American literary contacts such as J. B. Lippincott, Harper & Brothers, James T. Fields and R. H. Dana. There is more on his efforts at seeing his brother's books into print, and many letters prove how concerned he was over his own work in press. I have the impression he took more trouble over proofing and second thoughts than has hitherto been allowed. Such matters need sifting in future studies.

Comments on his own writing are sparse, apart from the occasional outburst at being misunderstood or woeful cries at the hard work of novel-spinning, but his comments to beginners in the trade are illuminating and unsparing. His response in 1870 to E. W. B. Nicholson, who had offered poetry to *St. Paul's Magazine*, is far from encouraging: "Such insight will no doubt come in time; but till it does come I fear you will have to suffer the sorrow of an unfulfilled ambition" (p. 494). Nicholson perhaps heeded the advice; he went on to become Bodley's librarian and founder of the Library Association. For such a busy man it is remarkable that Trollope devoted so much time and energy to advising others: Kate Field, Anna Steele, Cecilia Meetkerke, Austin Dobson—the list rolls on. The advice is generally standard: Trollope's old adage that a man should write because he has a story to tell and not because he has to tell a story, and that the best asset is a piece of cobbler's wax to stick him to the chair. The other standby is also very Trollopian: that by practice a man should achieve an easy style. He repeats it again and again. From Baden in 1878 he writes to his great friend, George William Rusden, writer, politician, and member of the Council of the University of Melbourne: "I am delighted to find that you speak with so much anxiety of the opus; first because I know that such a work cannot be done well without enthusiasm and a real throwing-of-oneself-into-it; and secondly from my conviction that in the fall of the leaf of a man's life nothing can make him happy but congenial work to do, or the reflection that congenial work has been well done" (p. 790). His long letter offers sound advice: labor to be accurate, but do not leave your reader behind—write to please. "No accuracy will make a book in these days succeed with the public, which is not written with a pleasing style." He recalls dozens of books about Australia, New Zealand, South Africa—earnest, informed, but oh so dull: "Not one of them is known to the world, or is worth the labor of reading, because the writers, though they have known their subjects, have not known how to write a book. Every page with them is a toil to the reader. Not one of them has the art of telling a story . . . ." Trollope had the art right enough, though he denied it in the *Autobiography* and

Living at a Gallop 225

dissembled a good deal of the time about how seriously he took the whole business.

Again Trollope insists on spontaneity in the telling and not so much polish "that the raciness of the narrative should be injured by little attentions which will smell of the oil." He presses the point to Rusden:

A man telling his story while the facts are fresh in his mind never mounts himself upon stilts. If by previous training he has learned the use of words he can tell his tale judiciously but yet quickly. The long training will have given him the power:—the freshness will give him the life. Changes after that will so often destroy the life! The author himself pondering over his own sentence, will desire polish,— and still more polish—But the reader coming after him, and dashing over his page, will unconsciously find that the polished words are unnatural. The grating of the file will annoy his ears, the smell of the oil will offend his nose. Then he will declare that the book is nothing. [p. 792]

Seductive, dangerous advice, no doubt, perhaps bordering on the cynical, but totally honest and revealing all the same. A postscript adds, "Yesterday I completed my 80th tale; not all what you would call novels, but of various lengths—I doubt whether a greater mass of prose fiction ever came from one pen—" (p. 792).

His correspondence with Rusden from Australian sources is a great boon, as is other talk on book matters with Blackwood, Smith and the Chapmans, and letters to other publishers including the Bentleys, William Isbister, Alexander Strahan and James Virtue. Among these the letters to John Blackwood are particularly valuable, as Hall's introduction indicates. One example—another case of Trollope's concern with other people's work—will suffice. After reading Lord Brougham's autobiography in manuscript, Trollope recommended calling in a strong-minded editor "with full editorial power, so that the errors may be corrected, and the confusion reduced from the present Chaos to fair literary order" (p. 527). An editor was duly found and over several months Trollope continued to pursue the matter.

Also newly illuminated here are the unhappy period Trollope spent on the board of Chapman and Hall, his devoted service to the Royal Literary Fund, and his lecturing up and down the country.[11] Trollope on the platform is best known for a speech on the Bulgarian atrocities, when Thomas Hardy was in the audience and observed the chairman vainly tugging at Trollope's coattails when his time was up to make him stop talking. Trollope offers his own account of another speech in a letter to G. H. Lewes in 1864: "My lecture at Bury went off magnificently. I went there in a carriage with a marquis, who talked all the way about the state of his stomach—which was very grand; and the room was quite full, and the people applauded with thoroughly good nature, only they did so in the wrong places;—and two or three Lady Janes told me afterwards that it was quite nice;—so that I was, as you see, quite in a little paradise of terrestrial Gods & Goddesses" (p. 250). Trollope had a very realistic notion of his own worth but hated self-advertisement (one reason he is a difficult subject for biography) and kept his guard up most of the time, so it is refreshing to read a letter like this. Other friends besides Lewes had the benefit of the unselfconscious, uncensoring Trollope— men friends, of course, like Escott, his first biographer, and John Everett Millais. During his sojourn with his younger son, Fred, he wrote to Millais in June 1875 one of those spontaneous letters which offer insight into the man's gentler side. He begins with a familiar grouch at having missed seeing his friend's paintings at the Royal Academy show (he was a devoted viewer) and declares roundly how he likes a man to be honestly proud of his work. Next he gossips about the Garrick and one old sinner who "always makes the place disagreeable to me" and who drove Charley Taylor[12] away: "If I find when I return that I cannot get a decent rubber there, I shall be driven among the ponderosities of the Athenaeum where I can neither smoke nor have a glass of sherry and bitters" (p. 659). This leads to a lyrical reflection on the rough life of the outback and, typically, the routine he has made for himself:

I write for four hours a day, then ride after sheep or chop wood or roam about in the endless forest up to my knees in mud. I eat a great deal of mutton, smoke a great deal of tobacco, and drink a moderate amount of brandy and water. At night I read, and before work in the morning I play with my grandchildren—of whom I have two and a third coming. Fred, my son here, is always on horseback and seems to me to have more troubles on his back than any human being I ever came across. I shall be miserable when I leave him because I do not know how I can look forward to seeing him again without again making this long journey. I do not dislike the journey, or the sea, or the hardship. But I was 60 the other day, and at that age a man has no right to look forward to making many more voyages round the world. [p. 659]

Such a letter with its cross-currents of irritation and tenderness, its firm grip on life's challenges, and its wistful anxiety as to the future seems typical of the creator of characters like Mr. Harding and Archdeacon Grantly.

Toward the '80s he began to go downhill rapidly with asthma and angina. To William Blackwood he wrote despondently from Harting in July 1881: "I have done my going from home, and shall be here all the autumn,—or in a better place" (p. 913). Henceforth his letters become preoccupied with the round of doctors and prescriptions. Still, with typical courage he embarked on exhausting research in Ireland for a new novel, *The Landleaguers,* left unfinished at his death. His letters from Ireland to Rose and Harry are among the most tender he wrote. Besides them Hall wisely includes a coda in the anxious exchanges between his brother and his son as the novelist lay in a coma.

Gaps remain to be filled in Trollope's story. The letters shed little fresh light on his adolescence and early manhood in London, or his time in Ireland. Rose is still a figure in the shadows, and nothing new is added to our knowledge of his relationship with Kate Field. However, the letters undeniably advance our acquaintance with Trollope the man and the writer. Here also are helpfully extensive chronologies, together with appendices embracing Trollope's Commonplace Book, 1835-1840, a proposed history of world literature, and a section on his reading aloud. The definitive biography is yet to be written, but this edition of the letters raises expectations for the work Hall is currently preparing.

Notes

1. Bradford Allen Booth, *The Letters of Anthony Trollope* (London: Oxford Univ. Press, 1951), p. vii.

2. *Selected Works of Anthony Trollope*, N. John Hall, gen. ed. (New York: Arno Press, 1981). There are thirty-six items in the series with introductions by eminent Trollopians. Among works they make available are: *The Macdermots of Ballycloran* (1847), Trollope's long out of print first book; *La Vendée* (1858); *Harry Heathcote of Gangoil* (1874); *An Eye for an Eye* (1879); and*The Landleaguers* (1884), published posthumously. The collection also brings together useful compilations such as *Miscellaneous Essays and Reviews*, *Writings for Saint Paul's Magazine* and *Collected Short Stories*.

3. *Victorian Fiction, A Second Guide to Research*, ed. George H. Ford (New York: Modern Language Association, 1978), p. 143.

4. Michael Sadleir, *Trollope, A Commentary* (London: Constable, 1927); C. P. Snow, *Trollope, His Life and Art* (London: Macmillan, 1975); James Pope Hennessy, *Anthony Trollope* (London: Jonathan Cape, 1971).

5. "Trollope the Person," *Trollope Centenary Essays*, ed. John Halperin (London: Macmillan, 1982), p. 142.

6. Booth, *Letters*, xxi.

7. Robert Ashley, *Wilkie Collins* (London: Arthur Barker, 1952), p. 105; Julian Hawthorne, *Shapes That Pass, Memories of Old Days* (London: John Murray, 1928), p. 167; James Payn, *Some Literary Recollections* (London: Smith, Elder, 1884), p. 167; Walter Sichel, *The Sands of Time, Recollections and Reflections* (London: Hutchinson, 1923), p. 217. These and many more contemporary views of Trollope will be available in my forthcoming *Anthony Trollope: Interviews and Recollections* published by Macmillan Press.

8. W. Lucas Collins, "The *Autobiography* of Anthony Trollope," *Blackwood's Magazine*, 134 (November 1883), 591.

9. See R. H. Super, *Trollope in the Post Office* (Ann Arbor: Univ. of Michigan Press, 1981) and Coral Lansbury, *The Reasonable Man, Trollope's Legal Fiction* (Princeton: Princeton Univ. Press, 1981).

10. Sir John Tilley, *London to Tokyo* (London: Hutchinson, 1942), p. 8.

11. See R. H. Super, "Trollope at the Royal Literary Fund," *Nineteenth-Century Fiction*, XXXVII, 3 (December, 1982), 316-28.

12. Sir Charles Taylor (1817-76), sportsman and close Garrick Club friend, described by Trollope as "a man rough of tongue, brusque in manners, odious to those who dislike him, somewhat inclined to tyranny, he is the prince of friends, honest as the sun, and as open-handed as Charity itself" (Trollope, *An Autobiography*, 2 vols. [London: Blackwood, 1883], I, 200). Hall notes that Edmund Yates applied this characterization to Trollope himself. It was used earlier by Lucas Collins in his *Blackwood's* article (see note 8, above).

Styron and Evil

Robert K. Morris

John Kenny Crane. *The Root of All Evil: The Thematic Unity of William Styron's Fiction.* Columbia: University of South Carolina Press, 1984. ix, 168 pp.

This past spring, Winthrop College in Rock Hill, South Carolina, held a symposium entitled "William Styron: Novelist and Public Figure." The timing was felicitous, coming a few months before Styron's sixty-first birthday and thirty-five years after the publication of *Lie Down in Darkness*, the novel that launched him on his way to becoming the novelist and public figure that the three-day convocation honored. Other novelists, along with poets, critics, and scholars, both from America and abroad, attended the event. The symposium was a fitting and proper interlude in the life of one of our finest novelists, for as well as celebrating a writer of international stature, it suggested in its very conception that the idea of American literature is generally alive and well: an idea that Styron has maintained repeatedly in a public voice grown more and more articulate over the years.

I am not speaking only of Styron's voice in fiction — though his novels are the things that have secured his fame and given weight to his eloquence — but the letters and essays he has written over the years, the activities and controversies he has been engaged in, the appearances he has made, and, not least, the dozens of interviews he has granted. Styron may well be the most frequently interviewed contemporary American novelist. Certainly he is among the most approachable, ready to talk about almost anything presented to his multifaceted mind, though his preference has naturally been to discuss how his books get written and what they are about. Why Styron is so approachable when many other writers are not is due in part to his being outgoing, gregarious, unaffected and generous to a fault with his time. But I think he possesses an even rarer trait — a compulsive interest in people which I would call "civilizing," in every sense of the word, and humanistic.

Styron's concern for them — on and off the page, and for the page itself — is positively old-fashioned. For some reason, he still believes novels should be about ideas *and* people. Nabokov, Pynchon, Barth, Heller, the latter Mailer, and Roth, good as they are, even great when they are that, have often tended to be so fired by technique that their protagonists have simmered somewhere on a back burner, eventually becoming ingredients in gamey intellectual and historical stews. They are human factors in witty, fearful, and bizarre plots, or in problems and puzzles. They are seldom human beings, however. Indeed, since dismantling, dehumanization, disintegration, and death are the essential alliteration of so many contemporary novels, it is difficult these days to find protagonists who are even thinly disguised as human beings.

The message is loud and clear enough. Perhaps such animals are an endangered species. Perhaps we are just bundles of paranoia, sex, violence: dupes, pawns, death-wishers, and all those other things you might find in the nastier sections of a thesaurus. Of course, there is a catch here, a Catch-22 plus, for anyone beginning with the premise that we are not human beings hasn't far to go to prove it. The fallacy in logic is called "begging the question," and while it makes for shaky dialectics, it undeniably makes for solid fiction.

We still scan "shit kickers" like gothics and sci-fis and thrillers and capers and mysteries in order to escape, but when we are glutted with such fancies, we pore over a "real" book to discover that we can't escape! We pay handsomely — both in coin and mental anguish — to read about our alienated, manipulated, fragmented, repressed, sick, and fearful selves for the same reason that our best novelists write about such things to begin with. We believe it. And if we are what they tell us we are, we have no one but ourselves to blame for having gotten that way. The structures and systems human beings created to run their lives have turned them into the non-human beings who now run the non-human systems and structures. The mere non-logic of question-begging leads to the more frightening dialectic of self-fulfilling prophecy, just as surely as one twentieth-century war has led to another, just as surely as crackpot racial theories have led to slavery and Auschwitz, to apartheid and "tolerable and acceptable" violations of human rights, just as surely as those dazzling light displays over Hiroshima and Nagasaki may lead to Nuclear Winter. One needn't search far to find interesting scenarios to depict our loss of humanity, or, for that matter, the end of it.

What has been uncommon these days has been to write novels with human beings at the center, and all these other dismantling, disintegrating, dehumanizing, deadly things at the peripheries. And if I seem to have strayed for a moment from talking about William Styron, it is to return to him with the sense of this difference in mind. Styron strikes me as a writer who has always been concerned with doing more than shaping characters into something "round" — a term that embraces any number of fictional heroines and heroes from Pamela to Mme. Bovary to Isabel Archer; from Mr. Pickwick to Ahab to Nat Turner — a term that immediately shows, by its examples, its limitations.

From the first, Styron's genius created round charactes of depth and complexity whose force and presence came from our recognition of them as more than real-life people — a comparison formulated by E. M. Forster that has always struck me as something of a critical kindness. (How many "real-life people" do we know who actually have the "depth and complexity" of fictional characters?) To call Styron's personae "larger than life," however, would simply exchange one cliché for another. Yet the singular obsession that binds Peyton Loftis, Cass Kinsolving, Mannix, Nat, Stingo, and Sophie together goes beyond the ordinary — if not beyond that to the metaphysical — and that obsession is their drive to complete themselves as human beings, despite the incessant whispers or howls of the world about them that the idea of humanity doesn't really exist, and that even if it did it would be impossible to extract a human ideal from it.

While the wish may be father to the thought, readers of Styron know that the thought has not always spawned the deed. For one thing, becoming human in Styron's fictional world means creating one's own order in it, not being enslaved by another's that tries to cancel the human out. For another, the weaknesses and/or deficiencies of Styron's characters make them go at the humanizing process in a hit-or-miss fashion. But go at it they do: some longer than others. They are galvanized to choose, to change, to find order, to become human; and when they lose the will for that, they of course lose touch with humanity, enslave themselves, negate themselves: as, notably, do Peyton and Sophie. Seen this way, suicides are not gratuitous in Styron, or derivative of Southern Gothic, or simply good old jolly *Grand Guignol*. They are willful acts of surrender to the will, declines into the willessness that annihilates everything but the final choice — which is to choose to choose no longer. Peyton's choice. Sophie's choice. Not gratuitous, yet clearly different from Cass's choice, Mannix's choice, Nat's choice, or Stingo's choice. What, really, in their most embracing world view, are all of Styron's novels but studies in choice — an artistic wrestling with our most basic anxiety that shapes either the chaos or order we create?

Styron's novels are about dozens of other things as well; but for me his apparent need more deeply to examine the philosophy of choice, or psychology of choice, or the anatomy of choice, marks his continued growth as a writer and thinker. As his own view of the problems which novels can undertake has matured, his art has matured as well. With maturation has come expansion. Styron has swelled the backdrop of his novels, has widened their scope, always keeping at their centers his protagonists' confrontations with choice, but moving them into remoter areas of darkness that *Lie Down in Darkness* — amazing first novel that it is, amazing *novel* that it is — only hinted at. Peyton's suicide spoke sadly and eloquently to a silent generation, but her final tragic choice doesn't really evolve from anything beyond her control or not of her own making. The Loftises may be cursed, but the curse is familial, not universal. For as the war-weary world turned — World War II is contemporary with the frame of the novel, the Korean War with its publication — an upper-class white southern family's decline must seem a very small curse indeed.

Lie Down in Darkness may still be Styron's most lyric, gut-wrenching book, since most readers can relate to its characters' range of experiences, if not to the experiences themselves. But Styron was never to write that sort of novel again. By "that sort," I mean one in which his protagonists were allowed avenues of escape — alcohol, sex, religion, suicide — to flee from the choices that define their humanity. (Even Sophie's suicide — to which I'll return — is not on the same order as Peyton's.) After *Lie Down in Darkness* there is no more escape in Styron. Choice is forced; change is forced; becoming human is forced on everyone. The next four novels are ultimately about not escaping choices, and about the transformation brought on by choosing.

The Long March is the first of these novels of transformation. We are still in the South, but not in the southern ethos. The earlier conflict, set within the family whose function should be to support and humanize, has been transferred to a larger area of concern — the military, whose very reason for existence is to dehumanize. The totalitarianism of Templeton, the awareness of Culver, the rebellion of Mannix make for the conflict in *The Long March* and its themes. I shan't take sides as to who is the novel's hero. The question still seems pretty much up in the air, and here it is beside the point. The point is that both Culver and Mannix survive the militaristic malignancy of Templeton and come away from the ordeal asserting their humanity.

Templeton is the first real malignant being in Styron — the progenitor of Mason Flagg in *Set This House on Fire*, Epps and Moore in *Nat Turner*, Höss and Jemand von Niemand in *Sophie's Choice* — the first of the authoritarian power figures who seek, directly or indirectly, to enslave the bodies and wills of others. Templeton is the first of such figures, but he is the least compelling. They grow worse as the ideologies that generate them grow worse: malignancies that history has excised again and again but has never eradicated. Mason Flagg stands for nearly everything that was wrong with America in the fifties and for everything that may be wrong with us still: our waste, greed, meretriciousness, insensitivity, carelessness, power lust, death wish. Epps and Moore — the intellect and brute nature of racism — are the rotten pillars on which southern slavery sat for hundreds of years, an institution that denied the black man's humanity, poisoned his soul, drove him to despair and murder. And Höss and Herr Somebody/Nobody — the last name Styron's brilliant crystallization of the anonymity and pervasiveness of Nazi malignancy — symbolize the Holocaust that didn't stop at enslaving will and body, but went on systematically to exterminate both.

Domination. Enslavement. Extermination. *The Long March* and *Set This House on Fire. Nat Turner. Sophie's Choice.* Critics recognize that Styron keeps coming back to the same ideas, and they want to know why. Styron knows why, or rather doesn't know why one man must exercise power over another to rob him of his freedom, his right to choose, his humanity. His novels are thus attempts to understand the malignancy in us. Sometimes such malignancy is of lesser degree, sometimes greater, sometimes so great that it is incomprehensible and absolute, though man's imagination throughout his very short history continues to transcend itself in finding greater evil to surpass lesser. Evil: one of our endlessly renewable resources. What was the Crucifixion and subsequent persecution of Christians compared to the Crusades and the Inquisition? What was the Inquisition compared to the institution of southern slavery? What in human history has compared to the Nazi concentration camps; and what to the extermination of 14 million Jews, Poles, Gypsies and others? What will compare to the annihilation of hundreds of millions, should the stupid fear and hatred of one power for another produce a second holocaust?

To understand evil — even after it has left its grim mark on the world — is hopefully to prevent its occurring again: certainly to make us aware of it so that we can speak out against it. For this reason alone, Styron's books are valuable portraits of the faces of evil. But they are novels, if I may repeat myself, concerned with ideas *and* human beings. Ideologies — whether good or evil — flower, but they are rooted in man, who alone is capable of choosing one or the other. But why one and not the other? Styron has answered the question many ways: not as a metaphysician, psychologist, sociologist, theologian or literary critic, but as a novelist. If the answers have an overall design, he has obligingly left it to his commentators to find it.

John Kenny Crane believes they do, and he has written a significant study that deals with much of what I've been discussing above, and more. The title of Crane's book — *The Root of All Evil: The Thematic Unity of William Styron's Fiction* — tells a good deal about it. Previous critics of Styron who have thought along Crane's lines but who have never actually thought all of them through, will find in his book a summation of most of the important ones — if not of *the* most important ones. I don't know that the book will really change our ideas about what Styron has done in fiction. I do know it will bring into focus many critical ideas that are diffused throughout the best criticism of Styron's novels. By this I don't mean to suggest that Crane is trudging over well-plowed fields or turning over familiar ground. He is very much his own man, fresh and individual in approach, accomplished in style, first-rate in scholarship. On top of it all, Crane's book has the distinction — incredible as it may seem at this late date in Styron criticism — of being the first full-length study of Styron by a single hand. Thus Crane brings to bear his own unifying vision of the unity he is discussing.

Crane's vision, along with his method, is retrospective. His study begins with a long, ambitious analysis of *Sophie's Choice* in which he argues for its thematic unity, identifying prominent themes in the novel which stand by themselves but which also cohere to clarify Styron's ideas of good and evil. From Styron's most recent novel, Crane works back to the earlier ones, though without being enslaved by chronology. He devotes sizeable chapters to each of Styron's books, seeking interrelationships among them, and in no way finding them inferior (because anterior) spin-offs of *Sophie's Choice*.

Crane's approach is astute and viable. Looking backward, we can see that Styron's first three novels are not simply preliminary exercises for *Nat Turner* and *Sophie's Choice*. But it's unlikely that the passionate, poetic, driven twenty-six-year-old writer of *Lie Down in Darkness* could have commanded the technique to write the more mature works, or put as much in them. The multi-layered construction of *Nat Turner* is extremely complex; that of *Sophie's Choice* the most complex. For the three patterns of action — Stingo's growth as a man and artist; Sophie's Auschwitz experience; Sophie's and Nathan's story — all conspire to the same end of confronting evil, understanding it, rejecting it. But the patterns are sewn together seamlessly, as, I think, is much of Crane's thesis. What exactly is "the root of all evil" according to Crane? Evil begins in the "solitary" man, who has "lost any sense of relationship or responsibility to his fellow man." Without these, he can demean, humble, crush, manipulate, dominate, enslave: "forcing fortune" at every turn to "realize" the "promise" he has made himself. The ends, in other words, serve the means. In such a world there is no room for humanity, because the "solitary" sees it only as an impediment to his realization." Crane sums up in the middle of his opening chapter:

As the ironies of Fortune are exposed and misunderstood, as promises are not realized, as attempts to give Fortune a push or kick prove useless, the human heart becomes hardened. It begins to isolate itself in a tacit belief that only oneself has been so treated, and the ability to feel guilt for one's actions is diminished. To my mind the root of all evil in Styron's universe is the inability to feel guilt for one's actions.

Further to support this contention, Crane brings in two other factors in his chain of reasoning: lying and God. The lack of belief in the latter presumes the legitimacy of the former. As Alyosha Karamazov exclaims in a book that also says much about evil: Without God everything is permitted! I expect, however, for Crane's argument to hold, that God — either as the One who looks on evil and refuses to encounter it, or as a non-entity entirely — needn't come in for all the brickbats when evil occurs in the world. Our moral code was around before God, and, no thanks to Him, still hovers about us like annoying batches of summer mosquitoes. Lies to perpetrate and condone slavery; to foster anti-Semitism and set in motion "the final solution"; to rationalize Hiroshima certainly bear on evil. But we still, to my mind, return to the matter of choice. To lie without a sense of guilt is to be without anxiety; to be without anxiety means that you've abnegated all but a single choice, and that means you are less than human. The fault, dear Brutus . . . The fault is ours, not God's. "At Auschwitz," Stingo ponders, as he walks along the beach at the end of *Sophie's Choice*, "tell me, where was God?" And the answer comes back. "Where was man?"

Obviously somewhere, else Styron would not go on writing the books he does in search of him. Those who do suffer *Angst* — the Kierkegaardian "either/or" that covers much of what Crane and I are talking about — become the first to reclaim their lost humanity: Mannix, Cass, Nat, Sophie, Stingo. Most dramatically the last three. *Angst* transfigures Nat as it does Sophie. He carries on his shoulders hundreds of years of oppression, she a thousand of guilt. Nat, forced to choose, murders and becomes more human in that act than he ever was as a slave without choice. Sophie chooses, and even in committing one child to the gas chamber, she too becomes more human than before. She has, in Crane's words, made a "transfer": i.e., "man's ability to imagine himself in the position of the recipient of the evil his own lack of guilt enables him to produce, tolerate, ignore." Sophie's suicide is also a kind of "transfer." It is a confession of guilt, of the family curse, and in this respect it is like Peyton's. It is not "the end," however. Peyton's leap renews no one, but Sophie's death renews Stingo, who is truly, literally, one of Styron's reborn. Stingo will now pass on what he has learned to the world in all the pages of *Sophie's Choice*. And its readers? Certainly if we were all endowed with this vision, this ability to act out "transfer," such evil as we know from the myth of Eden to the present might never have existed.

That, substantially, is Crane's thesis in *The Root of All Evil*, and it is a strong one. I am not always happy with his terminology — which does border on jargon — but the expert way in which he handles Styron's themes, and the countless examples he gives to support their appearance in all of Styron's novels perhaps pardon the necessary shorthand. The elusive horror that is evil needs to be confined before it is dissected. Crane cages it as well as any critic to date. The book is a fine interpretation of Styron's books and a splendid present to a novelist who has made us so aware of evil in our time.

Five Feminist Studies of Shakespeare

Burton Hatlen

Linda Bamber, *Comic Women, Tragic Men: A Study of Gender and Genre in Shakespeare*. Stanford: Stanford University Press, 1982. 211 pp.

Irene G. Dash, *Wooing, Wedding, and Power: Women in Shakespeare's Plays*. New York: Columbia University Press, 1981. xiii, 295 pp.

Peter Erickson, *Patriarchal Structures in Shakespeare's Drama*. Berkeley: University of California Press, 1985. xii, 209 pp.

Marilyn French, *Shakespeare's Division of Experience*. New York: Summit Books, 1981. 376 pp.

Marianne L. Novy, *Love's Argument: Gender Relations in Shakespeare*. Chapel Hill: University of North Carolina Press, 1984. xi, 237 pp.

Some Shakespearean scholars still see Marxist or Freudian or Feminist "readings" of Shakespeare as exercises in willful perversity. Such readings, the defenders of "traditional" scholarship protest, rest on a fundamental misapprehension: a refusal to accept Shakespeare as he is, and an insistence upon projecting onto his text the critic's own beliefs. Thus G. E. Bentley, in a recent essay on *King Lear*, summons the spectre of an imaginary scholarly article that begins, " 'I believe that Shakespeare was a subtle advocate of Women's Lib, ahead of his time. And for this reason in *King Lear* the armies of France are led by General Cordelia. And for the same reason the end of *The Taming of the Shrew* must necessarily be ironic.' "

Bentley admits that "books and articles displaying preconceptions such as these . . . are really not very numerous." But he then proceeds to accuse almost all modern critics of projecting their own self-image onto Shakespeare. The Victorians, says Bentley, "evidently conceived of Shakespeare as Alfred Lord Tennyson with a somewhat shorter beard." So too, while "it is easy for us to see that he was not Alfred Lord Tennyson, . . . I wonder if it is as easy for us to perceive that he was not Sigmund Freud either. A great deal of Shakespeare criticism, alas, reveals to the reader more about the critic than it reveals about William Shakespeare."[1] Implicit in Bentley's acerbic comments are some assumptions that seem worth uncovering. In essence, Bentley assumes that with a little effort we can come to know Shakespeare as he was "in himself," and that we can come to read Shakespeare in his own terms. Indeed, historical scholarship has for the last century dedicated itself to the task of assembling information about the political and social circumstances and the religious and philosophical beliefs of the Elizabethans, in the assumption that once we have assembled enough information of this sort we will be able to read Shakespeare as an Elizabethan would have read him, and in accordance with the author's own presumed intentions. To an historical scholar like Bentley, then, the options seem clear: you can devote yourself to the pursuit of the truth about how Shakespeare and his contemporaries lived and what they believed, or you can project your opinions onto Shakespeare's plays. The former seems, to the historical scholar, an activity worthy of serious human beings. The latter does not.

Yet the position I have here ascribed to the historical scholar already seems like an anachronism. A few academics still split "fact" from "opinion" and "scholarship" from "criticism" in this way, but for most contemporary students of literature these distinctions themselves have come to seem misleading. What has happened? The names of Freud and Marx, both mentioned by Bentley with considerable scorn, offer us a clue. From a Freudian or Marxist perspective, the aspirations of the historical scholar to recover the past as it was "in itself" and to read Shakespeare "in his own terms" are merely positivist illusions.

Feminist Studies of Shakespeare 243

To Marx and Freud, all thinking is necessarily constrained by its context: by a network of class relationships within which we find ourselves (Marx), or by a congery of more or less mythological images of the Other—images first born out of intrafamilial struggles for gratification and/or autonomy, but shaping our perception even as "mature" adults (Freud). If our thinking is constrained by our own life circumstances and the ideological preconceptions of our own society, then it follows that we can never grasp Shakespeare's plays or other works of literature "in themselves." Beguiled by the assumption that all literary commentary is trying to recover the author's presumed intentions, the historical scholar concludes that the Freudian critic must have succumbed to a naive belief that Shakespeare had somehow intuited and accepted the doctrines of psychoanalysis. But the Freudian or Marxist or Feminist critic responds that the true naif here is the historical scholar, who assumes that we can reconstruct and inhabit the "Elizabethan worldview." To the Freudian or Marxist or Feminist critic, we *have no choice* except to read Shakespeare in our own terms. And any critic who fails to recognize this fact is simply blind to the way the social and psychological circumstances of the perceiver *always* shape what we perceive.

On this score, the by now long history of Shakespeare interpretation, by actors and directors as well as by scholars, seems to support the Freudian/Marxist/Feminist position. As Bentley himself admits, the Victorians tended to read Shakespeare in Victorian terms. They saw the playwright as primarily a creator of memorable "characters," and they saw these "characters" as shaped chiefly by the moral choices which they made. Thus the "tragic flaw" reading of Shakespeare's tragedies: by and large the Victorians seem to have convinced themselves that by "hamartia" Aristotle meant a *moral* defect, for the Victorians wanted to believe that anyone who suffers must be morally inferior to other people. Such a reading of Shakespeare was obviously appropriate to a society which assumed that the possession of great wealth must testify to some inherent moral superiority, and that the poor must deserve to be poor. But in 1904, A.C. Bradley, the last of the great Victorians and the first of the great Moderns, pushed the "character"-centered reading of Shakespeare to its limits, at which point he discovered that the hypothesis of the "tragic flaw" simply won't suffice to account for what happens in *Hamlet,* or even in *Macbeth.*[2] This recognition of the inadequacy of a "character"-centered reading of Shakespeare coincided with the flowering of historical relativism, in books like Henry Adams' *Mont-Saint-Michel and Chartres,* and the writings of Dilthey, Croce, et. al. Thus was born the "historical" emphasis which dominated Shakespearean scholarship in the first half of our century. Scholars like E.M.W. Tillyard, Theodore Spencer, and Patrick Cruttwell sought to read Shakespeare's plays as products of a determinate historical moment, a set of cultural circumstances very different from the one we ourselves live in, and they deliberately set out to reconstruct these circumstances. However, beguiled by a dream of "scientific" objectivity, these historical scholars saw no need to address the question of how the scholar's *own* situation might affect what he or she sees in Shakespeare's plays. Rather such scholars have assumed that their own historical consciousness has allowed them to escape from history, thereby permitting them to read Shakespeare in seventeenth-century rather than in twentieth-century terms. Conversely, they have assumed that any interpretation of Shakespeare which has been visibly shaped by the critic's own historical situation is *ipso facto* invalid.

But an awareness of the way historical circumstances define the "horizon" within which we live must sooner or later become self-reflexive. Thus in the last two decades the claim to "objectivity" characteristic of most twentieth-century scholarship has increasingly given way, in Shakespeare studies as in literary studies generally, to a critical discourse which begins by spelling out where the critic is coming from, what kind of assumptions the critic is bringing to the text. A symptomatic moment here is Cruttwell's 1960 preface to the second edition of *The Shakespearean Moment.*[3] Because his book emphasizes the artistic richness of the Anglo-Catholic world view, the author tells us, many of his readers had assumed that he himself must be an Anglo-Catholic. But in fact, he says in

Feminist Studies of Shakespeare

his preface, he was not and is not an Anglo-Catholic. In writing his book, he had merely been trying to "get inside" the "Shakespearean moment," and to do so he had tried to put himself in the position of an Elizabethan Anglo-Catholic. This peculiar split consciousness (the unkind might call it hypocrisy) is becoming rare in contemporary Shakespeare studies. There is still a thriving school of Christian exegesis, but nowadays the exponents of this school are usually themselves avowed Christians. (Here G. Wilson Knight offers a worthy precedent. His Christian readings of Shakespeare were unabashedly the product of a powerful if idiosyncratic religious commitment.) So too, we have by now well established traditions of Marxist and Freudian "readings" of Shakespeare. As the five books here under review attest, a body of explicitly Feminist Shakespeare scholarship is also beginning to accrue. The complaints of Bentley and other like-minded traditionalists seem, in the face of the rising flood of explicitly ideological Shakespeare "readings," merely petulant. Marxist and Freudian and Feminist scholarship is *here*, whether the traditionalists like it or not. Furthermore, as my comments have already suggested, I admire the willingness of this "new" scholarship to recognize the limits of the critic's own perspective. For if historical criticism spoke for the consciousness of the first half of the twentieth century, a "committed" criticism, a criticism which openly acknowledges its own presuppositions, speaks for our *own* historical moment.

However, a criticism which openly confesses its own presuppositions also raises some theoretic and practical issues which I would like to explore here. Since my concern here will be specifically Feminist criticism, I would like to begin by trying to establish precisely what makes a given critical analysis of Shakespeare "Feminist." On this score, five fundamental assumptions, all more or less consciously shared by the writers of the books under review, seem to me crucial. First, all Feminist critics (but, obviously, not *only* Feminist critics), assume that gender relationships shape the character of human existence as deeply as—if not more deeply than—any other single force. Second (and now we are starting to enter specifically Feminist territories), Feminist critics assume that gender relationships are always inherently political—i.e., that to understand the relationship between a woman and a man we must look at the modalities of power which allow one to control the other. Third, all Feminist critics assume that at least in Western culture these inequalities of power have consistently issued in a legally and culturally sanctioned domination of men over women. Fourth, Feminist critics assume that the effects of these patterns of gender relationship infuse all the cultural products of any given historical epoch, so that any analysis of a cultural phenomenon which fails to take "sexual politics" into consideration will necessarily remain incomplete. Yet a principled anti-Feminist might accept all four theoretic and historical assumptions which I have thus far laid out. The way of thinking which I am here describing becomes "Feminist" only when it is supplemented by a fifth assumption, an explicitly *moral* assumption: that inequalities of power are *wrong*, and that the domination of one human group by another inevitably warps the humanity of both groups, instilling habits of self-denigration in the subordinate group and a blindness to their own limits among members of the dominant group.

All critics who accept the five Feminist premises laid out above must, as they turn their attention to Shakespeare, address certain key questions. The first of these is the question of the degree to which Shakespeare shared the Feminist critic's analysis of the forces shaping human life. That is, does the politics of gender relations occupy a central position in Shakespeare's plays? All Feminist critics assume that the answer to this question is "yes" —indeed, any Feminist critic who answered "no" to this question would presumably turn to some other writer. Further, the rich range of male and female roles which we see in Shakespeare's plays and the power he ascribes to male/female relations in shaping human life whether for good (*As You Like It, The Merchant of Venice*) or for ill (*Othello, Troilus and Cressida*) offer strong support for the idea that Shakespeare did indeed share the first of the five assumptions which I have listed above. And scenes like the exchange between Emilia and Desdemona in Act IV of *Othello* (the "willow scene") suggest that Shakespeare at least intermittently recognized the political

Feminist Studies of Shakespeare

dimensions of the relationship between women and men. But at this point some more difficult questions begin to emerge: To what extent do the plays of Shakespeare simply "reflect" the way gender roles worked within the society in which he lived? And to what extent do these plays offer a conscious *analysis* of the politics of gender relationships? On this question the authors—Feminists all—of the five books under review begin to distribute themselves across a broad range of positions, from the belief that Shakespeare more or less unconsciously gives voice to the gender stereotypes of his age, to a confident declaration that Shakespeare saw through all the sexist assumptions of the period. Still more divisive is yet another question: to what extent did Shakespeare share the values of modern Feminists? That is, did he see all forms of domination, especially the domination of men over women, as inherently wrong? Here the concerns of the Feminist critics collide with the work of several generations of historical scholars, most of whom have insisted that Shakespeare, like "everybody" in the Renaissance, believed in the great Chain of Being—and thus, presumably, in the "natural" right of men to rule over women. Some of the authors under review tacitly accept the view of Tillyard et al. on this subject. Others insist that Shakespeare "must have" shared the Feminist belief that domination always distorts the humanity both of the ruler and the ruled. On this question too, then, Feminist critics divide into two opposed camps.

I shall now attempt to chart the ways in which the five books under review have responded to the fundamental questions which, I have here proposed, any Feminist reading of Shakespeare must sooner or later address. At one extreme we find Irene Dash, who valiantly insists that Shakespeare shared both the gender-centered world view and the egalitarian moral values of the modern Feminist:

By creating confident, attractive, independent women whom we like, [Shakespeare] questions the wisdom of a power structure that insists they relinquish personal freedom. Some of his dramas question accepted patterns of behavior. Some stress the value of mutual respect between a man and a woman. Some reveal the confusion in a woman's mind when she seeks to understand the limits of her world. Occasionally, a drama documents the tragedy of a woman who loses her way and her sense of self when she seeks to conform. To hear his voice, however, one must recognize the individuality and three-dimensional quality of his women characters. Like the men, the women too respond to a variety of forces in their environment and are troubled by the world they see. But that world differs from the one perceived by men. [p. 5]

The opening sentences of this passage seem more confident than the final sentences: If the world preceived by men differs from the world perceived by women, we might begin to wonder whether Shakespeare's mind can really be as "large-mannered" as Dash would like to believe. Indeed, a contradiction seems on the verge of surfacing here. But Dash pushes away this contradiction, for she wants to claim for Shakespeare a position "beyond gender": "Shakespeare's plays show the diversity of the mind of a sixteenth-century man whose understanding of the human condition extended beyond his own sex and beyond his own time" (p. 6). The view of Shakespeare implicit in this statement may owe something to Virginia Woolf's belief that the imagination, especially the Elizabethan imagination, is androgynous. In any case, Dash clearly wants to find in Shakespeare an ideological ally, a Great Mind who shares her Feminist commitments.

To justify her claim that Shakespeare's vision transcends the limitations of his epoch and his gender, Dash points briefly to the "extraordinary circumstance" of Elizabeth's rule. Ultimately, however, the position which Dash stakes out is grounded less in historical data than in certain premises about the nature of art itself. In brief, Dash has accepted a "humanist" (or more specifically an Arnoldian) conception of great art as a vehicle for universal wisdom—a wisdom which "sees life steadily and sees it whole." And since no wise human being could, Dash believes, accept a patriarchal social system, she is confident that Shakespeare "must have" rejected patriarchy. But at the same time, Dash cannot avoid seeing how plays like *The Taming of the Shrew* have been used to justify patriarchy. It follows that any apparently patriarchal element in a Shakespearean play "must have" been put there by someone else: specifically, by generations of sexist actors and directors and scholars who have systematically distorted what Shakespeare wrote, in an attempt to turn him into a spokesman for patriarchy. Dash's project, then, is to rescue Shakespeare from his heirs, and to restore to us an "original" Shakespeare, immaculately free of all patriarchal prejudices. Indeed, Dash demonstrates beyond much doubt that Shakespeare's various revisers and interpreters have superimposed on the original text certain sexist stereotypes: her examples from theater history are both persuasive and interesting. Yet her fundamental assumption— that Shakespeare himself was immune to the influence of such stereotypes—remains unproved. Indeed, her book does not even try to argue this premise: rather it simply proposes, as an article of faith, that Shakespeare, as a great artist, must necessarily also have been a wise man, and thereafter "must have" been able to recognize the intellectual and moral emptiness of a patriarchal ideology.[4]

Marilyn French's already widely influential book, *Shakespeare's Division of Experience*, locates itself at the opposite pole from Dash's book. French makes no assumptions about Shakespeare's universal humanity, and she recognizes that the pursuit of presumed parallels between Shakespeare's view of things and the beliefs of modern Feminists is an exercise in futility. Instead she argues that the institutions and ideologies of western civilization are all grounded in a view of life as an interaction among three principles: the masculine principle ("associated with prowess and ownership, with physical courage, assertiveness, authority, independence, and the right, rights, and legitimacy"), the "outlaw feminine principle" ("associated with darkness, chaos, flesh, the sinister, magic and above all, sexuality"), and the "inlaw feminine principle" ("founded on the ability to give birth, it includes qualities like nutritiveness, compassion, mercy, and the ability to create felicity") (pp. 21-24). French proposes to trace the way those principles interact in Shakespeare's plays. Thus, she neatly sidesteps the question of whether Shakespeare accepted or rejected the tenets of patriarchy. Rather she sees the plays as dramatizing certain attitudes endemic not only to Elizabethan society but to our own as well. French does not spend much time talking about Shakespeare's "greatness." But implicitly her book suggests that Shakespeare is worth our attention not because he transcends "his own sex and his own time," but because his art allows the interplay among French's three principles an unusually full development. Thus French need not even consider the question of how *conscious* Shakespeare may or may not have been of the effects of gender role stereotypes on human beings, or the question of what his own beliefs on male/female relationships may have been. Rather than talking about Shakespeare's presumed beliefs and intentions, she focuses on what these plays *do*: how they dramatize the interaction among her three quasi-archetypal principles, and how the relationships among these principles change in the course of Shakespeare's career.

In a maneuver of central importance to Feminist commentary on Shakespeare, furthermore, French maintains that gender issues work themselves out in these plays primarily in generic terms. In Shakespeare's tragedies, says French, the masculine principle rules:

In tragedy, even those tragedies that focus on a love story, the focus and the weight are on power. Different kinds of power may war against each other; or the major figure may have an external goal that requires power or authority; or various figures or factions may make war on each other fighting for the single seat of power. Tragedy has plot. It may also have subplots, but these are parallels or illuminations of the major plot, rather than elaborations around themes. And because tragedy is linear, externally oriented, and concerned with the individual (individualism is the extremest form of transcendence of nature), it is necessarily disintegrative. This paradox lies within the masculine principle itself, which, cherishing the individual and his transcendent goal of establishing something within time that will outlast time, inevitably leads to death. [p. 38]

In comedy, on the other hand, the feminine principle, at least the "inlaw feminine" principle, rules:

Feminist Studies of Shakespeare

Shakespearean comedy is feminine: it aims at continuation, procreation; it is concerned with an entire community more than with one individual; it is accepting rather than transcendent, for although it ends with marriage or the promise of marriage, which is a masculine permanency, transcendent in its guarantee of happiness ever after, the plays end with the moment of exaltation, the moment of communal harmony, and do not depict the actual marriage situation. Comedy is circular, tied to nature and eternal recurrence. [p. 37]

In the space where gender and genre patterns intersect, however, French finally rediscovers "Shakespeare the man." For in following the evolution of comic and tragic formal structures through Shakespeare's work, French discovers an increasing inclination on his part to question the masculine principle's claim to legitimate authority, paralleled by an increasing horror of the outlaw feminine principle. Then in *King Lear* and *Antony and Cleopatra*, French argues, Shakespeare begins to explore the possibility of a reconciliation of the masculine and the "inlaw" feminine principle, a process that climaxes in the final romances. Thus French does finally arrive at some hypotheses about "Shakespeare the man." But the Shakespeare who emerges from French's book is no "premature Feminist," nor is he a timeless universal genius. Rather he is a man caught up in and wrestling with what it means to live in a gendered world; and French's Shakespeare confronts issues of gender not directly, as a political activist or a social theorist might do, but as a playwright whose immediate concern is the dramatic possibilities of comic and tragic formal patterns.

In *Comic Women, Tragic Men*, Linda Bamber presses the gender/genre relationship even further than does French. To Shakespeare, Bamber proposes, what happens to men is inherently tragic, and what happens to women is inherently comic. Borrowing her terminology from Simone de Beauvoir, Bamber argues that Shakespeare, as a man, naturally ascribes Selfhood to his male characters, but sees his women characters as Other. To live as a Self is, ultimately, to live tragically: to confront the limits and the mortality of the Self. In a Shakespearean tragedy we watch the anguished epic of a Self that claims an absolute significance which the world refuses to grant it. In a Shakespearean comedy, on the other hand, the Self escapes tragedy by surrendering itself to the Other. Thus in comedy the feminine principle may seem to rule. But even in comedy, Bamber insists, women remain Other: "The Self is unique, the Other is typical. In tragedy we value the hero for being unique, but in comedy we value those who are content to be ordinary. The comedies deal with our problems as if they were ordinary difficulties rather than issues of life and death. The Otherness of the heroine makes her difficulties seem ordinary even to herself; she is gifted with the true comic perspective" (pp. 39-40). Bamber thus rejects not only Dash's conception of Shakespeare's vision as "universal" but also French's theory that Shakespeare's work moves toward a reconciliation of the masculine and feminine principles. If Self and Other are the primary categories of experience (and this idea can be traced back through de Beauvoir and Sartre to, ultimately, Hegel), and if gender is always a primary attribute of the Self, then any male writer *must* perceive the female as Other. Conversely, if we want a literary experience of the Self as Woman, we must turn to women writers. The male writer may reach out to his Other, try to understand her, try even to incorporate parts of what she represents into himself. But nevertheless she remains always Other. To Bamber, thus, the world remains irreducibly gendered—and genred. And for Bamber the key to an understanding of these plays is in a recognition of the way Shakespeare's vision of life is distinctively *male*.

As here formulated, Bamber's position may seem to verge on Feminist separatism. Yet Bamber's insistence that Shakespeare's view of the world is inherently masculine allows her, paradoxically, to affirm the enduring value of these plays. Here is, Bamber proposes, a male writer who in the course of his life became more and more determined to confront the limitations of male selfhood, and more and more eager, especially in plays like *Athony and Cleopatra* and the romances, to reach out to the Other. To Bamber, as to French, the greatness of Shakespeare lies in his courage: his willingness to let the Self/Other dialectic work itself out in his writings (and,

Feminist Studies of Shakespeare

presumably, in his life), and his willingness to push at the limits of the various definitions of selfhood which his culture offered him. As such, the reading of Shakespeare can be, Bamber implies, a powerful educational experience, for women as well as for men. For a women needs to know how her own Other (i.e., men) sees her, and Shakespeare's plays offer women an unusually free and spacious development of the male vision of things. Of course, it also follows that a woman who accepts as "true" and as fully adequate Shakespeare's perception of what it means to be a woman would be making a major mistake. For such a woman would be accepting as final a definition of herself as Other, and so she would be denying herself any possibility of living as a Self. But, conversely, a man reading Doris Lessing (in whom woman appears as Self and man as Other) would be in the same position as a woman reading Shakespeare—and perhaps men should read Lessing for the same reason that women should read Shakespeare. Bamber writes, she declares, as a heterosexual woman, a woman who wants to reach out to her Other, who wants her Other to reach out to her. And in its confidence that life is, as Buber said, meeting, that we grow through reaching out to, opening ourselves to, the Other, Bamber's book proudly reaffirms the dialectical vision of life born out of the work of Hegel and Marx, and descending to us through Sartre and de Beauvoir.[5]

Dash's, French's, and Bamber's books are all at this point a few years old. This review originally set out to discuss only the new books by Marianne Novy and Peter Erickson; but I have included these three earlier books because Novy's and Erickson's books seem to me fully intelligible only when seen as extensions of certain possibilities opened up by French and Bamber, and as deliberate attempts to avoid the dead-end represented by Dash's book. Dash's inability to make a convincing case for the traditional humanist model of Shakespeare as a "universal" genius, transcending both his sex and his epoch, appears to have exhausted one impulse in Feminist criticism: the impulse to enlist Shakespeare in "our cause," to demonstrate that he was a Feminist without knowing it. French and Bamber make it clear that a Feminist criticism need not limit itself to the alternatives of "proving" that Shakespeare was "really" a Feminist or condemning him as simply a misogynist. Yet the critical methods to which French and Bamber commit themselves are also open to some question. In committing herself to a discussion of all of Shakespeare's plays, French gives short shrift to the complexities of the individual plays. She pays the penalty of articulating a powerful thesis: that in the end her book begins to seem too formulaic, more interested in the interplay of her three overriding principles than in the way Shakesperean comedy and tragedy work in practice, and more interested in these general generic patterns than in the unique formal designs of the various individual plays. Moreover, French never directly addresses the question of whether the three "principles" whose interworking she pursues are primarily social phenomena working in the institutions of Elizabethan England and merely "reflected" in Shakespeare's plays, or whether they are psychological phenomena working within Shakespeare's own mind. Further, Bamber's arguments raise serious doubts about whether the "reconciliation" between the masculine and the feminine principles which French finds in the later plays actually occurs. Thus at the very least, French's general thesis needs to be tested, elaborated, and (perhaps) revised.

Rather than trying to talk about the entire Shakespearean *oeuvre*, Bamber focuses on a few specific plays; and her readings of these plays are often acutely sensitive. However, I find myself wondering whether her Self/Other schemata may insufficiently acknowledge the dramatic character of the Shakespearean experience. Bamber chooses to read Shakespeare as essentially a poet, and to see the plays as an expression of the poet's personal vision of things. Yet drama is a collaborative art in a way that poetry is not. When I am watching a production of *Antony and Cleopatra*, I am engaged not only with Shakespeare but with the actor playing Antony, the actress playing Cleopatra, etc. Even if we accept Bamber's contention that Shakespeare *wrote* Cleopatra as Other, we must also recognize that the actress playing Cleopatra may project into the role a strong sense of Self. I suspect Bamber herself would be reluctant to tell Zoe

Caldwell that her interpretation of the role is "wrong," or to tell the men and women in the audience that they are "wrong" to respond to the Cleopatra which they see on the stage as a living, speaking female Self. That is, the real question here may be, not how Shakespeare saw Cleopatra, but how many and what kind of interpretive possibilities he wrote into the role. The fact that Cleopatra was originally played by a boy is here of only marginal relevance. For any play, to remain stageworthy, must open itself to a variety of actors. In any performance of the play that we are likely to see, Cleopatra will almost certainly be played by a woman, and as so played the role can be both convincing and moving. Somehow, Shakespeare has written lines which a woman can convincingly speak, has created a role which a woman can inhabit. This fact raises the question of whether in the theater the Self/Other dichotomy might become, in some measure at least, irrelevant. And if that is possible, then the absolute Self/Other distinction which Bamber predicates may need to be reconsidered.

The two most recent books of the group under review, Marianne Novy's *Love's Argument* and Peter Erickson's *Patriarchal Structures in Shakespeare's Drama*, move beyond Dash, French and Bamber in a variety of ways, especially by trying to build some bridges between Feminist criticism and certain other currents in contemporary Shakespeare studies. Thus Novy, in her opening chapter, invokes what has been perhaps the single most influential study of Shakespeare published in the last quarter century: Norman Rabkin's *Shakespeare and the Common Understanding*.[6] Rabkin proposed that Shakespeare's dramaturgy is characterized above all by "complementarity," a capacity to hold in solution two or more different, even incompatible ways of explaining a phenomenon. (Rabkin's own acknowledged indebtedness to Keats' concept of negative capability should be obvious.) Thus it is perfectly possible to read *Romeo and Juliet* as a play about how fate rules over human life ("star-crossed lovers"), or a play about the disastrous consequences of unbridled sexual passion (that is Friar Lawrence's interpretation of the meaning of these events), or as a play about the way a blind commitment to social convention leads the older generation to destroy their children (that is how Franco Zeffirelli read the play). Any one of these readings can be defended by reference to the text of the play; we misread the play only if we insist that one of these readings must be "right" and the others "wrong," for the play itself holds all of them in suspension. So too, Novy wonders whether the plays of Shakespeare might hold in suspension at least two ways of looking at gender relations. The terms which Novy offers to denote the two perspectives in question are "mutuality" and "patriarchy." "Patriarchy," says Novy, "literally means the rule of husbands over wives and men in general over women." As for mutuality, "while the word does not necessarily imply equality or inequality, it implies sharing and companionship, recognition of the activity and subjectivity of both partners" (p. 4). In any given play by Shakespeare, Novy argues, both these perspectives will be at work. One character may speak for the patriarchal perspective (Lear, for example); another will embody and speak for the possibility of mutuality (Cordelia, for example). But neither character "speaks for Shakespeare." Rather if we want to find Shakespeare within the play, we must find him in the *interaction among* all the perspectives here at work.

The individual plays of Shakespeare, rather than inviting a single, unambiguous response, evoke from us, Novy also suggests, a range of conflicting emotions, and thereby offer the audience a way of mediating these conflicts. At this point, Novy's critical method begins to open out toward "reader-response" criticism. In *The Taming of the Shrew*, for example, Novy feels no need to choose between the traditional reading of the play as affirming the rightful authority of men over women and Dash's belief that the play celebrates Kate's self-assertion. Rather, Novy argues,

> the ambiguous combination of patriarchy and play in *The Taming of the Shrew* helps it appeal to spectators who are divided among and within themselves in their attitudes toward marriage. In a time of social transition when Renaissance England felt conflict not only between contrasting images of marriage but also between nostalgia

Feminist Studies of Shakespeare

for an older order and a new awareness of individuality, inner passions, and outer chaos, the game element in *The Shrew* sets up a protected space where imagination permits the enjoyment of both energy and form, while the dangers of violence, tyranny, deadening submission, and resentment magically disappear. The game context permits Petruchio and Katherine to modulate from antagonists to co-creators of a new world to ruler and subject, and encourages the spectators to see as most important whichever pair of roles they choose and consider the others as "only a game." [p. 62]

By shifting the emphasis from the author's presumed "worldview" to the viewer/reader's response, Novy moves in a significant way beyond both French and Bamber. To these earlier critics, the key issue was, still, how *Shakespeare* perceived the world. But in Novy's book the issue instead becomes the ways in which the plays hold a mirror up to the men and women who came (and still come) to see these plays, allowing us all to see ourselves more clearly. Novy's method also allows her to absorb into a Feminist analysis such matters as the ways in which characters in the play move into and out of "spectator" roles, and the ways in which the movement of male actors into and out of female roles and the movement of female characters into and out of male roles affect our response to these plays. In the sheer scope of its concerns, coupled with its adroit avoidance of all varieties of reductivism, Novy's book seems to me the most useful Feminist study of Shakespeare published to date.

If Novy seeks to build a bridge between Feminist criticism and the work of Rabkin and of the reader-response theorists, Peter Erickson tries to establish an explicit line between Feminist criticism and the Psychoanalytic tradition. The primary link between Erickson's book and the Psychoanalytic tradition is Coppélia Kahn's *Man's Estate: Masculine Identity in Shakespeare.*[7] I wavered for some time over whether to include Kahn's book in this review; for Kahn herself is certainly a Feminist, and her book recognizes the ways in which the male sense of identity first emerges through a process of separation from the mother, and later through an insistence on the difference between "manhood" and "womanhood." Yet Kahn's book concerns itself only peripherally with the ways male bonding and the male sense of self affect women; rather she chooses to focus on the problematics of male selfhood itself. In these respects Kahn's book belongs more properly to the lively tradition of Psychoanalytic studies of Shakespeare than to the Feminist tradition which I have here tried to trace. Yet the phenomena of male self-definition and male bonding which Kahn explores obviously have implications for male/female relations, and it is these issues that Erickson chooses to explore: "The main focus here is on the political and psychological implications of male ties as the basis for patriarchal power by which men control women, whether ruthlessly or benevolently. The key issue to be addressed is the tendency of male characters to have primary attachment and loyalty to men rather than to women" (p. 6). As the tone of this quotation suggests, Erickson is less interested than is Novy in the possibilities of freedom which Shakespeare plays open up within a patriarchal social order, and more interested than she is in the way these plays reflect and even reproduce the repressive characteristics of that social order. Further, in his concern with specifically psychological patterns at work within these plays, Erickson returns to a concern with "Shakespeare the man" which critics like Novy and even French and Bamber had already moved beyond. And towards "Shakespeare the man" the one male critic in this group is, as we shall see, considerably more ambivalent than are any of the female critics.

Erickson's emphasis on patriarchal psychological patterns in Shakespeare makes his book seem at times like an "unmasking" of Shakespeare as just another sexist male. This problem is most apparent in the first chapter of Erickson's book, an almost willfully wrong-headed discussion of *As You Like It*, designed to prove that the sense of freedom and possibility which generations of play-goers and readers have seen in Rosalind is only an illusion:

As You Like It enacts two rites . . . . First, Shakespeare has the social structure ultimately contain female energy . . . . We have too easily accepted the formulation that says that Shakespeare in the mature history plays concentrates on masculine development whereas in the mature festive comedies he gives women their due by allowing them to play the central role. *As You Like It* is primarily a defensive action against female power rather than a celebration of it. Second, Shakespeare portrays an ideal male community based on "sacred pity." This idealized vision of relationships between men can be seen as sentimental and unrealistic, but . . . Shakespeare is here thoroughly engaged and endorses the idealization. These two elements—female vitality kept manageable and male power kept loving—provided a resolution that at this particular moment was "As Shakespeare Liked It." [p. 37]

The problem here is that Erickson seems totally insensitive to the multiple ironies of what seems to me Shakespeare's most subtly and pervasively ironic play. He remains, for example, entirely blind to the way in which, in the first Arden Forest scene, the Duke's own overblown language, not to mention the acerbic background comments of Jaques as quoted by Amiens, implicitly defines the picture of a chaste male utopia as a pastoral fantasy. Indeed, Erickson simply doesn't know how to read comedy. Yet as applied to the tragedies, his analysis of the ways socially sanctioned patterns of male bonding affect the life circumstances of women and the relationships between men and women can be enormously illuminating; and his central chapter on *Hamlet, Othello*, and *King Lear* seems to me perhaps the most brilliant single passage in any of these books. Furthermore, Erickson, like French, Bamber, and Novy, sees a distinct progression in Shakespeare's work, climaxing in *Antony and Cleopatra* (a key text for all these critics), which makes, says this critic, "a decisive break with the conventions of male bonding" (p. 11), and which achieves a vision of "mutuality" (p. 143) unprecedented in Shakespeare's work. The grim dogmatism apparent in Erickson's discussion of *As You Like It* does not, then, persist throughout his book. But the very unevenness of the book demonstrates that Feminist analysis is not a fool-proof "method," but rather (still) an adventure into only half-charted territories—and thus should warn us that there are some swamps out there.

Can we distill from the five books under review some

conclusions about the point at which Feminist criticism of Shakespeare has, as of 1985, arrived? First, it seems safe to say that Feminist criticism has gotten a long way past G. E. Bentley's crude stereotype of the "Women's Libber," as quoted in my opening paragraph. Dash's book demonstrates that even as late as the early 1980s, some Feminist critics were still motivated at least in part by a desire to enlist Shakespeare in their cause. But the other books under review show that for most contemporary Feminist critics the key issue is no longer the correctness or incorrectness of what Shakespeare believed about gender relationship. Rather the authors of these four books, whatever the differences among them noted above, all agree that the plays of Shakespeare are most usefully read, not as an exposition of timeless truths, but rather as (in the words of Ezra Pound, speaking of his *Cantos*) a "record of struggle": in this case, of a struggle to come to terms with the realities of gender relations, as they have been shaped by three millenia of Western social history. Further, all four authors agree that the overall curve of Shakespeare's career shows that he moved forward from an acceptance of the patterns of gender relations established by his society, toward an increasing willingness to question traditional notions of male and female roles. And all of these critics—although to varying degrees, with Novy standing at one pole and Erickson at the other—are less interested in "what Shakespeare believed" than they are in the ways these plays encode certain fundamental patterns of human social life.

The key word in the last sentence of the previous paragraph, "encode," comes to us from semiotics; and all the critical texts under discussion have been affected in some measure by the semiotic revolution. In this respect these books move away from the issue of what Shakespeare "intended," what his plays "mean," to the issue of what the plays *do*. If social life is itself essentially a symbolic enactment of power relations, then the dramatic performance takes its place within that process, as a particularly concentrated (because intentionally symbolic, consciously mimetic) instance of processes at work everywhere in human experience. The key questions then become: what *kinds* of power relationships does this play mime? And *how* does it enact these relationships? Thus the emphasis on genre in the new Feminist criticism. For to this "new" criticism, genres are something more than a set of boxes into which we seek to cram certain phenomena. Even as late as Northrop Frye, critics often assumed that once they had categorized a certain text as a romance or whatever, they had "explained" it. But Feminist criticism sets out to explain the social function of the various literary genres themselves, thereby allowing us to recognize that literary genres work rather like other kinds of social institutions. That is, they serve as traditionally sanctioned ways of structuring human relationships—or, at least, of structuring the terms in which we see such relationships. In opening up the question of the social function of literary genres, the new Feminist criticism of Shakespeare has moved boldly into a rich new territory—and has moved far beyond (for example) Feminist commentary on Milton, which still wastes inordinate energy in denunciations of Milton himself for his presumed "sexism." Rather than merely complaining about Shakespeare's opinions, French, Bamber, Novy, and (except for some lapses) Erickson have instead set out to show how Shakespeare's plays can help us to understand the dynamics of patriarchy, and how a Feminist consciousness can enrich our sense of what is happening in these plays. And in their willingness to honor the claims both of Shakespeare's own text and of the twentieth-century experiences which inevitably shape our apprehension of what Shakespeare wrote, these books can serve, I believe, as exemplars of what Feminist criticism can become.

Have the books under review exhausted the possibilities of a Feminist analysis of Shakespeare? Not in the least, for as I move from Dash's book to Erickson's, I have a sense that I am watching not so much certain questions being "answered" as a cluster of problems becoming steadily "deeper," as each successive critic tries to refine the terms of analysis employed by previous critics and/or tries to absorb new materials into the ongoing project of a Feminist analysis of Shakespeare. As a consequence, these critics also give us some clues as to where Feminist criticism might go from here. Novy's book, for example, suggests that Feminist criticism might want to reach out toward a lively critical tradition (I am thinking, for example, of Michael Goldman and John Russell Brown and J. L. Styan[8]) which has emphasized the "play as play"—as, that is, a text *for performance*. How does a systematic attempt to understand how these plays work *in the theater* affect our sense of the way gender issues here manifest themselves? Erickson's insistence on the repressive effects of patriarchy also seems to invite an exploration of the relationship between gender oppression and other kinds of oppression. Someone, I find myself thinking, should attempt a systematic merger of Feminist and Marxist analysis, to elucidate the ways in which gender oppression and *class oppression* here interact.

In addition to indicating some ways in which Feminist criticism might reach out to other critical traditions, the books under review also, I believe, point to some ways in which Feminist criticism might continue to refine its own distinctive categories of analysis. For example, while French, Bamber, Novy, and Erickson all agree that in the course of Shakespeare's career he increasingly questions traditional gender stereotypes, none of them offers an hypothesis as to *why* this happens. The assumption of an "organic" development toward a higher and higher degree of "maturity" seems a little too pat; and I suppose that my inherent suspicion of such "psychological" explanations is clear by now. Yet if we do not hypothesize such a psychological development in "Shakespeare the man," how do we account for the relative openness of *Antony and Cleopatra*? A recognition of the thematic impact of genre might be useful here. Could there perhaps be some connection between the relatively radical view of gender apparent in *Antony and Cleopatra* and the fact that it is a *classical* play? Here Feminist critics might usefully consult certain recent books which have looked at the Roman plays as a distinct sub-genre.[9] So too, the constant overlay of genre upon genre in Shakespeare's plays offers additional possibilities of analysis. For example, for many decades the plays that we call romances (Shakespeare himself probably never thought of applying this word to a play—in his time a "romance" was printed prose narrative) were called tragicomedies, and perhaps we need to look long and hard at

Feminist Studies of Shakespeare

the way comic and tragic elements here interfuse. And what happens if we read *A Midsummer Night's Dream* as a comic version of *Romeo and Juliet*, or *Romeo and Juliet* as a tragic version of *Dream*? Finally, the questions of how *conscious* these plays are of the meaning of the gender relationships therein dramatized and of how they do or do not instill a critical consciousness of such issues in us deserve more consideration. French waffles on this crucial issue; the other critics edge around it. I think the issue needs to be addressed directly, and again I think that genre may be the key: as one genre presses in upon another, it becomes increasingly impossible for us to accept the tragic world as "real" and "true," or to think of the comic world as merely a domain of light-hearted play. In Shakespeare (the only great dramatist to be wholly at home both in comedy and tragedy—witness Jonson's dreary tragedies) the interplay between comedy and tragedy renders both genres problematic. And the overall curve of Shakespeare's career is best understood, I believe, as a systematic exploration of the problematics of these genres—an exploration which leads him to ask questions about many of the social patterns which had become encoded within these dramatic forms, including not only patterns of gender relationship but also patterns of class relationship. The five books under review do not, then, exhaust the possibilities of a Feminist criticism of Shakespeare. However, they unquestionably serve to open up the territory, and they generously invite us to join in the exploration of that territory.[10]

Notes

1. G. E. Bentley, "Shakespeare, The King's Company, and *King Lear*," in *On King Lear*, ed. Lawrence Danson (Princeton: Princeton Univ. Press, 1981), pp. 47-49.

2. A. C. Bradley, *Shakespearean Tragedy* (Cleveland: Meridian Books, 1961), esp. Lecture One.

3. Patrick Cruttwell, *The Shakespearean Moment and its Place in the Poetry of the 17th Century* (New York: Random House, 1960).

4. A similar attempt to enlist Shakespeare in the Feminist cause seems to be at work in Juliet Dusinberre, *Shakespeare and the Nature of Women* (London: Macmillan, 1975). Dusinberre's book represents the first major

attempt to look at Shakespeare from a contemporary Feminist perspective, but her interpretive method is open to serious question.

5. Bamber's book is much indebted to Leslie A. Fiedler, *The Stranger in Shakespeare* (New York: Stein and Day, 1973), esp. pp. 43-81. Fiedler's book should have an honored place in any core collection of Feminist studies of Shakespeare.

6. Norman Rabkin, *Shakespeare and the Common Understanding* (New York: The Free Press, 1967).

7. Coppélia Kahn, *Man's Estate: Masculine Identity in Shakespeare* (Berkeley: Univ. of California Press, 1981).

8. Michael Goldman, *The Actor's Freedom: Toward a Theory of Drama* (New York: The Viking Press, 1975) and *Acting and Action in Shakespeare* (Princeton: Princeton Univ. Press, 1985); J. Russell Brown, *Shakespeare in Performance: An Introduction Through Six Major Plays* (New York: Harcourt Brace Jovanovich, 1976); J. L. Styan, *Shakespeare's Stagecraft* (Cambridge: Cambridge Univ. Press, 1971).

9. Maurice Charney, *Shakespeare's Roman Plays* (Cambridge: Harvard Univ. Press, 1961); Judah Stampfer, *The Tragic Engagement: A Study of Shakespeare's Classical Tragedies* (New York: Funk and Wagnalls, 1968); and J. L. Simons, *Shakespeare's Pagan World: The Roman Tragedies* (Charlottesville: Univ. Press of Virginia, 1973).

10. Readers who want to assemble a reasonably complete collection of current Feminist commentary on Shakespeare should add, to the books reviewed here or cited in my notes, two important recent collections of critical essays: *The Woman's Part: Feminist Criticism of Shakespeare*, ed. Carolyn Ruth Swift Lenz, Gayle Greene, and Carol Thomas Neely (Urbana: Univ. of Illinois Press, 1980); and *Shakespeare's "Rough Magic": Renaissance Essays in Honor of C. L. Barber*, ed. Peter Erickson and Coppélia Kahn (Newark: Univ. of Delaware Press, 1985). The bibliographies in *The Woman's Part* provide a useful guide to pertinent critical commentary on individual plays.

Popular Criticism

Martin Roth

David Geherin, *The American Private Eye: The Image in Fiction.* New York: Frederick Ungar Publishing Company, 1985. 228 pp.

Sinda Gregory, *Private Investigations: The Novels of Dashiell Hammett.* Carbondale: Southern Illinois University Press, 1985. 204 pp.

The topic for me here is popular fiction, and the pairing of these two books is efficient and provocative. In theory, popular fiction is a relative object; it can only be identified as such in opposition to an other called art or serious or good fiction. Without the other there is a danger that they may both become just writing. From the perspective of the "critical study," the opposition between art and pop is the difference between the work (or the work developing into canon) and the genre as units of treatment. Of these two books, one, *The American Private Eye: The Image in Fiction,* is content to let the writing it discusses remain popular and addresses it *through* an invocation of genre. The other, *Private Investigations: The Novels of Dashiell Hammett,* makes the opposite move; Sinda Gregory claims her subject (Hammett's longer fiction) as art, *against* an invocation of genre. Her argument is not clear because it is never openly made, but apparently Hammett's writing has been misconstrued as popular and is in fact either art or a confusing intermediate category (see Julian Symons's *Mortal Consequences*): popular fiction that both performs and transcends its genre and is for that reason either art fiction or a cut below art fiction—this is the kind of taxonomy that emerges when you try to box this particular compass.

David Geherin's project seems to me to be on the right track, but it also seems scandalously banal in conception and expression. Perhaps that is the appropriate complementary aesthetic for the treatment of the work as genre, but it often feels like the result of a familiar kind of contagion, as the original writing takes over the commentary in a spontaneous celebration of unity: "Ex-con Mal Ourney, for example, the protagonist of *Green Ice*, is a man whose toughness is demanded by virtue of his crusade to put an end to the 'crime breeders,' the big crooks who rope in the little ones. In the battle against the forces of the underworld, toughness is an absolute necessity" (p. 31). *The American Private Eye* is a book by a professor of English at Eastern Michigan University, published by the Frederick Ungar Publishing Company, but it reads like a pulp fanzine, like hype. It is easy to distinguish its uncritical adulation from criticism; in serious critical studies, however, well-written hype is indistinguishable from criticism. At any rate, I knew as soon as I began to read in Geherin's book that it could only be exposed and damaged by the kinds of judgment I had been commissioned to make.

Sinda Gregory's book is intelligent, perceptive and well-written, but I don't believe in it. It seems to me to be essentially tautological, insofar as it filters Hammett through a kind of academic literary study that is designed to produce exactly the kind of product that emerges—a work about works that transcend their context, background, genre. The art and seriousness that is ultimately deposited to Hammett's account are not necessarily qualities of the work in question. There is a haunting sense that they have been produced at the site of the critical study, just as the critical articulation of themes is often the only place in a work's extended domain where thematization occurs. Gregory's type of study (which denies the power of genre) is itself a genre (the most popular in American academic publishing); and this does raise again the question of art and pop, of the unique work and the repetitive genre, with a self-reflexive vengeance. Considerations like these are conventionally mooted, and probably properly so, but the combination and accomplishments of these two studies posed them irresistibly for me. The books are not even studies: Geherin's studies nothing, as its simple inability to denote endlessly demonstrates; Gregory's may be studying only the implications of its genre.

What focused my attention while reading Gregory was the idea of the tautology of authorship. This circuit has been sharpened by film studies, where, if you decide to treat Raoul Walsh as an artist, he becomes an artist before your eyes. This process fascinates me, seeming simultaneously to be a phoney project and the way that artists are generally constructed. There really is no thesis in *Private Investigations* except for the excellence of Hammett. The judgment that *"The Maltese Falcon* is a brilliantly unified novel" (p. 88) that integrates the incompleteness of the novels that preceded it seems to belong to its place in the sequence of review. Judgments like this, by now, lie in wait around the perimeters of the enterprises ready to attach themselves to the first appropriate work that comes along.

The contents of artistry, according to established criticism, are theme, character and self-reflexivity. Character is what really differentiates the art from the pop novel. Popular fiction throws up nominal characters or stereotypes, while the challenge of art is an interior legitimacy that is true and glorious. Gregory keeps asserting that Hammett has really created character (a proposition I wouldn't know how to argue for or against) and then both opens and closes this coffer of treasures by going on to claim that his artistic intention was to produce characters that are inaccessible in order to signify psychological mystery—so that we are back where the genre left off: "Ned [Beaumont] remains even more elusive than his predecessors. To some extent, this creation of a man of mystery is intended for mystery—the mystery of emotions, motivations, and actions" (p. 116). On an intuitive level, this line of argument felt perverse because Gregory radically undercharacterizes Brigid O'Shaughnessy who is, in my opinion, the richest and most various character in Hammett and ignores what are, to me, Sam Spade's most striking characteristics—his rage and his infantile defiance.

Like theme, self-reflexivity is of indeterminate location. If "the whole saga of Gabrielle Leggett is so outrageous and excessive that it could be read as a darkly humorous parody of the trials and tribulations of popular fiction and film" (p. 75), we understand that that is a good state for *The Dain Curse* to be in. But this seems to me to be the central work of all popular fiction. Detective novels reproduce norms that are instantaneously parodies of norms and, in the eyes of criticism, that is their shame. But criticism can redeem shame whenever it wants to by claiming that the parody was deliberate, instructive, and, ultimately, moral, although the surfaces of the shameful and the salutary text do not reflect much of a difference.

Studies like Gregory's are also cumbersome because the work in question is always being seen against a background of other similar works that it has "transcended"—that it is both the same as and utterly different from. Theoretically, many subtle measurements are always being made. While these are generally empty rhetorical moves (rather like a sportscaster changing synonyms for "won" or "beat"), the style has regularly to alternate among three orders of judgment: the conventional, the generic but transformed, and the original and unique. The distinctions are neither conceptually nor specifically clear, and the network of assumptions tangles if you breathe too hard. Genre also has a way of getting its revenge, of sneaking back in, as in the case of character that is thematically the absence of character. If the Continental Op signifies anonymity and mystery—anonymity and mystery written in the space of a fiction of rich and complex interiority—why is that not the stamp of a mystery fiction where authorship is indifferent—why is that not the significance of genre?

What is so gloriously fraudulent about both Gregory's and Geherin's studies is that the background that makes everything work, *the genre*, is simply not there, because the genre (whether mystery fiction, detective fiction or hard-boiled detective fiction) has never been adequately constituted by these or any other study that I know of. Genre really only has credit as a more or less adequate collection of texts assembled for study. Articles and books on detective fiction, however, have, from the beginning, asserted the genre as known, as an intuitively accessible body of moves and information. The map of genre

Popular Criticism 269

in Tzvetan Todorov's "Typology of Detective Fiction"[1] is wonderfully lucid and economical, but I have no idea where it came from other than a dream of genre. This is not to say that it is not as absolutely or roughly correct as it feels, but I have no communicable way of knowing that is so. In an age that distrusts the transcendental, ideal or normative definitions are highly valued, although we have had good reason to be suspicious of them ever since Aristotle, in *The Poetics*, defined the ideal by choosing as the ideal to define a single play which he then reproduced as genre.

Should the generic be a code-word for the most "popular" or the "best" (which are themselves often code-words for "my favorite") single or several works, which are then generalized accordingly? But if so, doesn't this contaminate the thriving business of differentiating the better and the best from the ordinary or generic? On the other hand, can genre be intuited from our drugged pleasure reading? Can we distinguish in our intuitive conceptions of genre what we have ourselves noticed from the form's PR: echoes and paraphrases of what the works, authors and commentators have asked us to think on the form's behalf?

At the center of genre there is a distinction between "classical" and "hard-boiled" detective fiction which by now seems both historically and conceptually unassailable. In Gregory's study it rests on metaphysical strata—an ultimate order to things as opposed to a universal absurdism. But hard-boiled cases get solved and classical cases get opened with appalling regularity. Classical cases may be stamped with a seal of logical finality, but even soft commentary exposes that as arbitrary and not logical; and many are not: the Father Brown stories, to take a well-known example. A hint from Todorov discussing the explained Gothic tale is in order here; he points out that the rational explanation in these tales is far more cumbersome than the simple allegation of a miracle would have been. Classical detective fictions may take place in an orderly universe, but their openings are regularly filled with echoes of the Gothic supernatural—William Hope Hodgson had a detective called Carnacki the Ghost-finder who only took on cases where the presence of the supernatural appeared certain. The crime is repeatedly identified as a supernatural event, a miracle, and the detective as a wizard. A criticism that notices only that these traces are eventually dispelled and does not try to account for their active presence will not, I think, get very far in its account of genre.

Gregory says that the revelatory scene at the end of *Red Harvest* "is also deliberately evasive about making the point with which nearly every hard-boiled novel concludes: that the violence and brutality of the detective have been vindicated by his unmasking a criminal even more violent and brutal than himself" (p. 39). Surely Gregory has not counted? The prissy correction is very much in order, for it covers a far more debilitating confusion— that the genre is not known in a way that would allow statements like this to be made. If I think of her statement, I intuitively reject it: I think of the endings of *The Maltese Falcon* and *The Glass Key*, or the ending of *Farewell My Lovely* where Marlowe schizophrenically arranges for the murder of Velma at the hands of her old lover. I do believe, however, that such a conclusion to criticism is part of the moralistic "art-sell" for a remarkably violent and sadistic novel [*Red Harvest*] by Dashiell Hammett that is in constant danger of being confused with a line of remarkably popular generic novels.

Gender analysis is as hard to find as genre analysis in a body of material that cries out for it because it victimizes and villainizes its women so constantly. Gregory refuses to open the subject. In a fiction where criminals turn out to be lovers, where Sam Spade can just happen to discover that the woman who is bewitching him sexually also happens to be an absolutely amoral and callow murderer who can therefore be put away in prison for many years—to comment on the incrimination of strong women by this form only through a morality that reasserts patriarchal values offends me. The form has a number of outrageous gender truths that it tells; in Geherin, detectives "chivalrously take the rap for crimes committed by the women they love" (p. 49). But in order for them to do so, the women must first be guilty. Hard-boiled detective fiction is a genre that is devoted to criminalizing or entrapping women. Geherin's

Popular Criticism

unabashed and unreconstructed sexism—"More challenging to his creative imagination are the spicy descriptions of female pulchritude that are the centerpiece of each Turner story" (pp. 58-59)—quite took my breath away. In his praise of this writer's style, he lists a series of euphemisms for the female breasts "which tax his imagination to the utmost as he ogles the women," and he seems, for a moment, brilliantly, on the verge of defining style itself as adolescent erotic circumlocution.

Popular fiction contains casual and intense violence; art fiction does not—it contains the theme of violence. But the line between violence or sadistic hardness that is proper to popular fiction and the subtly detached quotation of sadistic hardness for the purpose of framing and therefore exposing it morally (which is only allowable in art) is often too elusive for me. What should not be elusive is the pornographic energy of the terrible beating Ned Beaumont receives in *The Glass Key* by an ape-like man who plays him like a yo-yo; but this is also instantly thematized and sublimated in Gregory: "Beaumont's ability to control his destiny is limited, partially because of his own nature but more fundamentally because the world is simply overpoweringly destructive in *The Glass Key*" (p. 134).

I find this behavior (which permeates criticism) both seductive and terrifying: taking the texts' word for it and reproducing that as your own, passing on the texts' defensive postures as judgment, wisdom or truth. Interpretation only means having a different place from what you are reporting on—and if there is no need for a different place then there is no need for reporting. There is no interpretation in either of these books. Gregory and Geherin accept and promulgate almost everything the works and the "genre" say in their own behalf—the alibis, rationalizations, self-glorifications, idealizations—and we are left in a world where violence is symbolic or metaphysical, where cold control and manipulation are the necessary armor against a cruel and unjust world, and where self-loathing and masochism are a passionate desire for justice and the fulfillment of a quest. I really do not object to hard-boiled detective fiction; I just wish that someone would tell it a little like the way it is for me.

Note

1. Tzvetan Todorov, "The Typology of Detective Fiction," *The Poetics of Prose* (Ithaca: Cornell Univ. Press, 1977), pp. 42-52.

A Book for a Parlour-Window

O M Brack, Jr.

Laurence Sterne. *The Life and Opinions of Tristram Shandy, Gentleman.* Vols. 1-2: The Text, edited by Melvyn New and Joan New; vol. 3: The Notes, edited by Melvyn New with Richard A. Davies and W. G. Day. Gainesville: University Presses of Florida, 1978-84. Vols. 1-2: 966 pp.; vol. 3: vi, 572 pp.

That *Tristram Shandy* could become an instantaneous success in York and London, soon spreading to the rest of England, to Great Britain, Europe, and America, continues to be a source of amazement. On several occasions I have read the first two volumes through, trying to shut out what I know about the remaining seven, in hopes that I might reconstruct how readers in the winter of 1760 responded to the book. This "with fifty other points left yet unravelled, you may endeavour to solve if you have time;——but I tell you before-hand it will be vain" since no one "could pretend to come within a league of the truth" (p. 180.23-28). In spite of Tristram's warning in the penultimate paragraph to Volume II our imagination plays on this, as it does on the forty-six-year-old clergyman who wrote the novel. Literary historians and critics tend to be evolutionists rather than creationists, preferring authors to show early signs of genius and a development from early, simpler forms to later, more complex ones—like Shakespeare, Henry James, or James Joyce, with a clear line of development from *Dubliners,* to *Stephen Hero,* to *A Portrait of the Artist as a Young Man,* to *Ulysses,* to *Finnegans Wake.* Sterne's other great work, *A Sentimental Journey through France and Italy,* grows out of *Tristram Shandy* in what appears to be a predictable fashion, but who would have predicted *Tristram Shandy* from the author's earlier writing?

In fact there are few known earlier writings, two sermons published locally in 1747 and 1750, a poem in the *Gentleman's*

Magazine of July 1743, and contributions to the local newspapers on various political topics. Then in December 1758, in response to a debate over preferments in the Church of York, Sterne began *A Political Romance*. The small book of sixty pages was printed in York in January 1759 by Caesar Ward but was suppressed and never went on sale, the "copies committed to the Flames." Only six copies are known to have survived.[1] But Sterne had discovered his talent as an author. He may have begun work on the manuscript he called "The Life and Opinions of Tristram Shandy" upon completing *A Political Romance*, and certainly was at work on it by early March. In any case on 23 May 1759 he sent the manuscript of the first volume to Robert Dodsley. "The Plan," he wrote, "is a most extensive one,——taking in, not only, the Weak part of the Sciences, in which the true point of Ridicule lies——but every Thing else, which I find Laugh-at-able in my way——"[2] Dodsley answered the letter in June and declined the volume. All indications are that this version of *Tristram Shandy* was different from the one we know.

Much of our knowledge of the original plan comes from the letter of an unidentified gentleman who visited Sterne in June. Sterne sat up all night with his visitor going over a manuscript "more than would make four such Volumes as those two he has published," and revealing his design "to take in all Ranks and Professions, and to laugh them out of their Absurdities.... A System of Education is to be exhibited, and thoroughly discussed; for forming his future Hero, I have recommended a private Tutor, and names no less a Person than the great and learned Dr. W[arburton]: Polemical Divines are to come in for a Slap. An Allegory has been run up on the Writers on the Book of Job.... A Groupe of mighty Champions in Literature is convened at Shandy-Hall" (p. 818). Some parts of this design can still be recognized in *Tristram Shandy*, but Sterne reported to an unidentified correspondent in the summer of 1759 that "I have Burn'd More wit, then I have publish'd." By October, when he again wrote to Dodsley, he could declare, "All locality is taken out of this book——the satire general."[3] As Melvyn New has argued elsewhere, the "Fragment in the Manner of Rabelais," dates from this early period and provides another clue to what the original version of the novel was like, a satire on learning and sermon writers structured along the lines of *The Memoirs of Martinus Scriblerus* and heavily influenced by Rabelais and Swift, particularly the latter's *A Tale of a Tub*.[4] Even after what appears to have been extensive revision, the first twenty chapters as published contain a number of inconsistencies and unfulfilled promises. Neither Walter Shandy nor Uncle Toby is given the attributes which will come to dominate his character.

Whatever difficulties Sterne may have had in shaping the content of his work, he was clear about the form it should take in print. In a letter of 20 January 1759, probably addressed to Caesar Ward, printer of *A Political Romance,* Sterne warns, "That, at your Peril, you do not presume to alter or transpose one Word, nor rectify one false Spelling, nor so much as add or diminish one Comma or Tittle, in or to my *Romance:*——For if you do,——In case any of the Descendents of *Curl* should think fit to invade my Copy-Right, and print it over again in my Teeth, I may not be able, in a Court of Justice, to swear strictly to my own Child, after you had *so large a Share* in the begetting it." When Sterne wrote to Robert Dodsley 23 May 1759 hoping to interest him in publishing the volume, he tells him how it should be printed: "I think it will make a Volume in Octavo of about the Size of the Essay upon ingenious Tormenting, by Millar——that is, allowing the same Type & Margin." After Dodsley declined to publish the work in June, Sterne wrote to him about October asking him to sell the book in his shop and offering him the whole profits of the sale. "I propose, therefore, to print a lean edition, in two small volumes, of the size of Rasselas, and on the same paper and type, at my own expense. . . . The book shall be printed here, and the impression sent up to you; for as I live at York, and shall correct every proof myself, it shall go perfect into the world, and be printed in so creditable a way as to paper, type, &c., as to do no dishonour to you, who I know, never chuse to print a book meanly."[5]

That Sterne thought the form of his book important is further emphasized by the earliest known advertisement for it in the

London Chronicle and other London papers for 1 January 1760: "This day was Published, Printed on a superfine Writing Paper, and a new Letter, in two Volumes, price 5s. neatly bound, *The Life and Opinions of Tristram Shandy*."[6] On Christmas Day [?1760] Sterne writes from London to Stephen Croft, "I have been in such a continual hurry since the moment I arrived here . . . with my books," presumably the first edition of Volumes III and IV of *Tristram Shandy*, published 28 January 1761. In early January 1767 he writes, "I am all this week in Labour pains," with Volume IX of *Tristram Shandy* which was published 29 January. In fact Sterne was in London during the printing of the first editions of all of his works except for Volumes III and IV of his Sermons.[7]

The knowledge that Sterne supervised the first printing of his books should give the textual editor confidence that most readings in the copy-text are the author's. Of even greater value would be a manuscript, particularly the manuscript used by the printer. In the case of *Tristram Shandy*, unfortunately, the only manuscript which has survived is the Rabelaisian fragment. But for *A Sentimental Journey* there is an extant manuscript in Sterne's hand from which Volume I was printed; the manuscript for Volume II is now lost. In addition there is "a fair and generally accurate copy" of the entire manuscript of the work in an unidentified hand. This copy was made after Sterne had completed a fair copy in his own hand for the printer, but before he had made his final revisions. Since there are numerous changes in wording between the first edition and the carefully revised holograph manuscript, this is strong evidence that Sterne revised the proofs carefully. But as Gardner D. Stout, Jr., observes in his "Note on the Text" to his edition of *A Sentimental Journey*, problems remain.

Although many of the verbal changes could have been made only by Sterne, there are many more variants that could have been introduced just as readily in the printing house. "As we might expect," Sterne, in preparing the manuscript for the printer, was "in general, very careful about specifying accidentals, particularly where he intended dashes, italics, capitals, small capitals, for example, to express nuances of style

A Book for a Parlour-Window

or sense." Even though in general the formal details of the manuscript are followed in the first edition, there are exceptions. "Sterne evidently had the practice of the printing house in mind and tended to be careless or inconsistent about capitalization, pointing, and italics where he felt that his intentions were obvious and that the printer would normalize his manuscript in accord with them." In the absence of corrected proof sheets, Stout can only conclude that "Sterne's vital concern with the minutiae of punctuation and typography suggests that he may have made at least a few changes in accidentals," and he is left to assume that the many variants between the holograph printer's copy and the first edition "may be regarded as generally authorized even if not specifically authorial."[8] The choice of copy-text then is the first edition, which Stout felt required only a little more than forty minor emendations. I will return to this manuscript and its relevance to *Tristram Shandy* shortly.

Neither Stout in 1967 nor the News in 1978 waste time on theorizing about textual editing principles, but Greg and Bowers are clearly discernible as their model. The failure to mention the names of these two distinguished textual theorists is indicative of the sway they have held over textual editing. That the Greg-Bowers theory would come under attack could not be foreseen by the News at the time they were completing the text, but they can be held responsible for their lack of a complete understanding of the theory and their failure to apply consistently the principles they have adopted. This is to be an "authoritative" edition, we are told, and the term appears over and over. But wherein does the authority lie? It is on this point that the editors are confused and confusing.

In using the first edition [of *Tristram Shandy*] as copy-text, it has been accepted as the authority for accidentals. In those few instances where an accidental is emended, the change is based on the editor's judgment rather than the authority of another text, although the appearance of the new reading in subsequent lifetime editions has been recorded. Sterne's varied dash-lengths have been preserved, including the use of from two to five hyphens instead of dashes in the first editions of Volumes I and II. While hyphens were at times used by printers when they ran out of dash-lengths, I could find no pattern in *Tristram Shandy* which conclusively accounted for the hyphens as a printing-house phenomenon, and therefore assumed that the compositor was attempting to duplicate what he saw in the manuscript, a labor the London compositors were perhaps unwilling to undertake to indulge Sterne's whimsicality. [pp. 836-37]

Although the editors had hoped to escape the "tyranny of the copy-text," they have not succeeded (p. 832).[9] At the heart of this matter is a misunderstanding. Greg, after making his now classic distinction between "substantive" readings in the text, those that affect the author's meaning, and "accidentals," those that affect primarily the formal presentation, goes on to speak of scribes and compositors. "As regards substantive readings their aim may be assumed to be to produce exactly those of their copy, though they will doubtless sometimes depart from them accidentally and may even, for one reason or another, do so intentionally: as regards accidentals they will normally follow their own habits or inclination, though they may, for various reasons and to varying degrees, be influenced by their copy." Far from saying that the first edition is likely to reflect the author's manuscript, he thinks only that it will be closer than later editions. The choice of copy-text, Greg makes clear, is a "matter of convenience." The "authority" does not reside in the first edition just because it has been set from the author's manuscript or chosen as copy-text. It is the responsibility of the textual editor to learn as much as possible about the nature of the manuscript, its first printing, and subsequent transmission, and it is this knowledge, supported by evidence, from which authority derives. In Volume VIII, Chapter XXII, Trim is described: "Though it was the most serious despair in nature to the corporal——he could not forbear smiling" (p. 702.18-19). In the Textual Notes we are told that Ian Watt and Douglas Grant "print 'affair' which is perhaps a better reading though without authority" (p. 861). This suggests that "despair" has authority because it is in the copy-text, sense or non-sense. But if the editor feels that "despair" makes little sense in the context, he could, by familiarizing himself with the procedures in the printing house, drawing perhaps on John Smith's *The Printer's Grammar* (London, 1755), decide that here the compositor's memory lapsed and he set "despair" instead of a similar word, "affair."[10] Since authors presumably wish to make sense, but do not necessarily do so, the editor might wish to argue that the author, caught up in the feelings of his character at this point, described Trim's feelings as "despair" when the context demanded that he write "affair." All of this is hypothetical; I am not attempting to decide between the two possible readings since I am not at the moment qualified to make such a decision. The point is that the editor who has familiarized himself with the author's working habits, manuscripts, lifetime editions, printing-house procedures, etc., is qualified to make a decision and cannot abrogate his responsibility by attributing authority to one or the other exemplar of the text.[11] The editor must accept the responsibility for a decision *not* to emend just as he accepts the responsibility for a decision to emend. A cardinal rule of textual editing is to exhaust the bibliographical evidence before proceeding to emend the text—or *not* emend the text. The editors here have an extremely limited view of what constitutes bibliographical evidence.

One of the best features of this edition is the bibliographical descriptions of the lifetime editions of *Tristram Shandy*, twenty-seven items in all, by Kenneth Monkman, adding as it does useful details to his earlier essay in *The Library*.[12] Even if the examination of bibliographical evidence is confined to these twenty-seven items, there are problems. Ideal copy, a tricky concept in descriptive bibliography, has no place in textual editing. Modern editions must be produced from real books, often differing in one way or another from each other. The editors understand this insofar as they tell us that printer's copy consisted of photocopies of a particular set of the first edition of the novel. But what copy of the second edition was collated with the first? Are we to assume that other copies used in preparing the edition are the same as those described by Monkman? Press variants do exist, as a careful reading of Monkman's bibliography and the textual notes reveals, but copies are not distinguished and the variants do not appear in the textual apparatus where they might be expected.

The editors have chosen as copy-text for the "Memoire presenté a Messieurs les Docteurs de Sorbonne," not the first edition of *Tristram Shandy*, but Sterne's source, *Observations Importantes sur le Manuel des Accouchemens . . . Traduite du Latin de M. Henry de Deventer . . . Paris . . . M.DCC.XXXIV*. They argue, and I see no reason to disagree, that Sterne intended to make an accurate transcription of the text of the source and that "many of the differences between the text as printed by Deventer and the text as printed in *Tristram* represent simple errors of transcription at the first stage or composition at the second" and that "Sterne's emendations to *Deventer* are an important aspect of *Tristram*, one that can best be highlighted as part of the textual apparatus" (p. 939). The "essence of Sterne's satirical point," they argue, is that he could use verbatim an actual deliberation by the doctors of the Sorbonne. "This being the case, it is important to recognize the need for separating Sterne's function as a copyist from his function as artist, if he did transcribe the pages—or if the *Deventer* pages were used as printer's copy, for separating compositorial errors and printing-house practice from the text Sterne submitted" (p. 940). A discussion of variants follows, but variants from what? What copy of *Deventer* was used for comparison?

A similar problem arises with the "Abuses of Conscience" sermon, first preached in York Minster 29 July 1750, printed by Caesar Ward, and published 7 August. The editors compare the 1750 version with that found in *Tristram*, but there is no indication that multiple copies of the sermon were examined or which copy was used for the collation. Sterne's source for the Latin version of "Ernulphus's Curse" was probably Thomas Herne's edition of *Textus Roffensis* (Oxford, 1720) and the source for the English translation the *Gentleman's Magazine* for September 1745. Again no indication of copies. Are not all of these texts subject to the same bibliographical variations as the text of *Tristram*?

Choosing *Deventer*, the source, rather than the first edition of *Tristram*, is a daring decision, especially for an edition which follows an extremely conservative textual policy. Here the editors seem to have grasped the point of Greg's rationale—that one should attempt to bring his text as close to the author's intention as possible by trying to reconstruct printer's copy with, of course, any additions believed to have been made by the author in the process of printing the book. But by adopting the hyphens rather than dashes, we can only assume that the editors believe hyphens were in the manuscript and the compositor was following copy. It also means that the editors believe that Sterne began using hyphens for dashes in 1759, having apparently not used them previously, only to abandom them again for the remainder of his career. What was Sterne's practice in manuscript? He certainly did not use hyphens for dashes in the Rabelaisian Fragment, believed by New to have been written in 1759 as part of an early draft of *Tristram Shandy*. Sterne uses dashes in his letters and in the manuscript of *A Sentimental Journey*.[13] The explanation most likely to occur to an analytical bibliographer is that dash-lengths were in short supply in Ann Ward's printing shop, but this explanation is dismissed. What was Ann Ward's practice in other books? Monkman draws heavily on the evidence of other printing by Ward to support his contention that the first two volumes of *Tristram Shandy* were printed in York, and the editors speak of the uses of capitals in Ward's shop (pp. 947-48).[14]

What about the use of dashes? Although the printer's copy for the first two volumes of *Tristram Shandy* has not survived, there is a wealth of manuscript evidence, including a fragment from 1759, on which a decision about Sterne's practice might be made. If the editors really believe that this was Sterne's practice for a brief period, what is the significance of this fact?

A parallel instance is the italicizing of proper names in the first six volumes, a practice abandoned thereafter. The editors preserve this idiosyncracy as well. "Indications of discontinuity in the printing of *Tristram* may have significance in any critical reading of the work" (p. 838). They *may*, and they *might* have bibliographical significance as well. The habits of the printing house of William Strahan might provide a clue. As the editors are aware from the researches of Monkman, Strahan printed all of the first editions of *Tristram* beginning with Volume V. Had the break in style begun when Strahan took over the printing of *Tristram*—that is, beginning with Volume V—the change might have been attributed to the house style of the new printer. But it does not occur there; it appears only after Strahan had published Volumes V and VI as a unit. Volumes VII and VIII which appeared in January 1765, Monkman tells us, "contain a good many printer's errors."[15] No letter survives between 16 November 1764 and 16 March 1765, but in the 16 March letter to Garrick, Sterne apologizes for having not written, observing, "I lead such a life of dissipation I have never had a moment to myself which has not been broke in upon, by one engagement or impertinence or another."[16] Whether this statement refers only to the "few weeks" since he had written Robert Foley or to the period since his arrival in London at Christmas is debatable, but the evidence indicates that he did not spend much time over proofs to *Tristram Shandy*, suggesting that these volumes should be examined with a skeptical eye. What was Strahan's practice for other volumes printed at the same time? An examination of his ledgers in the British Library will provide a researcher with a list of titles. Immediately above the entry for Volumes VII and VIII of *Tristram Shandy*, for example, also dated February 1765, is the entry for the printing of 1000 copies of the third edition of Smollett's *Adventure of Peregrine Pickle*. Volume IX was published in January 1767, printed by Strahan, and entered in his ledger the same month.[17] Then on 27 February 1768 *A Sentimental Journey* was published, also printed by Strahan.

Very little printer's copy has survived for works printed before the nineteenth century. Most editors have only the printed texts, and perhaps a few letters never intended for publication, from which to construct their authors' habits of spelling and punctuation. Stout was certainly aware of his good fortune in having printer's copy when preparing his edition of *A Sentimental Journey*. When arguing for accepting the accidentals of the first edition rather than those in the manuscript, Stout observes that "Becket and De Hondt published Vols. V-IX of *Tristram Shandy* (1761-1767) and Vols. III and IV of the *Sermons* (1766). Sterne was thoroughly familiar with the normal practice of the printers they employed, and the accidentals in *A Sentimental Journey* accord closely with those in the later volumes of *Tristram Shandy*, particularly Vol. IX, which was published in 1767 (a year before the *Journey*)."[18] The connection that Stout fails to make is that the last volume of *Tristram* and the first volume of *A Sentimental Journey* resemble each other because they were products of the same printing house. William Strahan's usual habit was to make an entry in his ledger on the completion of printing a work. Under "Mr. Thomas Beckett" and dated "March 1768" is the following entry for the first edition of Volume I *only*: "Yorrick's Sentimental Journey, 14 sheets, No. 2750 @ £1:17:6 £26:5:0 Advertisements to the Subscribers No. 500 £0:5:0." That Strahan was responsible for only the first volume of the work is confirmed by an entry under April of the same year: "Yorrick's Sentimental Journey, Vol. 1st 2d Edit. 14 sheets No. 2000, @ £1:10:0 £21:0:0," and by an October 1769 entry for 2000 copies of "Vol. 1st 3d Edit."[19] There are some discrepancies between the ledger entry and the notation on the printer's copy—"13 Sheets / No 2500 / 150 fine"—pointing out the need for further study of the manuscript as a product of Strahan's printing house.[20] This need not, however, deflect us from the major point: that a careful comparison of this manuscript with the first edition of *A Sentimental Journey* can provide valuable information, not only on the printing of this work, but on the printing of the later volumes of *Tristram Shandy*.

As D. F. McKenzie observed a number of years ago, books are not printed in isolation; an individual volume must be studied in the context of the printing house in which it was produced, when this can be discovered, and in the context of what we know about the history of printing in a given period.[21] We should not try to reconstruct the printing house from the volume in our hand but examine the larger context, including such external evidence as printer's manuals. A printer's manual needs to be read critically, of course, since in some instances the author seems to be presenting the ideal practice of a printing house, rather than what must have been the confusing state of day-to-day practice. Nevertheless Smith's *The Printer's Grammar* provides valuable information for understanding the printing of *Tristram Shandy*. Smith notes that "By the Laws of Printing, indeed, a Compositor should abide by his Copy, and not vary from it, that he may clear himself, in case he should be charged with having made a fault. But this good law is now looked upon as obsolete, and most Authors expect the Printer to spell, point, and digest their Copy, that it may be intelligible and significant to the Reader; which is what a Compositor and the Corrector jointly have regard to, in Works of their own language." The compositor peruses his copy, "But before we actually begin to compose, we should be informed by the Author, or Master, after what manner our work is to be done; whether the old way, with Capitals to Substantives, and Italic to Proper names; or after the more neat practice, all in Roman, and Capitals to Proper names, and Emphatical words." But "if a work is to be done in the more modern and neater way, we pay no regard to put any thing in Italic but what is underscored in our Copy."[22] Might not William Strahan, proprietor of the "greatest printing house in London,"[23] decide to follow "the more modern and neater way," thus accounting for the shift to unitalicized proper names after Volume VI? "Running quotation marks in the left margin have been silently omitted," the News tells us (p. 837). Modernizing quotation marks has become common practice in scholarly editions, and I assume this is the reason the editors do so; otherwise their logic escapes me. Here there is no attempt to discuss Sterne's use of quotations in manuscript or printed texts as justification. The shift from lacing the quotation marks down the margin to the modern style occurs about mid-century and roughly coincides with the shift to a modern style of capitalization and italicization.[24] It is curious that James Aiken Work and Ian Watt make the later volumes coincide with the practice of italicizing proper names in the earlier ones, thereby creating an old-fashioned-looking text page. The News, typically, decide not to decide, although given their attitude toward quotation marks one might think they would make the earlier volumes coincide with the later. At the very least capitalization and italicization is a problem and it requires discussion in light of *all* of the bibliographical evidence available.

As Bertrand H. Bronson observes, "the generation schooled to capitalize nouns would go on writing in their habitual way."[25] Yet we know from surviving manuscripts that many authors accepted, or at least acquiesced in, the new style. James Thorpe's remark "that complaints against printers" do not necessarily "signify a concern about accidentals" is worth keeping in mind.[26] Perhaps the most memorable statement by an author on the treatment of accidentals is Mark Twain's comment to William Dean Howells on *A Connecticut Yankee*: "Yesterday Mr. Hall wrote that the printer's proof-reader was improving my punctuation for me, & I telegraphed orders to have him shot without giving him time to pray."[27] In spite of his numerous threats to printers and editors, Twain was often willing to have his wife and friends make substantial revisions in his works and even read proofs for him.[28] Sterne's oft-quoted statement to Caesar Ward in 1759 "That, at your Peril, you do not presume to alter or transpose one Word, nor rectify one false Spelling, nor so much as add or diminish one Comma or Tittle," cannot be accepted for every volume of his work, especially when it is contradicted by other evidence. Assuming that in fact he did attempt to control every detail of the printing of his works in York, no doubt his enthusiasm waned as the newness of authorship wore off, his health became increasingly uncertain, and time was required to play the literary lion. His flattering letter to Robert Dodsley of October 1759 also needs to be examined skeptically. After all, Sterne wants a favor. He wants Dodsley, one of the leading booksellers in London, to sell his book. What better way to persuade him than to praise his good taste in printing and reassure him that the first two volumes of *Tristram Shandy*, although printed in the provinces, meet Dodsley's high standards. It should be noted, at least as a curious coincidence, that Sterne chose Johnson's *Rasselas* as his model, a work of some popularity recently published by Dodsley, and (though this was probably unknown to Sterne) neatly printed by Strahan.[29]

Sterne scholars, by assuming on the evidence of the Caesar Ward and Robert Dodsley letters that Sterne controlled all aspects of the printing of his novel, accept as a given what is in reality very much in doubt. Perhaps the most extreme view of the sacredness of Sterne's text is an announcement of a reprint of *Tristram Shandy* which "unlike other editions . . . will reproduce the first edition in virtually all of its physical aspects: there will be a newly-created eighteenth-century typeface, preserving all the qualities of the original, spelling errors, errata, etc.—page for page, volume for volume as in the original, watermarked acid-free paper, hand-made, marble[d] leaves, and paper-covered board bindings as would have been available from an eighteenth-century bookbinder." Apparently various people in Toronto think that few people have access to first editions of *Tristram Shandy*, and that there will be "no way of conveying Sterne's total message, about his book" unless this expensive edition is purchased.[30] My heart goes out to eskimos and a few others who cannot read a first edition somewhere, and I wonder if they would not be better served by a facsimile reprint of the same high quality as those produced by the old Scolar Press. This gives new meaning to "tyranny of the copy-text" when editorial effort is spent trying to reproduce all the errors exactly. If we are to believe the editor of the recent Norton Critical Edition, it is only necessary to reproduce some copy of the first edition of each volume, amend "obvious errors, typographical or otherwise, it is usually impossible to tell," to have "An Authoritative Text."[31] In this Shandean world, Walter has triumphed, and textual criticism is needless.

The editors of the Florida Edition are cautious but make some emendations. Apart from the corrections of literals there seem to be fewer than twenty emendations, only four, I think, not made by previous editors, and about a dozen proposed emendations suggested, but not made, in the textual notes. I am cautious about suggesting the exact number because I find the textual apparatus confusing. The editors are aware of G. Thomas Tanselle's essay "Some Principles for Editorial Apparatus" but go their own way. Earlier New had warned, "My primary deviation is in my giving the historical collation within the list of emendations and not repeating the information in the historical collation list; I do not find this practice as inconvenient or confusing as Tanselle does."[32] The final statement in Tanselle's essay is worth quoting in full: "Only by being fully cognizant of the issues and problems involved in setting up an apparatus can an editor make those decisions which will establish his apparatus as a lasting contribution to literary study."[33] Tanselle's worthwhile goal in this essay is to standardize the form of a textual apparatus just as one or another form has come to be accepted for other kinds of documentation. Whatever theory is adopted for editing the text, the evidence must be readily understood by scholars familiar with the usual procedure for documenting scholarly editions.

At first glance, then, this apparatus seems to be set up along conventional lines, but the confusion in textual theory is reflected in the apparatus. After the List of Emendations and the Word Division table (divided into three categories) comes the Historical Collation, but since the history of the emendations is given in the List of Emendations and not in the Historical Collation, of what is the Historical Collation a history? It is, in fact, a list of all of the variants discovered in the course of collating but not used in emending the text. What is to be gained by this? But do not expect to find all of the variants in these three sections. Variants for the "Memoire presenté a Messieurs les Docteurs de Sorbonne," the "Abuses of Conscience" sermon, and "Ernulphus's Curse," not deemed important enough to make the List of Emendations, appear in separate appendices. Press variants between copies appear in textual notes without being reported in the apparatus. The editors have also departed from the standard form for reporting variants. At 85.2, for example, is "their] his"—meaning that the emendation originated with this edition. I find an entry without a siglum particularly confusing. At first "petite canulle] 1-6; *petite Canulle*" seems out of place in a List of Emendations since it looks as though no emendation has been made. The editors are in fact saying that they prefer the reading of the first six editions of *Tristram Shandy* to the Deventer copy-text. An attempt to reconstruct the copy-texts from this apparatus will be difficult indeed.

Most of the emendations to the text seem sensible enough, since many correct undisputed errors. Changing the copy-text reading "goals" from this accepted eighteenth-century spelling to "gaols" (p. 155.20) because of the confusion for modern readers is commendable. Since so much in this edition is relegated to numerous appendices I continue to be puzzled why the cross reference to "fifth chapter" (p. 130.16) is not corrected to "second chapter." True that "'fifth' may be a vestige of chapters later deleted" (p. 847), but would it not be better to discuss this in the introduction and the textual notes and have the correct reading in the text? Any reader not greatly familiar with the text is bound to be puzzled, as there is no siglum in the text suggesting that the reader look elsewhere. At several points in the text, emendations are made with the justification in the textual notes that they correct compositorial errors. (See pp. 237.10, 263.26, 356.15-16, 493.21, 575.8, for example.) On the whole, however, I find that not much allowance is made for compositorial error, the assumption being that every literal in the text might hold some secret Shandean meaning, no matter how much it looks like a typographical error to the uninitiated. The copy-text's misspelling of "Sulplice" (p. 602.28) for St. Sulpice "is preserved because of the likelihood that Sterne himself made the error, perhaps having the more common 'surplice' in mind" (p. 860). I would have thought it more likely that the compositor might have repeated the "l" in an unfamiliar word he was carrying in his head, but if Sterne wanted to preserve this spelling, what is the joke or allusion? In the copy-text *"La Battarelle"* appears twice in this form and twice as *"La Batterelle,"* but the editors accept the emendation of the second edition which makes all four references consistently *"La Battarelle"* (p. 856). *"Quedlingberg"* also appears as *"Quedlinberg"* and *"Quedlinburg"* (p. 852). Do the editors preserve the inconsistencies of the copy-text in the belief that Sterne had some reason for spelling this town in Saxony in a variety of ways? Perhaps there is a reason for these variant spellings, as there is for spelling "Avignon" or "Avignion,"[34] but the mere fact that they appear in the copy-text is not reason enough, given the editors' willingness to make corrections elsewhere, particularly when they can compare Sterne with his source.

So much for 1978. With the publication of the third volume in 1984, we have confusion worst confounded. New has now had time to think over editorial procedures for the first two volumes, his focus changed by reviewers, no doubt, and by the seductive overtures of post-structuralist literary theory. A full examination of the implications of his remarks would require another essay so I will content myself with pointing out only a few of the problems. I am uncertain, for example, what to make of the statement in the introduction to Volume 3 that "modern editors have proceeded in blissful unconcern about where they stand . . . in relation to their text" (p. 1), since I have been thinking, naively it seems, that this is the central problem to which textual criticism is directed. New now seems concerned to put as much distance as he can between what he erroneously labels "scientific" editors, such as Greg and Bowers, who are "naive" in thinking that they can establish a text which represents their author's intentions.[35] The modern critic, unable to distinguish between errors and correct readings, must abandon interpretation for elucidation. Having thus attempted to refute the textual theory, never entirely understood, which would give his decade of work in establishing a text of *Tristram Shandy* any meaning, the annotations are to set things right. Separating interpretation from elucidation turns out not to be an easy task, New tells us at great length—something editors have always known, although it does not hurt to be reminded of the annotator's duty, even when such hyperbolic words as "dangerous" and "treacherous" are used to describe it (pp. 9, 13).

At best the annotations demonstrate the many overlapping layers of thought that went into producing the novel, although the editors can now document rather fully what we all thought, that "Sterne's 'learned wit' almost always has more 'wit' and less 'learning' than we are led to believe," that *Tristram Shandy* is "liberally sprinkled with the names of authors he never read, books he knew little or nothing about, and technical details (from history and science in particular) that are not the indications of a universal genius but rather an inveterate index-reader" (p. 24). At worst the annotations are a raking together of everything the editors were able to discover and are badly in need of editorial intervention—even at the risk of dreaded and dangerous interpretation.

Just as every literal in the text is assumed to hold some potential secret meaning, every word is assumed to hold some potential sexual meaning. New quotes Robert Gorham Davis's comment that "Sterne . . . is as insistent as the most orthodox Freudian on the fact that for some imaginations at some times every straight object, every stick, candle, wick, nose can stand for the male genital, and every hole, slit, crevice and curve, for the female." New adds, "In this wilderness, as Sterne himself might have warned, the annotator had best proceed with caution" (p. 12). The reader should proceed with caution as well. I give one example. "By my fig!, I'll go no further" (p. 610.17) declares one of the mules being driven by the abbess and Margarita. On turning to the annotations we are sent from this use of "fig" in Chapter XXI to Chapter XLIII (p. 647.15 ff.) where Tristram buys figs and eggs from a gossip. The note for page 647.15, "I had figs enow," says only, "See above, n. to 610.17." We must understand, then, that the note for page 610.17 also applies to the use of "figs" for page 647.15. In descending order of probability the editors tell us that "Partridge suggests *pudendum muliebre*, but not as early as the eighteenth century; Sterne's usage in both instances, however, suggests that meaning may have been available to him." Then turning to the *OED* the editors suggest that "a type of anything small, valueless, or contemptible" or the Renaissance *fico*. "Far less likely," we are told is the *English Dialect Dictionary*'s "the droppings of a donkey" (Northumberland). Even Francis, the talking mule, was unable to make a *fico*, and I have trouble making any sense of this usage with the gossip. I do not find the first definition taken from the *OED* useful in either context, and the *EDD* entry makes no sense except for the mule, and little there. Are we to assume that Tristram is bargaining for sexual favors from the gossip, or that he is not because he has already had "enow"? What are the other meanings available to Sterne? There is the fruit, by far the most probable meaning regarding the gossip and highly probable in the case of the mule. The best explanation for the mule is to be found in a definition in the *OED (sb¹, 3b):* "*Farriery.* An excrescence on the frog of a horse's foot, somewhat resembling a fig." Among the sources cited is Chambers's *Cyclopedia* (1753). The note concludes with another cross reference to Volume III, Chapter XXXVIII (pp. 271.1-272.18) where we are sent back to the episode of the gossip. But I leave these bawdy interpretations to the reader.[36]

In the interest of providing context many of the annotations run on for pages. Again, to take only one example, when Sterne says, "As this revolution of the *Strasburgers* affairs is often spoken of, and little understood, I will, in ten words, says *Slawkenbergius*, give the world an explanation of it, and with it put an end to my tale" (p. 323.10-13). We are given two full pages of small print. "Sterne is accurate in saying the fall of Strasbourg was often spoken of," we are told, and then given quotations from an anonymous *The Politicks of the French King* (1689), William Ker's *Travels Through Flanders, Holland, Germany, Sweden and Denmark* (1693), Jeremy Collier's translation of Louis Moréri's *Dictionary* (1701), Voltaire's *Age of Lewis XIV* (Dublin, 1752), finally arriving at Gilbert Burnet's *Some Letters Containing an Account of . . . Travelling through Switzerland, Italy, Some Parts of Germany,* 2d ed. (Rotterdam, 1687) from which "Sterne seems to have borrowed his own particular account." At the end we are asked to see Franklin L. Ford's *Strasbourg in Transition: 1648-1789* (1958). I'm sure that other contemporaries commented on Strasbourg and this is only a selection. I suppose it is debatable how many citations a context makes, but would not the citation from Burnet and a "see also" or "cf." anonymous, Ker, Moréri, Voltaire, with a finishing flourish from Ford's modern account have accomplished the same thing in about twenty percent of the space? Even if the source for Sterne's remark had not been discovered, would it not have sufficed to say that Sterne was accurate? How many readers—scholars or beginning students— want a history of Strasbourg? After all, Sterne may not have known any of these sources and he may have known a dozen different ones. Since the entire context cannot be reconstructed anyway, why not exercise some editorial judgment and give the reader just what he needs to understand the passage? Volume VII, Chapter V is a "parodic rewriting" of Jean Aimar Piganiol de la Force's *Nouveau Voyage de France* (1724; Paris, 1755) and the editors have carefully rearranged the passages in French to parallel Sterne's development. But do the few people interested in this matter need the editors' English translation, which fills almost two pages? To gloss "that the nose must either fall off from the man, or the man inevitably fall off from his nose" (p. 307.21-23) our attention is directed to Petronius's *Satyricon* where there is a "similar observation about the size of Ascyltos' sexual organ." This is followed by the passage in Latin and two English translations, one from 1712 and another from 1959. We are given two translations, neither of them by the editors, for the motto from Epictetus on the title pages of Volumes I and II with no reference to Sterne's own free translation—"'Twas not by ideas,——by heaven! his life was put in jeopardy by words" (p. 101.1-2). All of this is tedious when taken to the extreme.

The first rule of the editors for annotating Sterne's language is to rely on the *OED*, turning to Johnson's *Dictionary* and the *English Dialect Dictionary* only when necessary, noting "every word that serves the *OED* as the initial, sole, or final illustration" (p. 10). True, many of these notes are not helpful to those who are simply reading the novel, but they are useful to scholars, particularly those interested in the history of the English language. Since they tend to be short they can be easily skipped over by those in search of more heady fare. The second rule strikes me as more controversial. The editors decided "to define no word recorded in the *Shorter Oxford English Dictionary*, which we took to be the desktop dictionary of a scholarly audience" (pp. 10-11). When *Humphry Clinker* was being edited for the Smollett edition by Thomas R. Preston we entertained the idea of adopting a similar rule. Somewhere in Smollett's novel is the legal term *mittimus*, and I can never remember what it means. I dig through the debris on my desk and find *Webster's New Collegiate Dictionary* (1977)—ah,

A Book for a Parlour-Window

mittimus, "a warrant of commitment to prison." Now I remember, but will I remember the next time I reread the novel? Probably not. Should the reader be asked to read through the annotations of the novel with a *Shorter Oxford English Dictionary* at the ready? I happen to think not.

No editor or group of editors can posit an audience exactly, but most of us have colleagues and students and understand the things they are likely to know. Most scholars—of literature—have little knowledge of legal and medical terminology, even if still in use, and probably know little about machinery or farming in the eighteenth century. As a city person I have often wondered about Walter's calculations on the Shandy ox-moor. Sterne tells us that his "father took pen and ink in hand, and set about calculating the simple expence of pareing and burning, and fencing in the *Ox-moor*" (p. 398.23-25). Fencing is clear, burning seems clear, but what about "pareing and burning"? For a gloss on this passage the editors give us a passage from one of Sterne's letters, "I was once such a puppy myself, as to pare, and burn." Under "Pare" in the *OED* ($v.^1$, 4a) the phrase "pare and burn" is given and defined as "to cut the turf to the depth of two or three inches, and burn it, in order to use the ashes for manure." This passage from *Tristram Shandy* is cited as an illustration. Later, when Obadiah hears of Bobby's death, he says, "we shall have a terrible piece of work of it stubbing the ox-moor" (p. 430.22-23). "Paring" and "stubbing" are not the same thing, as the *OED* informs us. "Stub" ($v.^1$, 4) is clearing the land by uprooting, with this passage from *Tristram Shandy* given as an illustration. The editors do not annotate these passages; the information on "pare and burn" and "stubbing" is available in *SOED*. Looking up these terms in a dictionary does help us understand the plans for the ox-moor but not Walter's calculations. Legal terms seem slighted—in the marriage settlement, for example (pp. 42-46). So much is made of Walter being "entirely a water-drinker" (p. 523.15) and Toby not being one—"I wish my uncle Toby had been a water-drinker; for then the thing had been accounted for" (p. 661.19-20)—that some explanation seems required at these points. The editors seem content when they have defined words not in the *SOED* and have documented Sterne's "scholarly" sources.

A vast amount of work has gone into compiling these annotations. I find them fulsome without being particularly helpful, but a final judgment must be made by Sterne scholars who use this edition over the years. New protests at great length about the need for the editors to remain neutral—to elucidate rather than interpret. But those familiar with New's *Laurence Sterne as Satirist* (1969) will recognize its earnest methodological shadow here. A cynical view is that all of the belabored theoretical questions in the introduction to Volume 3 are a justification for not making the hard decisions. You wonder how many eighteenth-century scholars, the ones with the *SOED*s on their desk, need two pages of quotations, strung together without comment, on Sterne's refusal to separate wit and judgment (p. 227.14-18 and n.). I have not, and will not, spend more than a decade studying *Tristram Shandy*, and I would like to be told what is pertinent by someone who has. Perhaps I am not attuned to fashionable literary theory, which is "flying over our heads like light clouds on a windy day, never to return more," or I simply want to believe with Martin C. Battestin that Richards gave place "to Wittgenstein, Wittgenstein to Levi-Strauss, Levi-Strauss to Shklovsky, Shklovsky to Poulet, Poulet to Derrida, and Derrida, with any luck, will soon give way to Common Sense."[37] The question of objectivity for the annotator is a longstanding one and, finally, unresolvable as New admits. The ideas raised in Arthur Friedman's old essay "Principles of Historical Annotation in Critical Editions of Modern Texts" still need consideration, and Battestin's "A Rationale of Literary Annotation: The Example of Fielding's Novels," in part an elaborate gloss on Friedman and in part self-justification, is useful.[38] It can be argued that Friedman's notes to his edition of Goldsmith are too austere and that Battestin is a bit too preoccupied with theological questions, but objections will be raised to any set of annotations. The point is that both editors accept responsibility for making decisions.

A Book for a Parlour-Window

For all of their wishy-washiness, the Florida editors have just as surely left their mark on *Tristram Shandy*, as if they had adopted a more clearly defined editorial policy. But a clearer editorial policy would have made the annotations much more useful for scholars of the late twentieth century. Instead of trying to provide some answers based on their years of research, we are handed a batch of ingredients and told to go off and make our own edition. In an ideal world this might happen. In the world we inhabit this third volume will greatly assist students looking for dissertation topics and will fill the pages of academic journals with notes by scholars attempting to do what the editors chose not to do. New argues that annotators like Battestin and Stout "work to inhibit all other readings" because, in spite of their attempts at objectivity, they in fact feel the necessity to provide their own closure for the work. This edition, however, "has provided the recognizable tools for multiple closures," leaving "the reader in a continuing state of mild irritability and unrest" (p. 6). Well, the editors have certainly left this reader in a state of irritability and unrest.

The indecisiveness of the annotations masquerading as literary theory appears in the edited text disguised as textual theory. No matter what textual theory is chosen, Greg-Bowers, a variation of it, or an entirely new theory, the full implications for editing this text with its peculiar problems must be carefully thought out, and the textual evidence presented in an acceptable form. In the process of developing an editorial procedure, *all* of the bibliographical evidence must be carefully examined. A careful study needs to be made of the printer's copy for volume one of *A Sentimental Journal*, for example, to understand what happened to Sterne's manuscripts in the printing house. Rather than just assuming that Sterne's typography is important, it needs to be studied carefully, perhaps along the lines of argument developed by D. F. McKenzie's "sociology of the text."[39] When all of the theoretical smoke at the end of Volume 2 and the beginning of Volume 3 is blown aside, the textual problem on one level is a simple one. Sterne appears to have seen the first edition of all nine volumes of *Tristram Shandy* through the press with varying degrees of care. The only major substantive variants occur in Volume V, which contains a new motto on the title page and two new sentences in the text. Sterne seems to have made a few corrections in Volumes I, II, and IV. Basically, then, the editors are correcting the first edition copy-text without having exhausted the bibliographical evidence in its widest sense. Users are bound to feel that some of the decisions are capricious and arbitrary. The text as edited is not likely to hurt scholarly study, but it must be lamented that the opportunity for a thorough examination of the text has been lost. It is hard to imagine that another edition of this scope will be attempted for a great while.

Users of the edition are likely to lament the absence of a thorough index and even more the lack of volume and chapter numbers in the running heads. Omitting the volume and chapter numbers makes the type pages of this edition look as much like the type pages of the first edition as possible, but the difficulty of referring to this edition is readily apparent when looking at the citations in this review.

This edition of *Tristram Shandy* represents a great deal of work by a number of people, and while it is the duty of a reviewer to point out short-comings and warn users of possible difficulties, I am grateful for the editors' contributions to furthering our understanding of this complex work. "A system, built upon the discoveries of a great many minds," Johnson reminds us, "is always of more strength, than what is produced by the mere workings of any one mind, which, of itself, can do little. There is not so poor a book in the world that would not be a prodigious effort were it wrought out entirely by a single mind, without the aid of prior investigators."[40] Among textual editors there is a good deal of talk about "authoritative" texts, texts that will stand the test of time, a hedge against our own ragged mortality. But I find myself turning again and again to a preface by R. B. McKerrow written in February 1910 on the completion of his edition of the works of Thomas Nashe.

In spite of the generous help of friends I part from this task leaving more difficulties unsolved, more allusions untraced than I hoped; but there are many problems upon which light comes only by chance. In time what has baffled me will no doubt yield to others. All my desire is that this edition of Nashe may prove to be a real advance upon its predecessors, and that it may form a better starting-point than there was before for future progress. He would indeed be foolish who should dream that any work of his in this kind could be final: he would, I think, be no well-willer to English scholarship who should even hope that it might be so.[41]

The editors can be pleased that they have joined the ranks of other distinguished editors who have increased our knowledge about this great comic novel.

Notes

1. Edward Simmen, "Sterne's *A Political Romance*: New Light From A Printer's Copy," *PBSA*, 64 (1970), 419-29; Arthur H. Cash, *Laurence Sterne: The Early & Middle Years* (London: Methuen, 1975), pp. 262-77.

2. Lewis Perry Curtis, ed., *Letters of Laurence Sterne* (1935; rpt. Oxford: Clarendon, 1965), p. 74.

3. *Letters*, pp. 77, 81.

4. Melvyn New, "Sterne's Rabelaisian Fragment: A Text From the Holograph Manuscript," *PMLA*, 87 (1972), 1083-92.

5. *Letters*, pp. 68, 74, 80-81.

6. See Kenneth Monkman, "The Bibliography of the Early Editions of *Tristram Shandy*," *Library*, 25, 5th ser. (1970), 14.

7. *Letters*, pp. 126, 294; Wilbur L. Cross, *The Life and Times of Laurence Sterne*, 3d ed. (New Haven: Yale Univ. Press, 1929), p. 371.

8. Laurence Sterne, *A Sentimental Journey Through France and Italy by Mr. Yorick*, ed. Gardner D. Stout, Jr. (Berkeley and Los Angeles: Univ. of California Press, 1967), pp. 55, 50-64.

9. The phrase is Sir Walter W. Greg's. See *The Collected Papers of Sir Walter W. Greg*, ed. J. C. Maxwell (Oxford: Clarendon, 1966), p. 382. The quotations below appear on pp. 376-77, 385.

10. "In composing we employ our eyes with the same agility as we do our hands; for we cast our eyes upon every letter we aim at, at the same moment we move our hands to take it up: neither do we lose our time in looking at our Copy for every word we compose; but take as many words into our memory as we can well retain" (p. 209). Smith makes clear that

this procedure is followed for printed copy and "such Manuscripts as are written fair," a "bad-written or intricate Copy requiring a much longer and closer application of the eye" (pp. 209-10). If the manuscript for *A Sentimental Journey* is typical, a compositor would not have had much difficulty reading it, suggesting that most of the changes were made deliberately by the compositor, with a few errors sprinkled in for good measure, no doubt. Philip Luckombe, *The History and Art of Printing* (London, 1771), repeats what Smith says, perhaps indicating only indolence, but more likely suggesting that Smith's descriptions of what went on in the printing house were still applicable.

11. "In using the first edition as copy-text, it has been accepted as the authority for accidentals. In those few instances where an accidental is emended, the change is based on the editor's judgment rather than the authority of another text" (p. 836).

12. Monkman, pp. 11-39.

13. I have not examined the manuscripts for *A Sentimental Journey* in the British Library and Morgan Library and rely on Stout's presentation of the evidence. Sterne seems to have used hyphens or a series of short dashes rather than the longer dash-lengths on very few occasions, usually in association with suppressed names. See Stout, *A Sentimental Journey*, pp. 113, 122, for example.

14. Monkman, pp. 12-22.

15. Monkman, p. 29.

16. *Letters*, p. 234.

17. B. L. Add. MS. 48802A, fols. 57, 70; Monkman, pp. 27-29. For a description of Strahan's ledgers, see O M Brack, Jr., "The Ledgers of William Strahan," in *Editing Eighteenth Century Texts*, ed. D. I. B. Smith (Toronto: Univ. of Toronto Press, 1968), pp. 59-77.

18. Stout, *A Sentimental Journey*, p. 52 n. 11.

19. B. L. Add. MS. 48803, fol. 17.

20. Stout, *A Sentimental Journey*, pp. 298-99.

21. D. F. McKenzie, "Printers of the Mind: Some Notes on Bibliographical Theories and Printing-House Practices," *SB*, 22 (1969), 1-75.

22. Smith, *The Printer's Grammar*, pp. 199, 201, 202.

23. The description is Samuel Johnson's. See *The Letters of Samuel Johnson*, ed. R. W. Chapman (Oxford: Clarendon, 1952), II, 23.

24. See Vivienne Mylne, "The Punctuation of Dialogue in Eighteenth-Century French and English Fiction," *Library*, 1, 6th ser. (1979), 43-61 and C. J. Mitchell, "Quotation Marks, National Compositorial Habits and False Imprints," *Library*, 5, 6th ser. (1983), 359-84.

25. Bertrand H. Bronson, *Printing as an Index of Taste in Eighteenth Century England* (New York: New York Public Library, 1958), p. 17.

26. James Thorpe, *Principles of Textual Criticism* (San Marino: Huntington Library, 1972), p. 141.

27. *Mark Twain-Howells Letters*, ed. Henry Nash Smith and William M. Gibson (Cambridge: Harvard Univ. Press, 1960), p. 610. For a good summary of authors' attitudes toward the spelling and pointing of their texts see Thorpe, Chapter V, pp. 131-70.

28. See Mark Twain, *The Prince and the Pauper*, ed. Victor Fischer and Lin Salamo (Berkeley and Los Angeles: Univ. of California Press, 1979), pp. 392-96; *A Connecticut Yankee in King Arthur's Court*, ed. Bernard L. Stein (Berkeley and Los Angeles: Univ. of California Press, 1979), pp. 580-85.

29. Gwin J. Kolb, "*Rasselas*: Purchase Price, Proprietors, and Printings," *SB*, 15 (1962), 256-59.

30. "Reproducing a Classic," *ASECS News Circular*, No. 55 (Winter 1985), p. [3]. Librarians purchasing this book might be accorded the same treatment as Twain's printer's proof-reader.

31. Laurence Sterne, *Tristram Shandy*, ed. Howard Anderson (New York: Norton, 1980), p. viii. The "authoritative" text begins with the accuracy of the title.

32. Melvyn New, "The Text of *Tristram Shandy*," in *Editing Eighteenth Century Novels*, ed. G. E. Bentley, Jr. (Toronto: Hakkert, 1975), p. 85 and n. 34.

33. G. Thomas Tanselle, "Some Principles for Editorial Apparatus," *SB*, 25 (1972), 88. New has been influenced by Stout's apparatus in *A Sentimental Journey* which he used when editing the Rabelaisian fragment. Stout requires a more complicated apparatus to record manuscript readings, but it is not as clear as it might be. There are entries without a sigla, for example.

34. In *Letters* the spelling is consistently "Avignon" (see pp. 291, 383, 392, 405).

35. "This unconcern [about where textual editors stand in relation to their text] has been of especial value to 'scientific' editors, those who have continued to posit the possibility of objectivity in literary editing, based upon certain

'rules' of procedure and selection" (pp. 1-2). "It is impossible to exclude individual judgement from editorial procedure: it operates of necessity in the all-important matter of the choice of copy-text and in the minor one of deciding what readings are possible and what are not. . . . it may not be too optimistic a belief that the judgement of an editor, fallible as it must necessarily be, is likely to bring us closer to what the author wrote than the enforcement of arbitrary rule" (Greg, "The Rationale of Copy-Text," p. 381). "It is true that less harm than usual may be caused to a text if the bibliographical method alone is narrowly followed; but for the real principles of editing, for the discipline that places editing as almost a creative art, bibliography is only one of a triad that also includes language study but above all literary criticism shaping the judgement within certain limits prescribed by bibliography and language. . . . I should prefer the taste and judgement of a Kittredge (wrong as he sometimes was), and of an Alexander, to the unskilled and therefore unscientific operation of a scientific method as if it were the whole answer to the problem and automatically relieved an editor of the necessity to use his critical judgement in any way. Bibliography can only help to prepare a text for the final operation. Bibliography is a good servant but a bad master" (Fredson Bowers, *Textual & Literary Criticism* [Cambridge: Cambridge Univ. Press, 1959], pp. 115-16).

36. As well as the following: "pudding's end" (p. 115.10), "vent" (p. 355.9-11), "seige" (p. 541.7-8), "mole" (p. 559.25-27), *Terra del Fuogo* (p. 669.13), "armour" (p. 739.14-15).

37. Martin C. Battestin, "A Rationale of Literary Annotation: The Example of Fielding's Novels," *SB*, 34 (1981), 2.

38. Arthur Friedman, "Principles of Historical Annotation in Critical Editions of Modern Texts," *English Institute Annual, 1941* (New York: Columbia Univ. Press, 1942), pp. 115-28; Battestin, pp. 1-22.

39. McKenzie advocates a "new and comprehensive sociology of the text," a general theory of textual criticism which would include the "history of the book, its architecture, and the visual language of typography." He rejects Greg's distinction between "substantives" and "accidentals" because he finds this distinction "has been utterly devisive, shattering any concept of the integrity of the book as an organic form." Since authorial intention has become attached to the "substantives," what Greg called "the author's meaning or the essence of his expression," recovery of this meaning has come to constitute the "ideal text." But McKenzie wishes to develop a line of argument "in which authorial control of the physical forms makes manifest the ideal, one in which the essence of a work's meaning is distilled in the detail of its formal presentation." See "Typography and Meaning: The Case of William Congreve," in *Buch und Buchhandel in Europa im achtzehnten Jahrhundert* (Proceedings of the Fifth Wolfenbütteler Symposium, 1-3 November 1977), ed. Giles Barber and Bernhard Fabian (Hamburg: Hauswedell, 1981), pp. 83-

84. The theory, not without its problems (see *PBSA*, 79 [1985], 125-27), has been worked out more carefully by McKenzie in his Panizzi Lectures delivered at the British Library in November and December 1985. Nicolas Barker's "Typography and the Meaning of Words: The Revolution in the Layout of Books in the Eighteenth Century" in the same volume (pp. 127-65) is a useful place to start for a study of Sterne's typography. The fact that *Tristram Shandy* was published in octavo rather than the usual duodecimo format for novels deserves some comment. Roger B. Moss in "Sterne's Punctuation," *Eighteenth-Century Studies*, 15 (Winter 1981-82), 179-200, has some interesting ideas about what he calls "Sterne's invented typography," but I am suspicious of a study which fails to indicate the edition it has used.

40. Boswell's *Life of Samuel Johnson*, ed. G. B. Hill and L. F. Powell (Oxford: Clarendon, 1934-50), I, 454.

41. *The Works of Thomas Nashe*, ed. Ronald B. McKerrow (1910; Oxford: Basil Blackwell, 1958), V, ix.

Contributors

JAMES L. BATTERSBY is Professor of English at The Ohio State University.

O M BRACK, JR., is Professor of English at Arizona State University.

ALASTAIR FOWLER is Regius Professor Emeritus of Rhetoric and English Literature at the University of Edinburgh and regularly Visiting Professor at the University of Virginia.

HARVEY GROSS is Professor of Comparative Literature at the State University of New York at Stony Brook.

BURTON HATLEN is Professor of English at the University of Maine at Orono.

DAVID H. JACKSON is Assistant Professor of English at Centenary College of Louisiana.

JOHN E. JORDAN is Professor of English at the University of California at Berkeley.

GERHARD JOSEPH is Professor of English at Lehman College and the Graduate School, CUNY.

SEYMOUR KLEINBERG is Professor of English at Long Island University.

DALE KRAMER is Professor of English at the University of Illinois at Urbana - Champaign.

JAMES MCLAVERTY is Lecturer in English at the University of Keele.

ROBERT K. MORRIS is Professor of English at the City College, CUNY.

BRENDA MURPHY is Associate Professor of English at St. Lawrence University.

JEFFREY C. ROBINSON is Associate Professor of English at the University of Colorado at Boulder.

MARTIN ROTH is Professor of English at the University of Minnesota.

P. G. SCOTT is Professor of English at the University of South Carolina.

R. C. TERRY is Professor of English at the University of Victoria.

JAMES THOMPSON is Associate Professor of English at the University of North Carolina at Chapel Hill.

DONALD GWYNN WATSON is Associate Professor of English at Florida International University.

JAMES L. W. WEST III is Professor of English at The Pennsylvania State University, and is co-editor of *Review*.